Annie Gray is a historian specialising in the history of food from around 1600 to the present day, conducting her research both in libraries and in kitchens. She has worked at Audley End, among other historical kitchens, and gives lectures all over the country. She has presented TV history documentaries including *Victorian Bakers* and *The Sweet Makers*, and appears on BBC Radio 4's *The Kitchen Cabinet*. She lives in East Anglia.

PRAISE FOR *VICTORY IN THE KITCHEN*:

'Deliciously entertaining ... This is popular history at its very best' *Daily Mail*

'Engaging ... appeals to three national obsessions: the preparation and presentation of food; the lost world of great households, above and below stairs; and the private life of a national hero, Churchill' *The Times*

'Recreates a corner of early twentieth-century domestic life ... Gray is an inventive researcher ... she likes to get close up to the everyday past' *Spectator*

PRAISE FOR *THE GREEDY QUEEN*:

'Zingy, fresh and unexpected: Annie Gray, the queen of food historians, finds her perfect subject. A book to devour' Lucy Worsley

'Had me at the first sentence' Nigel Slater

'Gray writes with great authority, verve and
c

'   *ectator*

C334588137

ALSO BY ANNIE GRAY

The Greedy Queen: Eating With Victoria
From the Alps to the Dales: 100 Years of Bettys
The Official Downton Abbey Cookbook

ANNIE GRAY

Victory
in the
Kitchen

The Life of Churchill's Cook

P

PROFILE BOOKS

This paperback edition first published in 2021

First published in Great Britain in 2020 by
PROFILE BOOKS LTD
29 Cloth Fair
London
ECIA 7JQ

www.profilebooks.com

Copyright © Annie Gray, 2020

10 9 8 7 6 5 4 3 2 1

Typeset in Dante by MacGuru Ltd
Printed and bound in Great Britain by
CPI Group (UK) Ltd, Croydon, CR0 4YY

The moral right of the author has been asserted.

All rights reserved. Without limiting the rights under copyright
reserved above, no part of this publication may be reproduced,
stored or introduced into a retrieval system, or transmitted, in any
form or by any means (electronic, mechanical, photocopying,
recording or otherwise), without the prior written permission of
both the copyright owner and the publisher of this book.

A CIP catalogue record for this book is available from the British
Library.

ISBN 978 1 78816 045 2
eISBN 978 1 78283 445 8

To SD and TD and most of all M

Contents

Introduction

One day in 1977, an elderly lady stood weeping in her bedsit kitchen, methodically shredding her memoir into tiny pieces and washing them down her sink. Her son-in-law and her daughter had told her that no one would be interested in her life. It was a bad time, tensions were high, and so she took the loose pages, written in slightly shaky, crabby handwriting, and watched as the blue ink ran, and the scraps of her life disappeared down the drain. That any of the pages survived was only due to her granddaughter, who discovered her, and saved twenty-six and a half pages, written and rewritten, crossed out and corrected, and which detailed the first fourteen years of the ninety-five she'd so far lived.

In some ways, they were right. This is a book about an ordinary woman, born and brought up in average conditions, and who had, on the face of it, a career like thousands of others. She'd been in service, like so many thousands of other women born in the late Victorian period, rising from scullery maid to cook, and eventually retiring, somewhat later than those brought up with the expectation of guaranteed pensions and a generally accepted retirement age. But this was also a woman to whom Winston Churchill, fresh from addressing the crowd on VE Day, said that he couldn't have achieved what he had without her.

Georgina Landemare worked for the Churchills from 1940 to 1954, the longest-serving of any of their domestic servants. They were, in turn, her longest employers. Her relationship with the family became one of friendship and respect, although she never forgot the ingrained line between servant and served. She was particularly close to Clementine Churchill, who valued her skills, her loyalty and her ability to turn out meals with minimum fuss despite rationing and the upheavals of war. In the course of her career she'd been Georgina Young, a schoolgirl; Georgie, a sweetheart and friend; Mrs Landemare, wife, mother and jobbing cook; and now she was known to the Churchill clan as 'Mrs Mar', an endearing mixture of nickname and the standard cook's honorific (cooks were always Mrs, regardless of marital status). She had been in daily personal contact with Clementine, a stalwart providing sustenance and delight to Winston, and, throughout the war years especially, a key element in his particular brand of dinner-table diplomacy, believing, as he so firmly did, that personal contact, especially over good food and wine, was the secret to political success.

Unfortunately, public history sometimes slips into a blur of great people doing great deeds: tales of the rich and famous, easy to research and easy to sell, for people have heard of them. In 2017 alone there were two major biographic films and a TV series with Winston Churchill as a key character. There are over a thousand books about him, which include titles such as *Hero of the Empire*,

An Unexpected Hero and *A Study in Greatness*: there is a definite theme. But look through the indexes of these books: even the magisterial multi-volume Martin Gilbert biography gives scant room to his domestic servants. Georgina does appear occasionally, but it's in passing, as a stock figure, vaguely imagined as a benevolent and buxom shadow, apron-clad among her pans. But great though Churchill may have been, his greatness was certainly made much more achievable by having someone on hand to pick up his pants – and cook his dinner.

Happily, this is not reflective of the wider historical discipline, and there's a thriving academic and popular interest in studying the lives of once marginalised figures, either because they reflect wider society or through the light they shed on specific events or better-known individuals.[1] The working classes, women, black and other minority ethnic groups are all being firmly (re)integrated into the historical narrative, whether in the form of biography, letters and diaries, or narrative history. This is particularly true when it comes to servants, for a long time dismissed as the subject of serious study. In the 1970s, when Georgina was writing down her experiences, domestic service was still a tense topic, something repudiated by the generation represented by Georgina's daughter, who had often been brought up with parents in service, but were now in a changing world, where it was increasingly seen as undesirable and not really to be talked of.

Domestic service remains deeply emotive, due either to family experience or simple modern politics. There are many excellent and nuanced studies of servant life, from the eighteenth century to the modern day, and a number of service wings at country houses are open with costumed interpreters or volunteers specifically tasked with tackling the tendency toward easy assumptions about servant life.[2] But media depictions, with some notable exceptions, still tend to emphasise either the cosy, nostalgic view, where over-stuffed houses were staffed by bobbing parlourmaids in black gowns with white caps; or the miserable, exploitative aspect, this time centred around young teenagers weeping as they scrubbed floors until their knees bled. At its peak, and although reliable statistics are impossible to obtain, domestic service was the single biggest employer of women in the UK. It's generally thought that it employed around 14 per cent of the working population by the beginning of the twentieth century. In the 1911 census, one in three women who gave their status as 'occupied' (i.e. having an occupation) was in service. This ignores all the women who had part-time jobs, took in laundry, went out to char, or who preferred, for reasons of status or social form, to state that they were unoccupied, and that their husbands or fathers could afford to keep them.[3] Service was, in short, a huge area, and very few women would live their lives without either being a servant or employing servants – sometimes both in the course of a life. Indeed, the history of service and that of women in the Victorian period through to the Second World War are so intertwined that it is inconceivable to consider one without the other. A study of domestic service is, in many ways, the study of all women at this time.[4]

Georgina's memoir was deeply political. She wrote

in response to her son-in-law's view of the past – through which she had lived – beginning with the words 'to my son-in-law, who always talks about the bad old days'. By the time she started writing, she had become, like many of those who worked predominantly in large establishments, and were career servants, rather reactionary. There should be no dichotomy between her view of herself as a servant who knew – and valued – her place, and the very real achievements of her life, during which she went from rural poverty to the top of her chosen profession; but for her daughter and son-in-law, the very fact that she'd been in service negated the value of her opinions. Her own words suggest that service, a profession that she'd had little choice but to enter, was nevertheless empowering: 'I feel I did give my whole life to the work I loved and enjoyed, and not only that but the most interesting people I served & liked who gave me the courage and inspired me to work hard and not to feel that I had no standing in life as a cook, but to feel on a par with other walks in life.' (The lack of grammar is her own.)

Researching the life of an unknown working-class woman in the late nineteenth and early to mid-twentieth century is not easy. Apart from the fragmentary memoir, which stops in about 1895, the evidence of Georgina's life and her career is hard to trace. I first came across her when idly browsing a cookery book collection, and came across a copy of Georgina's *Recipes from No.10*, which was published in 1958 with a foreword by Clementine Churchill. Through that, and talking to her granddaughter, Edwina (who, in her late 70s, is Britain's oldest Ironman competitor, and clearly follows in her grandmother's footsteps in terms of determination and longevity), I became hooked, and determined to tell the story of a woman whose very averageness at the start of her life was part of her appeal. Georgina's life was so much like that of so many other women, except that it was not: for she was one of only a handful of female society chefs in a profession dominated at its highest levels by men, and she remained part of the workforce throughout marriage and childrearing. Her life covers a time of enormous change in British food, from Edwardian excess to 1940s rationing, and into the era of frozen TV dinners and the wholefood movement. She cooked through all of it, gaining a reputation as 'a superb cook, combining the best of French and English skills'.[5] She was highly driven, highly motivated, very talented and determined. However, I would not be writing about her had she not had an equally driven, motivated, talented and determined final employer. Churchill continues to be central to the British sense of national identity, a figure of apparently endless fascination. There are books about all sorts of topics and people related to him. But, although you can read about his secretaries, his bodyguards and his nurses, the servants who fetched and carried, and served and cooked remain invisible. This is a start at filling that gap.

This is a book about Georgina Landemare. It's about her life, her times and some of her employers, including Winston and Clementine Churchill. It's about working-class life, and women's work and expectations, and it's about domestic service at the highest level. It's about

British food, and French influence, and the impact of war on the way we ate. It's the story of a woman who lived, loved and cooked her way through much of twentieth-century Britain, and, while her life is made more resonant by her relationship to her last employers, it remains, above all else, Georgina's story.

1

Beginnings

'German Kougelhof', from Georgina Landemare's 1930s hand-written recipe book. A yeast-risen, fortified bread. The version in Georgina's 1958 Recipes from No.10 *is sweeter – and smaller. The original text lacks punctuation: for ease of reading here it's been added in.*

> *2 lbs of flour, 1½ cup of butter, 8 whole eggs, 8 yolks, 4 oz sugar, 1¼ oz of yeast, ½ oz of cinnamon and grated lemon peel, salt, ½ pt of cream & Jordan almonds. First place butter in a pan, and work 10 minutes with the cinnamon, lemon peel, salt, sugar & fourth part of the flour, and 3 eggs should be added, and all worked well then add the rest of the flour, and eggs gradually, still continually [sic] to work the place with wooden spoon, when the whole has been used up, spread the paste out in the centre, add the yeast previously dissolved with salt & cream made tepid for the purpose. Work all well together, butter & put in splintered almonds in the mould, pour in mixture & prove. Bake a brown colour, and cover with cinnamon sugar.*[1]

Georgina was born Georgina Young, at the home of her maternal grandmother in the tiny village of Aldbury, in 1882. Nestled on the Hertfordshire-Buckinghamshire border, it looked to Tring, the nearest market town, for its residents' needs. Grouped around it were other small villages, and it was in one of these, Aston Clinton, that Georgina's parents lived at the time. These three places, nine miles apart, would form the backdrop to her early years, etching themselves on her memories. Despite a life mainly lived in London, her early years stayed with her, and when she looked back, she wrote of her rural beginnings with pride.

In the late nineteenth century, Tring was, as now, the main focus for the villages and hamlets surrounding it (many of which have since been swallowed by its later growth). It was a market town, with a population of around 4,000, and had, or was about to acquire, the usual set of resplendent Victorian amenities – town hall, museum, park – mainly paid for by the most significant local landowners, the Rothschilds.[2] The town had four mills, including the bluntly named New Mill, indicative of the second wave of industrial revolution, ongoing in Britain since the 1870s.[3] The British population was growing faster than it ever had before, with towns such as Salford, Leicester and Bradford booming off the back of industry. The major employer in Tring, however, was not one of the mills, but Tring Park, a country estate that employed around 300 people at its peak (and extended to over 5,000 acres). The Rothschilds had acquired it in 1872, after a disputed succession led to its sale, and subsequent purchase by Lionel de Rothschild (who gave it to his son, Nathaniel, normally known as Nathan). The ousted incumbents, who had simply been tenants, despite a hasty subscription organised by local tradespeople to raise the funds to help them buy the property, were reduced to buying a much less substantial (though still impressive) country house, Pendley Manor, which also employed a number of people in the area. Like so many towns of the era, rich landowners provided both jobs and welfare for the town, beautifying it with their philanthropic building works, holding yearly festivals in their grounds, and providing, through the custom of charitable giving, a measure of poor relief, at least for their immediate dependants. The period tends to be known for industrial growth, but this was also an era when country houses were significant employers, as the number of servants, both indoor and outdoor, deemed necessary for the smooth running of a household, increased. Domestic service remained the single biggest occupational group in Britain, and the influence of the aristocracy was considerable, even in urban districts such as Tring.

Aldbury and Aston Clinton were both satellite villages. Aston Clinton, which was the larger of the two, was also linked to the Rothschilds, for another branch of the family owned another house there, leaving Aldbury as one of the few settlements in the area without a resident Rothschild. Located one and a half miles to the northeast of Tring, instead of having one titled, ruling family, Aldbury had two influential gentry families, the Craufurds and the Woods. The village was small, having hardly changed in the previous fifty years. Most of its few hundred inhabitants were agricultural workers or straw-plaiters, and they supported three pubs, a grocer, a baker, a general shop and various tradespeople. There was also a small hotel at the station. Change, however, was afoot. In a sign of what was to come, in 1891 the two ruling families were joined by the Humphry Wards, interlopers (in that they came from Oxford and London) who in their turn would have a significant impact on life in the village.

Mary Humphry Ward was a pioneer of women's education, a promoter of education and social services in deprived areas, and a bestselling author, whose work dealt with social issues, religious doubt and difficult childhoods, with the inevitable late Victorian sprinkling of melodrama, murder and moralising endings. (She was also against women's suffrage, a factor that was instrumental in her lack of enduring fame.) It was her earnings, rather than those of her husband Thomas, an ex-Oxford academic turned *Times* art critic, that paid for the move to Aldbury. After they bought the main house in the village, Stocks House, from the Wood family (who moved a few doors down to Toms Hill), she set several of her books in and around Aldbury, vividly describing its environs:

> An elderly labourer was walking along the road which led to the village. To his right lay the allotment gardens just beginning to be alive with figures, and the voices of men and children. Beyond them, far ahead, rose the square tower of the church; to his left was the hill, and straight in front of him the

village, with its veils of smoke lightly brushed over
the trees, and its lines of cottages climbing the chalk
steeps behind it.[4]

The next thirty to forty years would see a quiet revolution in the way Aldbury, and many villages like in it
Britain, were populated and run. The wealthy gentry
families, who patronised the churches, organised the
village fetes and acted as godparents and sponsors to the
villagers, would still hold sway until the Second World
War – and in some cases beyond – but the migration of
people into and out of the village would accelerate as
traditional trades waxed and waned. The growth of
London, and the rise of dormitory towns, would eventually save all three from the decline that affected many
similar places. Even today, Aldbury supports a small
village shop and two pubs.

In 1882, however, Aston Clinton was still a sleepy
village, Tring a thriving market town and Aldbury a pic-
turesque, but poor, rural outpost. Although very little
survives of the memoir Georgina wrote in the 1970s, the
fragments that were saved cover her formative early
years, and the way of life she describes gives a vivid
picture of life in rural England in the mid- to late 1880s.
Britain was an urban nation, with 66 per cent of the population of England and Wales living in towns or cities of
areas of 3,000 inhabitants or above (this, therefore,
includes Tring, but not Aston Clinton or Aldbury). Nearly
9 million of the 26 million-strong population lived in or
near small villages or hamlets, and her experiences would
have been broadly familiar to people across the country.[5]

Georgina's background was what social campaigners and researchers Charles Booth and Seebohm Rowntree termed the 'affluent working class': in their analyses of Britain in the late nineteenth century, just over 51 per cent of the population fell into this category, making it the largest single group of people. Her paternal grandparents, the Youngs, had lived in Tring or its immediate suburbs since they were born. David, her grandfather, had started out in the usual profession for men of the area, as an agricultural labourer, marrying Elizabeth Tofield in the 1830s and immediately starting a family. By 1841 they had three children, and they would go on to have seven. Two of them were called Shadrack, a traditional Jewish name, although the family was Church of England. Records of the time show a significant number of Jewish names or spellings of names in Tring, usually from the working classes of the town, and generally on Church of England marriage banns – this may be linked to the presence of the Rothschilds. In the case of the Youngs, their first Shadrack died, aged 3, the month after he was baptised. The second lived into adulthood and married the equally Jewish-sounding Rebekah Wright, a neighbour from a few doors away, in a Church of England ceremony in 1871.

By the time Georgina knew her grandfather, he had become a gamekeeper, a thriving profession at the time as agricultural rents declined, and landowners devoted more and more of their holdings to pleasure. She remembered him fondly, describing him as 'a grand old man. He wore a moleskin waistcoat and white breeches and was the essence of kindness.' By the time of the 1881 census he was sufficiently senior to be living in Pendley Beeches, one of the more architecturally interesting of the various lodges attached to Pendley Manor.[6] At 65, he was still working, and looking after various members of his extended family, including his assorted grandchildren, who were frequent and protracted visitors. The various social surveys of the time were unanimous that the hardest point for any working-class family was when they had three or more children who were below working age. While married women could, and normally did, work, their earning power was almost always far less than that of a working man, and when they became mothers, they also had primary childcare responsibilities which took both time and energy. Children of school age needed feeding and clothing, but in the main could contribute little to the income of the household. One, very common, solution was to farm children out to grandparents. On census night three of Georgina's cousins, of various ages, were living at London Lodge with the Youngs. One was old enough to work – inevitably as an agricultural labourer – and the other two were still at school. It was a precarious existence, and David, like most other men of his class, never retired. He did, however, reach old age. Gamekeeping may have had the perk of a purpose-built, modern house, but it was nevertheless a dangerous profession. In 1891, six years after David's death, two of the under-gamekeepers at Pendley were shot by a poacher. It wasn't an isolated incident: rural poverty made for desperate men, and desperation and guns don't usually afford happy endings.

Georgina was less kind about Elizabeth, her paternal grandmother, who she said was mean – so much so that when her daughter-in-law was visiting she'd hunt for stale leftovers to feed her grandchildren, and never make them anything fresh. This may well have been pragmatism as much as meanness. Although by the 1880s the family lived in a well-built estate house and only had one school-age child to feed, they had moved around the area a great deal over the years, from Hastoe to New Mill, and, like most of the women in Tring, Elizabeth had plaited straw for extra income. Her children plaited too, or, like Mark, Georgina's father, got jobs connected with agriculture or in outdoor service: aged 15 he'd worked as a poultry boy on a local farm.

Straw-plaiting was one of those very specialist occupations that occupied a great number of people in a very small geographical area. There were straw-plaiters elsewhere in the UK, but the centres of the straw hat-making industry at the time were Luton and Dunstable. The latter even gave its name to the Dunstable bonnet – which in turn became the title of a 1765 folk song. Straw hats required plaited straw, and the area surrounding Luton and Dunstable became the straw-plaiting capital of Britain. The workhouses, corrective institutes and prisons (including, during the Napoleonic Wars, prisoner of war camps) provided cheap labour, but couldn't plait enough to meet demand. Plaiting was a huge industry, peaking in the early nineteenth century, but still a very significant employer during Georgina's childhood. Each village had its own plait style, and, before the Education Act of 1870 regulated and made compulsory schooling to the age of 12, the majority of children in and around Luton were educated at plait schools, where children of school age could learn to plait, and then sit plaiting, while learning the basics of reading, writing and arithmetic from a board in the middle of the room. It's likely that both of Georgina's grandmothers, and possibly her grandfathers, were educated in this way. Aldbury's plaiting school, which her maternal grandmother almost certainly attended, was on the main high street, and generations of Aldbury residents passed through it, gaining a haphazard education, but one that nevertheless provided the basics. One of its pupils' daughters later recalled that her 'mother could read easily but was very shy of anyone seeing her writing'.[7]

The main market for finished plaits was in Tring on a Friday (there was another at Ivinghoe, to the north), and plaiters would take their products down to the market and sell them to buyers on a weekly basis. The availability of relatively good-quality and well-paid work for women marked the area out. Even very small children could join in, snipping ends from the plaits or splitting the straws into plaitable strands. It helped to alleviate the ever-present risk of slipping below the poverty line, a line on or under which Booth and Rowntree reckoned around 27 per cent of the population lived at any one time (with considerable regional variation). A good plaiter could earn around 15 shillings a week – up to £40 a year. David, as a senior gamekeeper, was probably earning around £50 a year.[8] Add in the earnings of older children, especially since part-time school attendance was rife, and a family with children old enough to plait, even if not old enough to officially work, could count themselves very lucky indeed.

Mark Young, Georgina's father, left home at some point in the 1870s, finding work through the network of local connections, both among families of his parents' social status, and the families who habitually employed them. By 1881, he was working as a coachman for Cyril Flower, an MP who was married to Constance Rothschild, who, with her husband, maintained an establishment in London as well as spending significant amounts of time in Aston Clinton, near her parents. The family was well-connected, regularly hosting recitals, dinners and hunts. Constance's uncle, Nathan Rothschild, was firm friends with Winston Churchill's father Randolph, both personally and politically, and the Churchills were very much part of their 'set', and were frequently included in the social activities at Aston Clinton. In the mid-1880s, Randolph briefly became a significant statesman, but he was a controversial figure. Even as a house guest he was notoriously erratic, going missing at the start of a hunt once because he was locked in his room reading. Despite (or because of) this, Constance later remembered him as having 'promise of unusual intelligence and originality'. There may well have been a level of hindsight here: Queen Victoria's view a few years later was that Randolph was 'mad and odd and also has bad health'.[9]

Mark Young was listed as single and alone on census night in April 1881, an instance of official records giving only a partial glimpse at people's lives. Over in Aldbury, Mary Messider, Georgina's mother, had already returned home from her job in service, in preparation for her marriage to Mark in June of that year. Thereafter they would spend their time shuttling between Aston Clinton and London, where Mark had lodgings in Little Grosvenor Mews. The Mews was one of those areas that had started life as a planned development, and been rapidly infilled, mainly with stables and workshops. By the 1880s, it was crammed with horsey types like Mark: grooms, coachmen, stable-workers, saddle-makers, farriers, harness-makers and the like. Other domestic servants were there too, boarding out, and part of a large shifting population of household workers whose employers are hard to trace, and who weren't always permanent or live-in staff, contrary to the stereotypical picture of Victorian below-stairs life.

Mary was from Aldbury, and throughout her marriage she remained very close to her mother, Martha, who in turn also made a lasting impression on the young Georgina, as the family visited her regularly while they still lived in Aston Clinton. Martha is a dominant presence in Georgina's memoir, far more alive to her than her father's mother. Like Elizabeth Young, Martha was a straw-plaiter, as was her sister. In 1853 Martha had married Jesse Messider, who was variously a hostler for the local inn, an agricultural labourer and finally a coachman. Unlike Elizabeth, Martha continued to list her trade as a plaiter for most of her life, and her daughters all grew up in the trade as well. By the 1890s, however, plaiting was in terminal decline. Cheap imports, mainly from Japan, were flooding the market, and the foundation of the British Straw Plait Association in 1896 was a desperate attempt to counteract the fact that, after over 200 years, Hertfordshire's women were losing their livelihoods.

Like the Youngs, the Messiders moved around within the village, until finally settling 'above the rectory' (above in this case meaning further up the hill). Aldbury hadn't seen much new building since the late eighteenth century, and the house, which was typical of that era, was a low, two-storeyed whitewashed building, set at right angles to the road. A staircase that was barely more than a ladder led to the upstairs floor, and life took place mainly in the large downstairs room, which opened directly onto the garden. It, and the smaller cottage to which it was attached, were very convenient for those, like Jesse, employed by the Woods at Stocks House – or, after they sold Stocks to the Humphry Wards, Toms Hill. The houses in Aldbury were, in the main, basic. One inhabitant looked back from the comfort of the 1980s at her childhood in the early twentieth century, recalling that water had to be drawn from a well, while the toilet, which was at some distance from the house, was simply

a bucket with a wood surround and a high back. The top was removable and there was a handle which you had to pull to release lime into the bucket which, when full, had to be buried in the garden. If we used the toilet at night, we had to carry a lantern with a candle in it. It seems funny to sit in the kitchen now, by a nice fire, with a carpet on the floor, and think of those days.[10]

Village life centred around the two, later three, gentry families who owned the large houses. Like the Rothschilds, albeit on a much smaller scale, they employed a significant number of people, as well as funding village celebrations and organising charity. They also acted as godparents and sponsors to the village children: Georgina, like nearly all of her siblings, was born in Aldbury, for her mother returned to her own mother's house to give birth. She had both a Wood and a Craufurd as her godparents. Like Mark Young, working for the Rothschilds in Aston Clinton, in Aldbury those who went into service often gained their first positions through the network of local gentry and their connections. Mary Messider may well have been one of these, for she, like Mark, had left home to work in service, which was almost certainly how they'd met. Like Georgina many years later, Mary Messider worked at Chequers, then owned and occupied by the Russell-Astley family. She talked to her daughter of earthworks in the grounds, which she said had been built by Oliver Cromwell in the seventeenth century (they weren't, but there was a Cromwell connection, as one of his descendants married into the then resident family, bringing his significant art collection with them).

Both Mary and Mark's families remained close-knit as their children, and then grandchildren, moved away from the area. Mary was one of nine children, one of whom had died in infancy. Her sister Lizzie, who also entered service, became a lady's maid, and made many of Georgina's childhood dresses, while Mark's sister Lydia later delivered Georgina's daughter Yvonne. The highly localised nature of the families changed, however. The working-class diaspora, which was well underway in Mark and Mary's generation, gained pace with their children. In the 1930s, there were still Messiders in Aldbury (running the pub), but they were also scattered across not just Hertfordshire, but Lincolnshire and Yorkshire. Lizzie ended up in Newfoundland. Of course, workers had always migrated, especially when they became domestic servants, often settling far from their original homes. The end of the Victorian era and the early twentieth century saw a huge growth in other sectors, though, especially the service sector, which employed 45 per cent of the workforce in 1891. Retail alone accounted for 2.3 million jobs, and was booming, driven in part by department stores, the most desirable type of shop in which to work. Mary's siblings worked in domestic service, in transport or, in one case, as a policeman. Her children would, with the exception of Georgina, go into London trades all connected with the service industry.

Mary and Mark, too, would eventually leave the confines of Tring, Aston Clinton and Aldbury, and London was very much present in their lives. Their own family started with Georgina, in 1882, and they would go on to have five children. Even in her early years, Georgina shuttled between Buckinghamshire and London. Her schooling was haphazard, mainly based on Sunday School, and broken by the constant travelling, for the whole family spent the season in London with the Flowers, the rest of the year being spent in the country. Mark also went to Brecon regularly, where Cyril Flower was an MP until 1885, when he started representing the more convenient Luton.

One of the most evocative parts of Georgina's memoir details a trip from Aston Clinton to visit her maternal grandmother. The narrative is probably an amalgam of many such trips, taken over the first ten or so years of her life, while Mark was still employed by the Flowers. In it, she paints a vivid picture of her early childhood, albeit one seen with hindsight and a strong desire to make a political point about how it wasn't at all bad. In Georgina's narrative her brother, Algy (Algernon, younger by fifteen months), is toddling, and her sister Maud is in a pram, in which all of the children ended up in the course of the walk. Maud was four years younger than Georgina, and made an uneasy third in the close partnership she had with Algy. As she commented dryly in her memoir, 'Algy and I didn't relish her'.

It was six miles walking from Aston Clinton to Aldbury, but the trip was broken up, firstly and memorably by Tring Park, which had a fairly unique appeal: 'when we got to Tring Park, we stopped to see the kangaroos with their young in their pouches and that helped my mother'. The kangaroos, rather out of place in Hertfordshire, were part of the menagerie gathered by Walter Rothschild, Nathan's eldest son. Walter, though supposedly destined to follow the family path into banking, was entirely uninterested in finance and passionate about natural history. Initially encouraged, or at least funded, by his father, who, for his 21st birthday in 1889, paid for the building of a museum to house those of his specimens that weren't living, Walter employed collectors to bring specimens of everything from dead beetles to live tortoises from across the world. At Tring, his various live creatures roamed freely in the early 1880s, and spectators could see him training zebras to pull his carriage, as well as admiring the other exotic fauna around the park. Unfortunately, not all of his efforts were appreciated. Not only did his collection of edible dormice (*Glis glis*) escape (or were set free) to colonise the surrounding area, from which they have never been eradicated, and are now regarded as a pest, but the kangaroos jumped the ha-ha and dug up the flower garden, and the giant lizards ate all of the lilies.[11] The final straw came when a cassowary (a flightless bird, heavier than an emu, only slightly smaller than an ostrich, strikingly beautiful and, according to the *Guinness World Records* book, the deadliest bird in the world) chased Nathan round the garden. The animals, apart from the emus and rheas, were caged. But the trouble didn't end there, and a combination of dangerous creatures, his inability to manage the finances of the museum and his total lack of desire to settle down meant that Walter eventually found himself disinherited, although the million pounds he was left to live on meant that he was not as disadvantaged as he might have been – and he still assumed the title of Lord Rothschild of Tring, which was inalienable. He never married, and the museum was gifted to the nation after his death in 1937, becoming part of the Natural History Museum, and recognised for its world-class collections. The live animals, however, are long gone (apart from the *Glis glis*).

Next up on the family's route to Aldbury was the Youngs', where Grandmother Young's silk frocks and Grandfather Young's white breeches marked them out as having attained a certain level of grandeur in the young Georgina's eyes. As it was approaching early afternoon, 'after that we stopped for dinner as it was called in those days'. Dinner was the main meal of the day, regardless of class, but by the late nineteenth century the upper and middle classes had their dinner in the evening, while the working-class dinner remained around midday. The roots of the confusion, which still exists today, lay in the pattern of changing mealtimes from the Tudor to the Victorian periods. Dinner for the Tudors was in the morning, around 11 a.m., with a light breakfast beforehand, and a supper in early evening. By the early eighteenth century it had shifted forward by several hours, and throughout the Georgian period it gradually crept ever later. At the same time, class difference became more obvious: by the 1830s the upper classes ate around 7–8 p.m., the middle classes a few hours earlier, and the working-class meal remained just after midday. Lunch – or nuncheon, noonings, noon-shine and other glorious terms for it – made an appearance for the late dinner-eaters in the very early nineteenth century. Suppers still existed for early dinner-eaters, though tea would effectively become an alternative name for it (with what would eventually become known as afternoon tea slotting in for the lei-sured classes). The names and timings of meals became very class-dependent, though they also differed by region: generally, the more rural an area, the more likely dinner was to still be early. Nowhere was that more obvious than in country houses, where meals and their times were laid out for all to see. One early Edwardian household guide makes this very explicit, giving ideal timetables for all staff, which include servants' breakfast-time at 8 a.m., family breakfast at 9 a.m., family luncheon at 1.30 p.m., servants' dinner at 2 p.m., servants' tea at 4.30 p.m., the drawing room tea at 5 p.m., family dinner at 7 or 7.30 p.m., and servants' supper at 9 p.m. The author also includes the following:

> no mention is made of servants' lunchtime. It is usual for servants to have lunch, either bread and cheese or a piece of cake, about eleven o clock; but they should not be allowed to sit down to it as the morning hours are too precious. The cook should see that this meal is expeditiously despatched. Beer (if allowed at all) should not be taken at this lunch-time.[12]

It is a mark of Georgina's changing world view, and the milieu in which she later worked, that she looked back at a midday dinner as part of the past. By the 1970s, when she wrote her memoir, she was thoroughly urbanised: had she been living in many, more rural, parts of the country, she would still have found most people having breakfast, dinner and tea (or breakfast, lunch and tea, with dinner reserved for special occasions).

After this the party got going again, covering another mile or so before reaching Tring station, on the outskirts of Aldbury. It was one of the stations on the

London–Birmingham route, one of the earliest of the UK's railways, built during the first wave of 'railway mania' in 1837–8. Designated a first-class station, it was one of the few at which first-class and mail trains stopped, and its buildings, designed in 1838, were deemed of sufficient architectural merit for the plans to be exhibited at the Royal Academy Exhibition that year. The line itself had been the subject of a great deal of wrangling – Georgina was determined to emphasise the benevolence of local landowners in beautifying towns and helping the locals, suggesting that a 'kind benefactor' was responsible for the station – but the truth was rather murkier. The benefactor in this case was the people of Tring itself, who pushed for the station at Aldbury, rather than Pitstone, another three miles away. Throughout the building of the London–Birmingham line, landowners proved an obstacle. The line was routed away from several large estates, just to get the bill authorising it past their owners, who sat – and voted – in the House of Lords. Others simply asked for so much money to sell the land to the railway company that costs became prohibitive. The then owners of Pendley Manor, the Harcourts, were one such family, refusing to sell their land at Aldbury for the sum offered. The deadlock was only broken when a consortium of tradespeople, led by a local brewer, John Brown, not only raised the extra money but, according to one account, literally chased the offending Harcourt down in a pony and chaise to get him to agree to the sale. They also paid for the aptly named Station Road to get their goods from Tring to the new station. Cannily, Brown also built, next door to the station, the Harcourt Arms, adding it to his existing portfolio of pubs and hotels. By the time Georgina knew it, the Harcourts had left the area, and the building had been renamed the Royal Hotel.

The Tring part of the line was one of those feats of Victorian engineering that still remain impressive today. Because the line was designed with shallow curves and easy gradients, any hills had to be cut through. The Tring, or Cheddington, cutting is one of the largest on any major British railway, and was dug out entirely by hand. Six men died, thirty-seven were injured, and the contractor went bankrupt. Georgina's grandmother Messider recalled travelling through the cut in an open carriage, which was the third-class norm at the time it was built. Given they were renowned for their lack of comfort, she may not have entirely agreed with the contemporary account of the cut as 'one of the most stupendous cuttings to be found in the country ... The contemplation of this vast undertaking fills the mind with wonder and admiration.' The isolation of the area also impressed those who travelled through:

> at intervals are bridges carrying roads across the railway at a fearful height; whilst below all is still, save the occasional footsteps of the policemen on duty, or the distant sounds of an advancing train. The echoes in this place are very distinct, and whilst traversing its extent you seem shut out from all communication with the world, except these invisible mocking birds of your own voice.[13]

Georgina's recollection of the area, as she crossed the railway bridge on foot and headed toward Aldbury, was rather more prosaic: 'we would stop and pick the flowers on the way to make flower posies with dog daisies and harebells, till we got near the church'.

Finally, the family reached the Messiders' home, with Martha in situ, armed with tea and bread and butter and jam. Writing after a lifetime of cooking in other people's kitchens, Georgina's description concentrates on food provision, and she describes a way of living which would not have been out of place a hundred years before.

> She had been making her bread this day. Just by her gate was a sort of a shed and in it was an oven. So, she used to put in a faggot of wood and it would burn itself out. By that time the oven would be hot enough to cook the loaves and sometimes she would put in a rice pudding to start and I guess she would have to put on more faggots. Nothing was too much trouble for her.

Brick beehive ovens, of the sort she describes here, had been around since the Roman era, and remained in use in some areas into the twentieth century. Even some country houses still used them, despite the advent of cast iron ranges and, by the 1860s, gas ovens. (A faggot oven can still be seen in situ in the multi-period kitchen at Petworth, co-existing with gas ovens from the 1920s, and an even later 'Gloworm' solid fuel range.)

The principle was simple: faggots of wood were bundled tightly into the oven and lit. When they burned themselves down, the ash could be raked out, ready for cooking. In practice, it was hard to judge the temperature, and users had various ways to tell if an oven was ready for baking, ranging from the angle of the flames across the roof to putting flour or paper into the oven to see what colour it went. Striking a spark on the oven floor was another common method, and some cooks had particular pieces of brick or stone inside that changed colour when hot. More wood or, in coal-burning areas, coal could be added and lit as required, and in some cases a fire was kept permanently going, usually to one side and sometimes with a separate access door. Bread was cooked when the oven was at its hottest, with other items being added as the oven cooled. Making rice pudding, which takes several hours in a cooling oven, was an ideal way to use the heat, but other stories of such ovens in use around the same time also mention baked potatoes or slow-cook meats put in at the same time as the bread. Normally the oven had a door, but if not, fast-cooking biscuits or rusks could be placed in the doorway to cook and then removed and replaced with drying breadcrumbs or custards, meringues or baked apples.[14] Houses without ovens could in theory take their bread, pies and cakes to the bakers, which, in the case of the Aldbury bakery, was effectively a house with a decent oven and a front room given to selling. If a dwelling had the space, building an outdoor oven like that of the Messiders was a very practical solution.

Georgina recognised the primitive nature of her grandmother's equipment. Most of her food was boiled (or poached, in modern parlance):

Outside her kitchen door was a wall of bricks built
so as to stand a boiler on. She would put a black
boiler on and when boiling she would put in a net
with potatoes in, and also another with cabbage or
another veg. Now, what was in another cloth could
have been a suet pudding, with very little meat as it
was then dear to buy and grandfather's wage was
only 15 shillings a week. She kept chickens and they
found their own food. If anyone killed a pig it was
shared among neighbours. Whereas today it would
be an insult to give anyone a bit of pig's fry, it was
looked upon as a gesture of kindness, and so we
were brought up without luxuries and perhaps a
willingness to eat what we were given.

The interior of the Messider residence doubtless had
open fires, and may have had a basic range, but they
were probably small, and cooking outdoors on a separate boiler like this had the advantage of not super-heating
the house in summer. One-pot cookery of this type was
still happening in some areas (mainly East Anglia) in the
1950s, because it was deeply practical. Besides the cooked
food itself, the boiling liquid could also be used, forming
the basis for gravy, thickened with butter and flour, or
any number of stews or soups. One of the classic com-
binations was to cook dried peas at the same time as
boiling a ham: the salt and flavour from the ham seasoned the peas while cooking, and they were then
puréed, mixed with egg and any further seasonings
wanted, shaped into a pudding, put in a cloth and boiled
for a bit longer. The resulting pease pudding helped eke

out the more expensive ham, being both filling and reasonably nutritious.

This style of living and cooking would have been familiar to the majority of village and small town working-class dwellers. Although grocers, butchers, bakers and general shops were usually present, even in very small communities, their produce cost more than home-made or -grown items, and there were perennial fears about quality. Although a series of parliamentary acts in the 1860s and 1870s had made it illegal to adulterate food, and the quality had improved dramatically, many consumers still distrusted manufactured food, with bread one of the worst offenders. Big firms now habitually advertised based on purity and quality, and the late Victorian era would see a boom in catchily named branded goods, many of which are still going over a hundred years later. Worry over what wasn't included on the label persisted, though, often to the detriment of people's health: tinned meats, which provided a cheap, easily stored alternative to often fly-blown and expensive fresh meat, and which helped to add much-needed protein to poor diets, were derided as unwholesome and unpalatable. One 1874 author felt the need to painstakingly point out that, despite popular opinion, there were definitely no kangaroos and elephants and horses in the tinned Australian meat then entering the country.[15]

The result was that, if they could, people generally produced as much as possible themselves. Martha Messider, in common with much of the rural population, not only made her own bread, but she also gleaned for the wheat or barley she used for it, going out to the fields after the harvest had been taken in to pick up what was left, generally gathering enough for her own family's needs, and sometimes enough to provide for her extended family too.

Most rural dwellings had vegetable gardens, together with fruit trees if there was room, and many kept, as Martha did, chickens and sometimes pigs. Pig-killing day was, as is still the case in some parts of Europe, a big occasion. Travelling butchers often performed the task of slaughter, after which it would be suspended from a frame and cut up. Some cuts, namely hams and bacons, would be preserved through smoking or salting for use throughout the year, while others, especially the offal, needed to be eaten quickly. The pig's fry Georgina mentions consisted of the heart, liver, lights (lungs) and chitterlings (small intestines), and was a quick dish, easy to prepare on killing day, and which, given the size of a pig's innards, could easily supply half a small village. It hardly needed a recipe, but one mid-nineteenth-century author advises cutting the bits into slices, seasoning and flouring them, and frying them

> with some kind of grease in the frying pan. As the pieces are fried, place them on their dish to keep hot before the fire, and when all is done, throw some chopped onions and sage leaves into the pan, to be fried of a light colour; add a very little flour, pepper and salt, a gill of water, and a few drops of vinegar; boil up this gravy, and pour it over the pig's fry.[16]

Further produce would have been gathered from the wider landscape, and the woods and hills around Aldbury were full of plants (and animals) that could be used to swell the family pot. Mary's brother Jack, who worked for the Woods at Toms Hill, but lived with his parents and came home for meals, brought back mushrooms, cycling to and from work on a penny-farthing bicycle.[17]

Country life was hard, and the horses Mark loved and depended on for a living were starting to be replaced by cars. He was at one stage a postillion (riding carriage horses to drive them if there was no coachman, or if there were more than two horses), one of a number of positions that were to gradually disappear as formal, horse-led parades became scarcer. Unlike Mary, who loathed London and found it made her ill, he enjoyed London life, and sometime between 1884 and 1887 he left the Flowers and went to work instead for Sir Stephen (Stephanos) Ralli, a second-generation Greek merchant and one of the very few Victorian millionaires. It didn't work out, for Mary was ill in the smog, and was desperate to move back to the countryside. She may also have been worried about the perils of London life: in February 1886, the West End riots saw mobs of unemployed workers breaking windows and robbing shops in Piccadilly, and there were further clashes between police and protesters in November 1887.

The poor of the East End were already a source of both fascination and repulsion for the middle classes: 'slumming' was a short-lived craze, whereby wealthy men would tour the streets around Brick Lane, sometimes excitingly disguised as tramps, afterwards writing deliberately provocative accounts of their time in the dark underbelly of the capital. These accounts weren't exactly balanced: for example, although they give the impression of an opium den on every corner, all of the tales of opium eating seem to be based on one house, and there's no real evidence there was much beyond that.[18] Genuine, if occasional, violence, and the hyperbole of the media, did lead to fears of social revolution in some quarters, and while the monied classes made the most noise, respectable workers with families were hardly immune to feelings of tension.

London was seen by outsiders as a den of vice, ready to suck up the unwary, and even in upmarket Kensington, around which Georgina's own experiences of London would be centred, it was easy to wander too far and cross into some of the worst streets in the capital. Notting Dale, just west of Notting Hill and just north of North Kensington, was known as an area of 'piggeries and potteries', despite the best efforts of successive campaigners and officials to clear it, at least of the former. Here, twenty people occupied houses designed for one small family, sanitary provision was at its most basic, and life expectancy far below that of much of the rest of London. During the cholera epidemic of 1848, it had fallen to 11 years and 7 months (at birth), compared to 37 in the rest of London. While life expectancy statistics can be overly shocking – they are based on averages, and with infant mortality riding at almost 50 per cent in Notting Dale even in the good times, the total is pulled right down – such figures do give an idea of the conditions in the area. Charles Booth's Poverty Map of the late nineteenth century labels Notting Dale as 'vicious, semi-criminal'.[19]

By 1888, Mark was working as a coachman for a china merchant, Frederick Bower, at West Dean Park in Sussex. The major local landowner was the Duke of Richmond at Goodwood House, and the Goodwood races loomed large in the soundscape of the years Georgina spent at West Dean: 'Goodwood Race Course was nearby and no-one was allowed through our gate to go as it would have been a short cut but we used to go out and pick large yellow buttercups from the stream and listen to the shouting and excitement near the course.'

The estate provided the family with milk and vegetables, which was normal for employees of large houses. Generally, estate workers and tenants could buy skimmed milk from the estate dairy (the cream went to make butter), and excess vegetables were either sold or given away, along with limited amounts of game. Other treats were available, although not for the Youngs. Up above the racecourse was a hillfort called The Trundle, of which Georgina recalled, 'I think it was pigs that used to grub up truffles to eat. If this was true I don't know. Later on in life I learned what they were.' The Bowers seem to have been good employers: they allowed the three Young children to take a shortcut through the pleasure gardens to get to and from school, which they did twice a day, for they returned home for their midday dinner. Perpetually interested in food, the siblings then rushed back to school because 'many [pupils] came from a long way and couldn't go home for their dinner like us so they used to have soup provided from some good people. So we used to hurry back ... to have some of this if there was any left, [much] to the disgust of our parents.'

It was still hard going, with freezing winters and rooms which, while large and airy, were impossible to keep warm. Mary made endless rugs, and the family supplemented their coal with logs gathered from the nearby woods. She also brewed her own beer, a declining practice in the late nineteenth century, and Mark and his co-workers would stay up drinking into the small hours. They also frequented the local pub, where they were sufficiently well known that if Mr Bower rang for one of his staff, a message would go down to it to summon them back. In December 1888, another brother, Archibald (Archie), was born, the only one of Mary's children not to be born at her mother's house in Aldbury. In common with most Victorian children, the siblings were merely told that their mother was unwell and had no idea where this extra baby had come from.

In 1891, the Bower family moved to London, selling West Dean to a wealthy American. The Youngs moved with them, and this time they stayed for at least nine years. Georgina was 9 when they moved, but she would leave home before the family decamped to the countryside again, still working for the Bowers, now at Broomfield Hall in Egham. It was a pivotal period for her, not only because she was old enough to have adventures on her own (or, more often, with Algy), but also because she was finally settled long enough to attend school regularly in one place.

The Bowers lived at 73 Cromwell Road, in Kensington, a substantial seven-storey terrace surrounded by similarly large houses, with various mews and less-well-appointed dwellings in the streets around it. Between 1915 and 1916, Winston and Clementine Churchill lived at number 41, sharing with his brother Jack and his wife Gwendoline ('Goonie'), although Winston escaped to his mother's house in the less nouveaux-riches surrounds of Mayfair as much as possible.

The Youngs lived nearby in Ashburn Mews, running parallel to the railway tracks as they entered Gloucester Road underground station. The end of the road faced Bailey's Hotel, one of the more prestigious London hotels, catering especially to Americans with its 'ascending rooms' (lifts) and 300 bedrooms, with bathrooms on every floor. It was, unusually for the area, red brick, and one (American) guidebook of the time singled it out for its 'cosy, homelike atmosphere, which is enhanced by the rich and substantial surroundings', as well as its bar, fire escapes and sanitary provision.[20] It provided endless hours of people-watching for the Young siblings, with a highlight being the sudden arrival of the Sultan of Johore, Abu Bakar, in May 1895. Bakar was already suffering from severe kidney disease, and contracted pneumonia shortly after his arrival. Gravely ill, he nevertheless received a couple of royal visits, before dying in June.

Georgina and her siblings became known among the residents of the area, including a lady who used to give them farthing buns because she recognised the baby, Archie. Like so many children of their class at that time, they spent a lot of time out and about, either on organised excursions, such as the regular summer trip run by the Sunday School to Petersham Park, or by themselves. Their parents rarely participated in their outings, for Mark worked full-time, and Mary had Archie and the house to look after. She may also have been working part-time as a char, or taking in laundry, and their parents only took them out on bank holidays. However, even in his limited time, Georgina's father had already installed a life-long love of horses in her, taking her along to Hyde Park to watch the parades. Algy and Georgie were also known to the porter at the Royal Albert Hall, who used to let them in to sit in the gods and listen to the organ, and the Albert Memorial was a regular haunt for them, especially after church on a Sunday, when they would slide down the steps and spend any pennies they had in Kensington Gardens.

Spending much of their time around the streets of Kensington by no means meant that the Youngs were street urchins. The mews around Cromwell Road were not the slums of Notting Dale, and Georgina's family was very much part of the respectable working class. Booth categorised Ashburn Mews as being 'fairly comfortable, good ordinary earnings'.[21] Families who fell into this large category had their own codes of behaviour, well removed from the endless, angst-ridden outpourings of middle-class etiquette writers, but equally as rigid. The idea of respectability was paramount, and children were brought up strictly to be honest and clean. Being well-turned-out was hugely important, especially on Sundays – it was exactly the social milieu in which every person had an outfit that was 'Sunday best'. The Youngs were no different:

Dad was very particular how we was dressed, so he used to take us up to Goodge Street [and] Brompton Road to get coats, Maud and I. And my word if we got a spot of dirt on them he was furious. On school-days we had different shoes and they were all cleaned by me on Saturday and put away til Monday for school ... this was the routine of my home, perhaps a bit strict but it carried me all through my life, training others in cleanliness and also honesty and loyalty to our employers.

Punishment for transgressions was swift and often physical, and parents ruled as much by fear as anything else, instilling in their children a respect for authority, and a life of routine: ideal traits for going into the workplace later. There was a strong sense of belonging, which for the Kensington coterie was especially centred around churches: Georgina vividly remembered going back to someone's house with some school friends after church, only to be told that 'you don't go to St Paul's, Onslow Square', and to be turned away. As with most children, Georgina and Algy did not always live up to their parents' expectations, although they were largely successful in keeping most of their murkier adventures secret, covering up for each other as required. When Algy played truant from school and was caned, the two kept quiet. Food had enormous potential for trouble:

One Saturday, we were out with some friends and they took us to a German pastry shop where they used to spend their pocket money on the pastries of the day before, as the shop would be closing for the weekend. We hadn't much money as it was new to us. But they were so rich and full of cream and jam.

They didn't tell their parents about the wonders of cheap pastries until decades later, knowing spending money on frivolities wouldn't go down well. Their father did find out when they swapped their services, buying a bottle of whisky for one of the cooks in the upper-class terraces for lots of cakes, and was unequivocal in his banning them from ever doing it again. It didn't stop them, as a few years later they were buying rum for a lady they'd met in a biscuit shop. Again, cake was the bribe on offer, a kougelhopf, but this time their father went off to the lady responsible to upbraid her. (She told him what lovely children they were, which presumably mollified him, if only a little.)

By this point Georgina was 12 and had left school.[22] However, no sooner had she left than she promptly had to go back for a year, as the school leaving age changed. She was already interested in food, especially the rich, sugary kind, which was scarce at home. Although the diet of the very poor was relatively high in sugar after 1874, when the tax on it plummeted, making skimmed condensed milk, treacle and cheap jam part of the staples of everyday life, slightly more affluent members of the working class were able to spend their money on a more balanced diet. Money wasn't plentiful, Kensington shops were expensive and food was carefully planned, but Georgina's meals growing up contained both meat and vegetables, both of which tended to be rather lacking in the diets of those at the very bottom of society.

She recalled that oranges were always cheap, as was rice and suet, and also remembered her father buying an aitchbone of beef, and their eking it out to the very last morsel. Pastries, bought from shops whether stale at the end of the day or fresh in the morning, were often German, for German bakers were widespread, having fled political turmoil in their homeland in the late 1870s. Street vendors were plentiful: the muffin man of nursery rhyme lore was especially present on Sundays, selling hot muffins to people on the way to and from church, and the winkle man with periwinkles, to be eaten with vinegar by themselves or in a sandwich. Like most people, Georgina's mother shopped widely, knowing where was best value. Even for the middle classes, food provisioning could be problematic: Molly Hughes, a junior barrister's wife in the 1890s, started off shopping at Whiteleys, where everything could be ordered and was delivered. Georgina's family had shopped there occasionally in the late 1880s, before they moved to West Dean. Molly, who bought all her goods there, soon found 'that this easy way of buying had to be paid for by too high prices, so I determined to explore the neighbourhood, buy what I wanted, and bring it home myself'.[23] Unlike Mary Young, she found the whole experience 'fun', and was soon doling out advice to other shoppers as to what they could cook for their husbands to save them from endless cold mutton. Like Mary, she also took to making her own bread, finding it tasted better and was much more economical than buying it from a baker.

For Georgina, 1894 was a year of change. In November her mother was once again 'unwell', and returned to Aldbury to give birth to Evelina, the last of Mary and Mark's five children. In Mary's absence, Mark took the children to the pub, where they gorged themselves on gingerbread and biscuits before coming home on the top of the open top bus with no coats on. Georgina's resulting cold meant she was bedridden and fed a diet of onion gruel and Parrish's food (an iron supplement). She enjoyed school, but was legally able to leave, and she recognised that although 'I loved to read about different things that happened in the Reformation ... that wouldn't get me a living'. She left school when she was 13½, both to help her mother at home and to get a job and bring in some much-needed extra money. She embarked upon this next stage with some trepidation, not sure what she wanted to do but eager to get on and do it. Mark sat her down to impart some advice: be honest, never borrow money as it makes you enemies, and always be on time. Words, as Georgina agreed when she wrote them down eighty years later, a person could live by.

2

The Kitchen Hierarchy

'Eperlans sur Hâtelets à la Méteor', from Georgina Lande-mare's 1930s handwritten recipe book. Smelts are related to trout and salmon, and are eaten whole. The fish are stuffed before being rolled and deep fried and garnished with an orna-mental skewer (known as a hâtelet).

> *Clean some smelts, season them with raw chopped mush-rooms, lemon juice, parsley, oil, then place a boned anchovy filet in the centre of each boned smelt, roll up, fasten with a skewer, egg and crumb, and fry. When cooked put in a silver skewer in place of the other, serve sauce vel[outé].*[1]

In keeping with most of her contemporaries, Georgina started working as soon as she left school. Like most girls entering service, she did so gradually, building up from helping her mother at home to what she describes as simply running errands, but which was working-class shorthand for doing odd bits of work for odd bits of cash. While some, especially in rural areas, were packed off with their trunks to become live-in servants straight away, it was far more common to start off working from home, or to take a short-term position to test the waters.

Mothers played a pivotal role in setting their daughters up for the future: discipline, respectability and a certain level of deference were drilled into Victorian children by both parents, but when the time came to get a job, and to eventually leave home to go into live-in service, it was maternal networks that generally secured a child's first position, and mothers who checked that the position was suitable. There were many cases where mothers (and to a lesser extent fathers) visited their offspring and removed them from potentially abusive or exploitative situations.[2]

At 14, a child was deemed old enough to work, but one of the most striking things about reminiscences from the period is how innocent maids entering service were, not just about sex, but also about life more generally. They learned quickly, however, and by 16, by which time parental oversight had generally stopped, and ability to walk out of a job had been curtailed by the need for a good reference, most had not only worked out how to circumvent overly restrictive rules, but also, as Jean Rennie put it in her memoirs of life as a maid in the 1920s, 'learned to deal with any [boy] who had further ideas'.[3]

Georgina's mother duly organised her daughter's first job away from home, which came through her Sunday School teacher. She was offered a year-long post as a nursemaid, working under a nurse who doubled as a governess, and helping to look after five young children. In a section of the memoir heavily scored through,

Georgina wrote that she was 'overjoyed', changing this in a later version of the same story to simply say, 'of course I said yes'. She packed her clothing and went to work for Stephen Gwynn and his wife (and cousin), Mary Louisa. At the time Gwynn, who later became an MP in Ireland, supporting the nationalist cause as the debate over Home Rule raged, was a writer, having just returned from teaching Classics in France.[4] The family was probably the least socially elevated that Georgina would work for in her long career, but even so, decidedly better-off than the vast majority of servant-keeping households. Around 40 per cent of servants in late Victorian Britain worked in households that employed only one or two servants: only one in five worked in households employing more than three.[5] Career servants aimed at employment only within this top 20 per cent, and Georgina never sank below it.

The Gwynns had three boys and two girls, aged between 6 and 1. In addition to Georgina, there was the nurse-governess, Frances McGuire, presumably recruited through Stephen's family in Ireland, where she was born, along with a cook and one housemaid. In 1901, the latter two positions were occupied by two sisters, Emily and Mary-Anne Norman, from Devon. Country girls were reputed to be more malleable and harder-working than their urban counterparts, as well as often being cheaper – and it was also harder for them to run away, as the cost of a train fare home could be prohibitive. It was unlikely in this case they'd need to: Georgina found it to be a pleasant atmosphere, writing that, 'I liked Mr Gwynn very much, also the nurse, Miss

Maguire [sic].' Nurseries were set apart from the rest of the household, under the charge of a nurse, or nanny. As with the Gwynns, in modest households, nurse, nanny and governess could be one and the same person, and although the boys would have been sent to boarding school as soon as possible, girls tended to be educated at home for fear of corruption (and for cost purposes).

The late Victorian era was one of increasing worry over children, especially among the middle classes, and the nurse was a key figure in any household – usually the second servant to be taken on, after a maid-of-all-work (also known as a slavvy, which is entirely indicative of their very low status in the servant hierarchy). Prevailing wisdom held that children should live highly prescribed lives, fed only on bland foods for fear of exciting animal instincts (spicy food would clearly lead to sexual incontinence later in life), and with plenty of fresh air and exercise. There was a great deal of tension around the employment of nurses: on the one hand they were servants, and expected to carry out tasks, including changing nappies and lugging bath water upstairs, which no one who considered themselves genteel would do; but on the other, they were the most important influence on a young child's life, and came into regular contact with the parents.

The ideal was a well-trained professional of at least an upper-working-class background, but they were hard to come by. *Bow-Bells*, a self-proclaimed 'magazine of general literature for family reading', tried its best to encourage gentlewomen of reduced circumstance to consider employment in the nursery, with stories such as

'The Nurse-Maid's Place', wherein the young heroine, having been brought up in a nice middle-class way, but having unfortunately lost the money she was to inherit, goes to look for a job. Acknowledging the fall in status ('perhaps that might do, if I can swallow my pride'), she takes on a job looking after a motherless boy, bonds with him, and (inevitably) ends up marrying the widower. Given that he is described in less-than-glowing terms as 'weak and womanish', and that the story ends with the now married nursemaid thinking that 'I love both my babies – the young one and the old one – dearly', it's hardly the most persuasive piece of literature, and it's hard to imagine it convinced many ladies of genteel birth to try nursemaiding.[6]

In 1892, the Norland Institute was founded to train nannies and allow them to take advantage of that training, in combination with the desperation of the middle classes and gentry to find the right person to look after their children, to raise their status significantly. Norland nannies ate apart from the other servants, wore smart uniforms that reflected their gentlewomanly status and certainly did not carry out the various extra, housemaid-shaped duties that Georgina and Frances McGuire almost certainly did. The Gwynns would probably not have been able to afford a Norland nanny: a well-brought-up and eager young girl such as Georgina, and a slightly more experienced woman like Frances would have been paid around £8–10 p.a. and £15–18 p.a. respectively, and Norland ladies started at about £50 p.a. – and needed their own room and rather better food than would necessarily have been expected further below stairs.[7]

Working for the Gwynns as a nursemaid was an ideal starting job for Georgina, who was well used to looking after younger siblings and, as the first of them to go out to work, had a sense of responsibility toward her family that was highly developed. The bulk of her wages would have gone into the family pot, and she was very conscious of the importance of this in relieving some of the burden on her mother. The job also gave Georgina her first chance to travel beyond the confines of London, West Dean and Berkshire, and to meet others (mainly her employers) with experience of living across the world.

As a servant she was, to some extent, what Eric Horne, a country house butler who wrote his memoir of life in service in the 1920s, called 'live furniture'. Mrs Gwynn sent her to stay with her sister Jane in Bath, taking with her the baby, Madeline. Georgina later said that Jane's husband, Herbert Dumergue, was French; he wasn't, despite his name. Quite possibly she never met him.[8] Another sister, Florence, herself born in Switzerland, was married to an officer in the Indian army. The families shuttled between the less fashionable bits of Kensington (Brompton and Chelsea, essentially), Bath, where the sisters had been brought up, and the seaside resorts of southern England.

Following Georgina's stay in Bath, 'Mrs G took a house on the south coast' (near Lancing, just outside Worthing), 'this was a level crossing and it thrilled me to see the trains go through. We were at the sea every day and we were so pleased.' Mild drama and a life lesson followed, however: 'Neither Miss Maguire nor I could swim and one afternoon Miss Maguire got out of her depth and I went to her help, hence the result that someone spotted us and came to our rescue and then I made up my mind to swim and I have never looked back.' It was a typical response from Georgina, to spot a problem, find a solution, and thereafter determinedly pursue it. She never stopped swimming, and in later life she recounted swimming in the Serpentine, well before the opening of the Lido enabled women to officially swim in the waters of Hyde Park.[9]

Like many young servants away from home for the first time, Georgina missed her family. Unlike most employers, however, the Gwynns went out of their way to help alleviate this:

> Mrs Gwynn asked me one day 'are you happy away from your home?' I said I missed my mother and sister and brother. I said my mother has never seen the sea. So she said she'll see what she can do about that. Within a week my mother came down with Archie and he was quite a small boy toddling along.

Even on her low wages, Georgina managed to buy her mother 'a sort of shrimp broach, which she kept for many years'. She'd bought gifts for her mother on school trips and church outings as a child, but this was the first present from her own earnings: a pivotal moment as she prepared to leave home for good.

Eventually, the job ended. The Gwynns returned briefly to Ireland, and Georgina went back to Kensington. In 1898, Mark Young's employer, Frederick Bower, moved to one of the most upmarket streets in London, Kensington Palace Gardens. His wealth was steadily increasing, and he was by now worth nearly half a million pounds. Mark, Mary and their children took up new lodgings, as usual in the attached mews above the stables. Although they could be on separate roads at a short distance from the house they pertained to, mews houses were generally sited at the back of grand terraces, and consisted of only two or three storeys (one of which was a basement), versus the six or so of the main house. They were built around a ground-floor coach house and stable, with living quarters provided for the coachman above. They had their own entrances, off the road known simply as the 'mews', but in some cases connected with the service areas in the basement of the main house, and Georgina would have been very aware of the comings and goings of other staff around her.

Georgina, newly conscious of money, work and the future, was very aware that she was the only one of the five siblings who could, at that stage, earn their own living. The Bowers were planning a move to the country, which would mean the Youngs going too, unless Mark could find another position – but working for the Bowers evidently suited him, given he'd been in their service now for over a decade. Mark in his turn was worried about the rise of motor vehicles, and the slow but steady decline in his own trade. Londoners could easily call upon cabs, and the number of private individuals who maintained extensive stables, coaches and coachmen was declining. His eldest daughter, meanwhile, was thinking hard about what she wanted to do next. In the time she had known him, her father had only worked for the upper echelons of society – all new money, but lots of it, and with very little corner cutting, which was at times a characteristic of the more prestigiously titled (but sometimes poorer) aristocrats, trying to maintain appearances on a shoestring.

One man who would have loved the Bowers' lifestyle was Winston Churchill, then aged 24, and serving as an officer in the army in India. He and his mother Jennie (his father had died in 1895) were fairly typical of the lower ranks of the aristocracy, mixing with, and related to, others with more money and lavish lifestyles, desperate to have the same, yet without quite the income to manage it. They complained constantly and bitterly of their terrible poverty, Churchill writing in 1898 that 'the pinch of the whole matter is that we are damned poor'.[10] It was, of course, relative. His mother's income was around £5,000 a year, though she claimed it was half of that, easily enough to employ at least six servants according to guides of the time. Winston himself, meanwhile, just a few years later, was spending (not necessarily earning) around £1,400 p.a., nominally enough to keep three to four servants but, as was a determined pattern with him, he spent just a little bit more than he had, keeping two expensive manservants, and three somewhat cheaper women.[11] However, the working lives of those servants would, in all likelihood, be harder and worse paid, and were definitely much less prestigious – especially when it came to moving on – than those who worked for someone like Frederick Bower.

Georgina had an interview for a position in Queens-gate, either as a housemaid or another nursemaid, and, in a mark of how much thought she was putting into her career, rejected it: 'after seeing the Lady I said I am not going there to carry bath water up all those stairs'. Instead, she fell back on the usual staple of those between jobs, and did washing, presumably as a day char. Even many working-class households employed girls, usually young ones, as they were cheap, to help out with the washing: servants were by no means just the province of the firmly middle class, and charring while living at home was a very common way of earning money without fully entering the realm of domestic service. The whole family was on the lookout for opportunities for Georgina, conscious that she needed to get a move on. She considered doing a course at night school, but instead her mother's sister, Lizzie, offered to pay the transport costs to get her up to Brough, where she was living, and give her a holiday.

Lizzie had also gone into service, as a lady's maid. More prestigious than many servants, lady's maids were the personal servants of the lady (or, in most families, ladies) of the house. In large households, they were among the most senior staff, and because of their constant proximity to their employer, regarded with some suspicion by many of the others. At this level, they were sometimes French, usually of upper-working-class birth, and reasonably well-educated. Rosina Harrison, a lady's maid in the 1920s, chose that position because she wanted to travel, and was well aware that being the personal attendant to a very wealthy woman would enable her to do just that.[12] At the gentry level, where Aunt Lizzie was employed, such opportunities were rarer, and the lady's maid much more integrated into the household. Only very large establishments could divide their staff into upper and lower, separating them for meals and enforcing rigid hierarchies, and many lady's maids in smaller households doubled – as did pretty much all the staff – as housemaids, lighting fires, carrying bath water and answering doors just as much as darning lacy undergarments, writing letters and helping to dress their employers and their daughters (and female guests).

In 1894, Lizzie had married Albert Bell, an electrician who, by the time Georgina stayed with them a few years later, was working as an electrical engineer at Welton Hall, near Brough in Yorkshire. Lizzie gave her age at marriage as 29, knocking two years off her actual age, following it up in 1901 by losing another year. She was probably not consciously lying – it was still not uncommon for working-class children to grow up not being sure of their exact birth year. Albert had been born in 1872, and was nearly a decade her junior. He was a keen cricketer, and Georgina tells a story of his having been awarded twelve silver teaspoons and some sugar tongs by the cricket club. Dividing the spoons between them, his two sons waited until his back was turned and then cut the tongs in half and took one arm each.

The stay in Brough was instrumental for Georgina: the excuse that she needed a holiday was simply to get her in place for a good talking to. Whether it was felt that she was shirking her duties toward her family, or just that she needed help in deciding what to do next,

Lizzie and Mary had been colluding. Georgina's recollections do not, of course, hint that they may have been becoming exasperated with her continued lack of proper employment, but at some point during the holiday, Aunt Lizzie had a stern conversation with her. They discussed various options, and Georgina's interest in food must have come up. Her mother had been a kitchen maid, and service remained the most obvious route. Eventually, a vague idea of hereditary talent won out: 'my aunt was a very good baker and my mother was the same, so after a good talk I thought I might like cooking which involved a lot of hard work'. She returned to London, network of family and friends primed, ready to enter the kitchen.

Georgina's first cookery post was in Kensington Palace Gardens, doubtless gained through word of mouth among the servants – or from the Bowers themselves, and it was a characteristically large establishment: under pressure Georgina may have been, but she still managed to start as she meant to go on, avoiding households with less than six servants, roughly equating to at least £2,000 household income a year.[13] She was taken on as a scullery maid, the lowest of the ranks of kitchen staff (though still a fair step above the despised slavvys, or maids-of-all-work). She was interviewed, as was usual in larger households, by the housekeeper, who remarked that she was very young, but would take her, 'if I would do as I was told and not answer back'.

She was 'no.6' in the kitchen, with a cook and four maids above her, and probably around fourteen servants in total – according to *Cornhill Magazine* something that was achievable only if one had a yearly income of at least £10,000 p.a. Ideal guides can be misleading, however: before Randolph Churchill, Winston's father, died, he and Jennie employed around eight indoor servants plus at least a couple of coachmen or grooms on about £3,200 a year (though, like their son, they always spent more than they had).[14] They only had two in the kitchen though: six meant a very prestigious household indeed. At this level, scullery maids were generally at least 17 or 18 years old, and came with experience. Georgina must have come highly recommended, and acquitted herself well at her interview, for she was only 15, and hadn't worked in a kitchen before.[15]

The final paragraph that survives from her memoir gave the basics: 'Now I start my track of life. I started on ten pound a year, payable every quarter, two coarse aprons to clean the copper saucepans in.' She was up at 5 a.m., and in bed at 10 p.m. Her duties were those of all scullery maids: peeling and prepping vegetables, gutting, plucking and skinning game, washing up kitchen equipment (the dishes used by the family would have been cleaned elsewhere, as they were more delicate) and cleaning the large, copper batterie de cuisine, which all households of such standing possessed. Her final line contains a pride in a job well done that is reflected in other servant memoirs, even those written by maids who looked back with real anger: 'Although it was hard I liked it, and more so I liked to see my copper pans looking nice, and to see and to know all the uses of the small moulds. Today all that is no longer used.'

Copper was the standard material used for pans in high-end cooking, as it was conductive, as well as glorious when polished up. Pans were lined with tin, which needed to be regularly checked for signs of wear and tear, for there was a small risk of verdigris poisoning if acidic foods were left for too long in them. By the end of the nineteenth century there were pans for everything, as the second industrial revolution of the 1870s onwards had resulted in the ability to mass-manufacture copper goods as well as so many other items. The aspiring hostess could invest in a bewildering quantity of different moulds, to be used for everything it was possible to shape. There were moulds for meat mousses, vegetable purées, blancmanges both savoury and sweet, jellies, pies, puddings, ice creams, rice borders, fruit charlottes, cakes, biscuits and aspics. Foods were routinely piped or glazed, or threaded carefully onto skewers for cooking, to be replaced with nice, silver skewers, for serving. This was the ultimate era for food which no longer looked anything like its natural form.

She does not mention, and presumably escaped, one of the profound indignities visited upon servants, which was to be known by a different name, either because someone with the same Christian name was on the staff already, or because their own was deemed too elevated for a servant. Florence Wadlow, who worked in Kensington in 1929, found both a problem. She couldn't be called Florence, because that was the parlourmaid's name, so

they asked me what my second name was, and when I said 'Georgina' – well I couldn't be called Georgina. That was far too big a mouthful, and too smart really, for just a kitchen maid. So they called me 'Ena' and that took a bit of getting used to.[16]

Fortunately, Georgina Young's employers were rather more relaxed.

Kitchens in houses with staff catered for far more than just the family meals. Although dinner tends to be given the most emphasis in depictions of past dining, it was one among a series of meals that marked the passing of the day. If the establishment was big enough to divide servants into senior and junior, as was probably the case here, the cook could well be expected to produce four meals for the family, four for the servants, four for the upper servants, and any packed lunches for trips away required. They might also be called upon to make food for the nursery, although many nursery maids cooked food for their charges themselves.

Kitchen routine was remarkably similar from house to house. Margaret Thomas, a kitchen maid in Portman Square, described how

for news of what was to be cooked I was told I must read the slate. This had been 'passed' by the Lady in the morning: it was always written in French, so I spent most of my afternoons, until I got a working knowledge of the language, studying the cookery book, which gave the names of each dish in French as well as English.[17]

Primers were available, aimed more at mistresses with a rusty command of culinary French than their maids, but useful for both, which gave lists of dishes in French and English, and advised on compiling ideal menus in suitably elevated language. French was regarded as sophisticated and elegant, and French food the ultimate in fashionable cuisine. There was very little specific training, and maids who wished to advance had to watch, copy and learn. Jean Rennie, another London scullery maid in the early twentieth century, commented, 'I watched Chef very closely at every opportunity. Mrs Preston [a previous cook] had warned me, wherever I went ... she said everyone had their different ways, and my best way was to watch the different methods as I went on and pick the best of them for myself. So I did.'[18]

Cooks varied as much as the girls who worked under them. Some shared their knowledge, training their maids and correcting their mistakes, while others sent them from the room at pivotal moments so that their underlings couldn't usurp them. Many kept handwritten books of their recipes (some houses also had their own recipe books, which stayed at the house regardless of the cook). Nancy Jackman, another 1920s cook, was told in her first position that 'the cook's bible is her own private recipe book. Always remember that.'[19] Georgina's recipe book still survives, though the current iteration is not the original, for she gathered her recipes together and copied them out uniformly years later, by which time they were honed and perfected, as well as changed to suit an era that by then had seen a world war and was only just emerging from a worldwide economic depression.

Most young maids did not stay long in their first job. Scullery maids in particular were understandably eager to move on from being the first up, taking the other maids and the cook their cup of tea, keeping temperamental boilers and ranges alight and wrecking their hands with hot water, ice water, salted iced water (from ice cream), blood, guts, gore and the skin-blistering mixture of salt, sand and lemon used to get all that copper to gleam. The work was extremely physical, with certain tasks both repetitive and demanding – Edwardian food involved a phenomenal amount of sieving, for example, and while vegetables are easy to push through a drum sieve, puréeing rabbit in this way is decidedly more challenging. Margaret Powell, working in an eight-servant household in Hove between the wars, commented on making beef cake:

> the raw beef, generally a fillet, had to go through the mincer. This wasn't easy. But then I had to get it through a wire sieve, still raw, so you can imagine how long this took. I thought it was impossible when I first tried, but I found I could do it if I kept on long enough.[20]

Although middle-class writings of the time are full of concern over 'the servant problem', servants were still plentiful, cheap and easy to obtain, and, although technological advances had been made that would have made life below stairs considerably easier, employers were very slow to adopt things like gas (or even electric) ovens, electric whisks, food blenders and fridges. They were costly, didn't always work very well, and there was still a level of pride and patriotism attached to, for example, a spit-roast pheasant. The more staff, the fewer shortcuts: the royal kitchens didn't even buy baking powder until the very end of the nineteenth century, and jelly was still made by boiling down calves' feet, despite the ready availability of packet gelatine.[21] Scullery maids also sometimes carried out certain tasks that in other houses were the province of the housemaids: scrubbing the front steps (before breakfast, so that the family would never risk seeing a maid at work), shining shoes and, in Georgina's case, making up pull-down beds in the pantry for the other maids. Naturally, all the deep-cleaning work in the kitchen and associated areas also fell to the scullery maid, and they rapidly became adept at scrubbing stone floors, sanding and soaping wooden tables, black-leading ironwork on ranges and ovens and keeping storerooms scrupulously clean. Dressers were emptied and scrubbed on a weekly or bi-monthly basis, stores had to be checked, coal brought from the coal store and soot scraped out of the pipes and surrounds of the range.

Even fairly simple-seeming dishes required physical labour in the preparation. If ice cream, a standard late Victorian dessert dish, was being made, ice would be ordered in and delivered in large blocks. Bigger houses kept the delightfully named odd-men or odd-boys, who did a lot of the heavy work, and could be called upon to smash up the blocks for use, but in smaller establishments, such as Georgina's, that task once more fell to the scullery maid. She'd smash the ice, load the ice pail, add the salt and, under close supervision, turn the handle of the ice churn until the mix was frozen and could be pressed into a mould. The mould then sat in an ice cave, the equivalent of the modern freezer, a wooden chest with zinc- or lead-lined cupboards within it, and which itself needed to be loaded with yet more crushed ice and salt, and which then needed draining and cleaning after use.

After no more than two years, Georgina had learned enough, and was able to obtain a good enough reference, to move on. By 1901, she was working for Edward Dunbar Kilburn, co-owner of Schoene, Kilburn & Co., which was one of the most important firms in British India. It had started as a straight import/export business, diversifying into insurance, tea, navigation, electricity and a number of other areas. Kilburn was significant enough that he'd been offered (and turned down) a seat on the Viceroy's council, and, although he was in his late 70s by the time Georgina came to work for him, he remained well connected in the City.[22] He was, again, nouveaux-riches, a man who had made his money recently, and plenty of it, but who did not possess the titled antecedents or ingrained habits of the landed aristocracy.

Kilburn was mainly resident at 19 Gloucester Square, a late Georgian development of imposing terraces, with the inevitable mews behind, and a private garden for residents of the square in front. (Winston Churchill later bought a house in Sussex Square, the next square down. It was a good part of London.) Kilburn also owned Chancellor House in Tunbridge Wells, a large mansion

set back off Mount Ephraim in one of the most desirable areas of the town. Two adult daughters still lived
with him, along with his wife, Annie (or Anna). According to the census, he employed seven indoor servants: a
footman (who probably doubled as his valet), three
housemaids, a lady's maid, cook and Georgina, listed as
a 19-year-old kitchen maid, at the bottom of the list. The
cook, Mary Mitchell, was 33 and from Gloucestershire,
and the lower housemaid, May Soughter, was from
Lancing, scene of Georgina's happy seaside adventures
with the Gwynns a few years before. She was the same
age as Georgina, on a slightly different track, but working
her way up as steadily within her field as Georgina was
in the kitchen. Outside this, there was at least one coachman in the mews behind (then Devenport Mews, now
Radnor Mews).

The kitchen maid position was, on paper, a promotion, but since there probably wasn't a separate scullery
maid, Georgina's role would have remained similar. She
may well have benefitted from a man or day girl to do
the 'rough' work, and she would certainly have been not
only able, but encouraged, to play a more active role in
cooking. With two staff in the kitchen, the norm was for
the kitchen maid to have charge of the servants' food
completely, which meant making a great deal of plain,
but plentiful, economical dishes. London cooks rarely
baked their own bread, so breakfast, which would have
consisted of toast and preserves and probably porridge,
was hardly onerous, but servants' dinner, around midday,
was regarded as good training for a maid. Servants were
renowned for being ready complainers when it came to

their food, and could be just as demanding as the family who employed them.

Classic late Victorian and early Edwardian servants' fare was simply cooked meat, generally roasted or poached, with lots of potatoes and seasonal vegetables. Stews, steamed meat puddings and cheap fish such as herring or cod were savoury alternatives. Two courses were served, and the sweet was almost always a pudding, very occasionally a fruit pie if fruit was plentiful. The British standards of macaroni pudding, tapioca pudding, sago pudding, rice pudding and blancmange came into their own here, served with stewed fruit or preserves. They were cheap, wholesome and provided lots of calories for very little cost or effort – and, while monotonous after a while, they were, if well made, tasty enough for the discerning below-stairs palate.

Tea, later in the afternoon, was yet more toast and cake, generally fruit cake, with supper normally of bread and cheese. Beer was still sometimes consumed, especially by the menservants (or wine by butlers and other upper servants), but the ubiquitous drink was tea, along, of course, with water, which for employers had the massive advantage of being free. All the meals were supplemented with pickings from the family meals, although where leftovers ('cold meats') could be upcycled, they were. Cold roast meat could easily become rissoles, hashes or patties, or be pounded and potted to make sandwich fillings. Bones went for stock. Small amounts of uneaten food, however, were kept back, and maids tell stories variously of cupboards or buckets full of chicken legs and slices of pie, dainty cakes and uneaten stuffing balls, all regarded as the servants' prerogative, either for supper or, depending on the household, simple snacking throughout the day.

Number 19 Gloucester Square was a typical upmarket London terrace.[23] It had four main storeys, plus an attic floor for nurseries and servant bedrooms, and a basement that extended the full depth of the house, right out as far as the mews at the back. The standard layout was repeated across London, as well as in cities such as Hove, Bath, York, Norwich and Edinburgh, which had a preponderance of late Georgian and early Victorian housing. At the front, set into the pavement, was a coal hole (the distinctive, round, iron covers that are still found on many streets today), which emptied directly into a coal cellar set under the pavement itself and opened out onto a small 'area' or sunken courtyard between the house and the street, and which was accessed via steps set in iron railings. The area sometimes also held a beer cellar. Opening off the area within the house itself was a corridor leading to the service areas – literally, in this case, 'below stairs'. The well-lit front-facing rooms were the most prestigious (and visible, at least with a bit of effort, from the street), so were allocated for butlers and housekeepers, where kept. There were also china closets, linen closets, silver rooms and facilities for footmen and valets to carry out jobs such as brushing outer clothes, ironing newspapers (it stopped print coming off on genteel hands), cleaning plate and decanting wines.

Next came the servants' hall, usually a fairly small room with a grandiose title borrowed from larger establishments and country houses. It was used not just for eating, but as an all-purpose room in which any leisure time (rare) could be spent reading, darning or writing letters. In one of the basements beneath Brunswick Square in Hove the full set-up survives, complete with cupboards to hold servants' outer garments and storage for dining items. Beyond this, and providing light for the servants' hall, was usually another small area, which indicated the back of the main house upstairs. In most cases, toilet facilities were somewhere here, fairly basic, but by this point flushing.

Depending on the house, the main corridor usually continued past this second area, leading to the kitchens, which were strictly demarcated from the rest of the house: cooks were equal in status to (or just below) housekeepers, and regarded their demesne as sacred to them. It would have been double-height for ventilation, with daylight from a window onto the area as well as from above, with a clerestory window or top-light sitting like a greenhouse on top of the roof. The layout was absolutely standard: range on one wall, dresser on another, low sideboard with cupboards under the window, table in the middle. Although gas ranges were being fitted to new-build villas from the mid-century, many houses, such as Gloucester Square, which pre-dated gas ovens, retained early Victorian fixtures and fittings.

Central to the cooking facilities in such houses would have been a coal-fired cooking range, an enormous lump of cast iron with a central fire and ovens to either side. Roasting ovens were heated from the top, baking or pastry ovens from below, via a system of flues and pipes that carried the heat (and soot, hence the endless cleaning). Boiling and stewing was done on top, with the hottest spot being above the fire itself (there was a series of rings to lift off to expose the fire itself, and increase the heat). Cooks quickly got to know the top of their range, and cookery books of the time carry instructions to move pots to the back or sides of the range, expecting the reader to know that this means to a cooler spot. There might be an additional oven, boiler or, in the luckiest of kitchens, gas hobs as well, or the by-now increasingly old-fashioned coal-fired roasting range, with built-in smoke jack, driven by the draw from the fire, which turned a fan up the chimney, connected to a set of cogs and pulleys to turn a spit or series of spits. A door at one side of the kitchen opened onto a separate scullery lit only with 'borrowed light' from the kitchen itself, and fitted out with sinks, cupboards and a small fire for boiling water (or, even better, an actual water boiler). Larders, lined with marble or slate for meat and fish, or with wooden containers and shelves for dry goods, opened either out of the kitchen or were on the corridor just outside. There might then be a final area with a water pump, drainage and access to the back of the mews via steps that led to street level, where the stables and coach house were situated.

Basement service areas were very enclosed spaces, cut off from the rest of the house, and even from much daylight. Gas lighting was the norm, and some houses had electricity, but it wasn't exactly brilliant. Upstairs, candles remained in use, preferred to gas or electricity for reasons of tradition, cost and habit (upstairs chamber pots remained in use well into the mid-twentieth century, for much the same reason – plus, no lady wished to be seen popping into the water closet when she could simply float to her dressing room where no one knew what she was up to – and there were always servants on hand to empty them). Advice manuals of the time emphasised that giving servants access to too many nice things was not only unnecessary, but unfair, for they would not be used to them, and basements were habitually painted in off-beige ('drab'), and bedrooms in the same, with oilcloth or linoleum on the floor.[24] It was rare for kitchen staff to see the upstairs rooms: even if they had bedrooms in the attic, they were accessed by a back stairs in houses of this level. That said, many of the kitchen maids who recounted their lives in later years recalled being invited up to the dining room to see it laid out for special dinner parties, with white linen cloths, oodles of flowers, soft candlelight and highly polished silverware. It left a lasting impression.

The dinners given at this level of society were substantial, showy and involved several days of preparation. When guests were expected, which could be several times a week, the standard and number of dishes increased even more. Late Victorian and Edwardian food had reached a point of extreme elaboration, which, at its apogee, was a triumph of style over substance. The food could be – and sometimes was – delicious as well, but cookery books of the time, inevitably aimed at the newly minted middle classes and gentry, and highly aspirational, are often mind-boggling in the level of intricacy they require.

There were definite demarcations within the servant-employing classes, and it's hard to generalise about a household's diet based on recipe books that carry no guarantee that they were cooked from – or that if they were, that all of the recipes found equal favour. The traditional landed aristocracy favoured French cooks, if possible, cooking strictly French dishes, without the taint of English fashions, and in some cases, they still maintained a version of the old, multi-dish serving style, à la Française, wherein a number of dishes were presented simultaneously. They certainly did not reject culinary innovation, and the expense of purchasing and maintaining a top-notch set of copper moulds was an excellent way to display wealth when the results reached the table, but they integrated older food traditions with the new. There was something rather militant about keeping a coal-fired roasting range in good order and knowing that everything on the table was sourced from the estate – and was served in a style that did not disguise, but enhanced, the ingredients.

Sybil Lubbock, a grandchild of the earl of Harewood, wrote in horror from the 1930s about the earl's dinner conversation, asking 'what sheep will this be? to the butler, who could promptly respond with the age of the animal and the flock from which it came'. She 'hated to hear this sort of talk; if mutton had to be consumed I did not want to associate it with a sheep that had recently been alive'.[25] Georgina's employers, urban, monied and modern, were more likely to err toward Sybil's view than that of her grandfather. Cooks, as mentioned above, had their own books, containing recipes gleaned from books, from other cooks, from journals or magazines, from their employers and from their own heads. Every cook had to produce food that catered to their employer's tastes as well, altering ingredients or seasonings to suit, which inevitably meant changing printed recipes as they went along.

Books do give a flavour of the time, however, and, together with anecdotal evidence, it's possible to build up an idea of the style to which Edward Kilburn and his family would have been accustomed. They were, firstly, new money, and would have adopted the sequential dining style known as à la Russe. At least seven courses would have been served, plus dessert (seventeen courses was the norm at Blenheim, but that was excessive, even at the time).[26] The courses were rigid: hors d'oeuvres, soup, fish, entrées, joint with vegetables, sweets, savouries (and/or cheese) and dessert.[27] The fancier dishes, those that required the most time, equipment and sieving, were the savoury entrées and the sweets (known in some cases as sweet entremets, for the French, as ever, sounded just that little bit better bred). Well-established families, especially those with titles, tended to eat in a more old-fashioned, and often slightly plainer, way, with greater emphasis on roast meats, estate produce and silverware, and, as ever, older employers often favoured the food they had grown up with.

Having spent a large part of his life in India, Kilburn may well have developed a taste for the foods of the Raj, and the Anglo-Indian cooking style involving curries made with cucumber and apples, and kedgeree made with fresh fish and eggs, rather than the simpler lentil and rice dish that lay at its roots. The British in India rarely ate actual Indian food, but the hybrid cuisine that developed as a result of returning officials, merchants and soldiers did help to make Indian-ish food ubiquitous on British tables. Georgina and Mary Mitchell would have been expected to turn their hands to Anglo-Indian dishes, English classics, French food and a category of cookery that was in many ways undefinable, but which summed up the era: recherché cuisine.

Recherché dishes were the most elaborate and sophisticated things a kitchen could produce. The term originally simply applied to recipes felt to be rare or particularly interesting – in practice it came to be applied to anything modern, and therefore often had a decided whiff of new money about it (new money with exquisite taste, and a desire to eat French food, anyway). Those authors who were most enthusiastic about it were those who assumed their readers were working in a modern, well-equipped kitchen. As the term spread down from essentially professional books to those that aimed at the aspirational mistress with her trained-on-the-job English cook, other elements crept in, including a love of food colouring and a well-made aspic.

Those intricate little moulds, which Georgina so loved, were indispensable here, for food tended to be puréed, moulded, jellied and decorated to the extent that it was impossible to tell what it had once been. This was about control of nature, and woe betide the family who served, for example, a plain boiled tongue, when they could serve a tongue that had been boiled, minced, sieved, mixed with cream, aspic, cayenne and red food dye and used to mask a purée of veal, foie gras, truffles and egg, pressed into a tongue mould and steamed, before the lot was covered with aspic, dyed red and given a rice border, and a suitably ornamented hâtelet skewer was pushed through the whole.[28]

Agnes Marshall, who was responsible for that particular recipe, was a bestselling author who also ran a cookery school on Mortimer Street, catering both to maids and mistresses, and held a series of patents for kitchen equipment (including an ice cream maker that froze ice cream in three minutes but was made of zinc, so would have the unfortunate side effect of slowly poisoning the consumer). Marshall's recipe books, containing recipes devised by herself rather than plagiarised from others (relatively unusual at the time), were very popular, and she was one of the most iconic culinary figures of the age. The books were illustrated with line drawings of many of the dishes, and in layout and style were close to books written by leading male chefs, such as Charles Elmé Francatelli, briefly cook to Queen Victoria and careful never to let any potential reader forget it, and Alexis Soyer, leading light at the Reform Club and probably the most celebrated chef of the mid-Victorian period. They screamed professional cook, firmly moving away from the domesticity promoted by Isabella Beeton and her predecessors, whose books were underlain with the understanding that their readers, while employing servants, might very well also be cooking themselves.

Marshall's audience definitely employed (or were themselves) cooks and, while they were almost certainly

female, she, and they, were part of a growing movement
to promote women as chefs, and not merely substitutes
for more expensive and apparently more talented men.
The advice she gives in the back of the book on putting
together the various courses is brisk and pointed, and
ever-so-slightly fashionably francophile:

> It may be roughly set down as a first principle of
> sweet-serving that the last touch of a dinner should
> be at one both light and elegant. Like the final
> touches of a toilet, they should simply be relied
> upon to give that finish which crowns the whole
> effect. The aim of a properly constructed sweet is to
> convey to the palate the greatest possible amount of
> pleasure and taste, whilst it is in no way suggestive
> of nourishment or solidity, from which it will be
> seen that the average English tart is a fair example
> of precisely what a sweet should not be.[29]

However, her recipes belie her efforts: implicit within
them is the sense that the user is working in a slightly
understaffed kitchen, and that while there may be a
kitchen maid on hand to pound, purée, sieve and carefully cut out vegetable pieces with a shaped cutter, there
is also a need to use packets of ingredients, shortcuts
and patent ingredients (all, of course, available from
Marshall's School of Cookery and Show Rooms). As a
contrast, Garrett's *Encyclopaedia of Practical Cookery* (it's
not, very), which runs to eight volumes, predominantly
contains recipes where every stage is done from scratch.
It is much more suited to kitchens with at least three

staff members, with inclinations involving taste as well as looks.

Even more alien to modern tastes than some of Marshall's suggestions are those contained in the eye-wateringly nouveaux-riches *À La Mode Cookery*, by Harriet de Salis. The pictures are particularly terrifying, for nearly all of them involve specialist moulds and, since the plates are in colour, the full spectacle leaps out. A good example is 'Jugged Hare à La Surprise', which is a sweet comprising Genoese sponge hares (the recipe blithely starts 'butter some hare-moulds'), which are placed in baked almond paste jugs, over-piped in pink and filled with strawberry jam. The hare's eyes are made from dried cherries.[30] A dinner filled with such dishes would certainly have been spectacular, but it made for a great deal of work downstairs, and a large outlay on equipment that could only be used occasionally. How many families genuinely consumed such frivolities on a regular basis is impossible to tell – but the books did sell, so some, at least, of the contents must have been cooked.

Mary and Georgina were two among many thousands of cooks working in similar conditions and cooking similar food, across the country. They were a step above female cooks working on their own, or with one part-time assistant (a housemaid-cum-slavvy or a char), who were self-taught and whose repertoire was relatively basic. Such women were known as 'plain' cooks, not because their food was necessarily boring, but because it was unlikely to be French, or involve lengthy processes or the endless aspics and faff of the upper-class dinner table.[31] Instead, as Georgina's career progressed, she would have called herself a 'professed' cook, i.e. one for whom cooking was truly a profession, and who had learned by being apprenticed, working her way up from scullery to kitchen maid until she could gain a position as a cook. She probably stayed with Kilburn for another year or two. By the end of 1901, he had put Chancellor House on the market, and was permanently in London (it failed to sell, and was auctioned in 1903, eventually going to Rachel Beer, the 'first lady of Fleet Street', ex-editor-in-chief of *The Observer* and the *Sunday Times*, at a time when no other woman edited a national newspaper).

Her next employers were a couple who would play a pivotal role in Georgina's life. Sir Ian Hamilton was a career soldier, at the time chief of staff to General Kitchener. He and his wife, Jean, entertained a wide variety of dignitaries, including foreign princes, dukes, various royals and official ambassadors, and, as with Georgina's previous employers, they maintained a large staff at their London house, which was in Chesterfield Street. They also spent time at Tidworth Camp, staying in the former Tedworth House, where they also held dinner parties, including one in August 1905 for the Duke of Connaught, Edward VII's brother. Ian knew Winston Churchill very well, both from serving together and because Winston had written a book about him in the Boer War, and he became part of their regular dining circle. Jean was no fan, writing in December 1903 that he was 'always so full of mischief ... I always long to say something rude to Winston.'[32] However, as was often the case where Churchill was concerned, repeated exposure brought a change of opinion, and a month later, when forced to sit next to him, she (very) grudgingly came round:

> I laughed and said 'what a pleasant surprise for you', he looked fat and stupid and said nothing. He had only his cousin Francis (Lord Courson) on his other side though and condescended to make himself quite agreeable, even delightful; for the first time I felt how really attractive he could be, in a very dominating sort of way.[33]

The Hamiltons were part of a network of politicians, military officers and high-ranking civil servants who regularly wined and dined each other at their homes in London, and being taken seriously within their ranks was a crucial move for an aspiring politician. Winston had been well-trained in the potential of dinner-table diplomacy for achieving all sorts of ends, writing of his mother, Jennie, that 'in my interest she left no wire unpulled, no stone unturned, and no cutlet uncooked'.[34] She'd been instrumental in furthering his early career, in the army, in journalism and in politics, and he'd learned his lessons very well. Through the Hamiltons he would meet a wide circle of contacts. Through them, too, their senior kitchen maid would advance, working for many of the same circle through that all-important personal recommendation.

Jean kept an intermittent diary, making notes on her many luncheon parties, whether successful or 'detestable', often with seating plans so she could see who had been partnered with whom for later events. Some of her guests would have been familiar already to Georgina, including Mrs Humphry Ward from Aldbury, and members of the Ralli family. Things did not always go swimmingly, and she wrote in frustration in 1905 that

> yesterday went off very well too, in spite of bother about the hot water. I went into the kitchen at a quarter to seven a.m. and found the entire place empty, except the man I had instructed to look after the fires and see they were all right, the water in consequence was hot, and do I find it only requires proper fires in the morning, and all the worry we have been going through was for nothing at all – only the kitchen maids' lazy carelessness. These household matters do get on my nerves. I hate the machinery of life and constantly having to look after it.[35]

Despite this incident, Georgina must have impressed Jean. Although they rarely feature by name in her diaries, some of Jean's servants were significant in her life. She was prone to depression, and Ian was often away (the couple was childless until they adopted a son and daughter after the First World War), and she relied to a great deal on her relatives and her lady's maid, writing on one occasion that, 'I felt her to be a real friend.' Kitchen maids were a fair few steps down from lady's maids, who were in constant contact with their mistresses, but Georgina managed to rise above this, and when she left their service, in 1907, they remained in contact. She was lucky in the nature of her employers, and although her ability to forge contacts and gain the respect and liking of them was undoubtedly a mark of her own warm personality and culinary skills, she also seems to have picked good people to work for. Certainly, she could have done worse: Winston Churchill's father, Randolph, summed up his (old-fashioned and very aristocratic) attitude toward his servants when he wrote to his wife Jennie in 1891, 'tell Mary from me she is a fool & to forgive Billy. What does an occasional cook or housemaid matter?'[36]

In 1907, Georgina, now 25, made the move up to cook. She left the Hamiltons to work in Holland Park, still within Kensington and close to home, for an Italian-Greek merchant, Robert Allatini, and his wife Bronia.[37] One of their daughters, Rose, would go on to minor notoriety as a member of the Bloomsbury Group and writer of a novel called *Despised and Rejected*, which was banned in 1918 for a heady mixture of homosexuality and pacifism, neither exactly encouraged by the government at the time. They were Jewish, connected to the Rothschilds through business, and probably also knew the Rallis, Mark Young's employers in the 1880s, but, while both families had featured in Georgina's early life, it was equally possible she found her new post through the servant network. She may also have sought work through one of the more exclusive of the London domestic servant agencies: Mrs Hunt, Mrs Massey and the Regina Agency were the leading lights for finding the very best positions.[38] Georgina had now successfully worked her way from no.6 to no.1 in the kitchen, and had her own kitchen maid, in a six-servant household that habitually included Germans, Italians and Austrians among its staff. The Allatini family took holidays to the Isle of Wight.[39] They were cosmopolitan and very well off – Robert was worth £41,964 at his death in 1927.

Georgina may have followed in her mother and father's footsteps in entering domestic service, but she was the last of the family to do so. Domestic service remained the biggest employer of women until the Second World War, but in urban centres the service sector was increasing apace, with department stores, home furnishing companies and tea rooms competing for the middle-class market. None of Georgina's siblings would enter service, and she was the last of the family to follow that tried and tested route. Just as her mother had done before her, she also met her future spouse through her work. The first surviving photograph of Georgina was almost certainly taken to give to her fiancé: dressed in her finest, with a fur round her neck and a very jaunty striped and feathered hat, she is posed on a chair, looking somewhat wistfully into the middle distance. Snub-nosed, very pretty and slender, she has a determined set to her face. She's signed it 'Georgie'.[40] A new phase in her career beckoned now, for at some point in the preceding years she had met, and fallen in love with, a French chef, some twenty-three years her senior. On 22 November 1909, at Chelsea Register Office, she married him.

3

Paul

'Cervelles à la Connaught', from Georgina Landemare's 1930s handwritten recipe book. A very rich, mildly spiced and fruity brain stew.

> *Blanch and braise some brains then make a good sauce with the liquor of the brains, a little curry powder, a little tomato sauce and two tablespoons of mango chutney that has been cut up into dice, add lastly seasoning and 2 oz of cream, cut up the brains into small pieces and serve in the sauce.*[1]

In 1958, in her introduction to Georgina's cookery book, *Recipes from No.10*, Clementine Churchill described Georgina's 'husband, with whom she had worked for many years' as having been 'a renowned chef'. Yet Paul Landemare is an elusive man. Family legend surrounds him, but basic anecdotes have been fleshed out over the years with frustrating suppositions that don't hold up. He was 52 in 1909, with six children (though he gave his age as 50 on his marriage certificate). He was a widower – just – for his first wife, Ann (or Annette), had died the same year. He and Georgina would be together for twenty-three years, until his death in 1932 left her, in turn, a widow, at almost the same age he was when he married her.

Paul was born in Paris. His father, Mathurin François, came from Cherisy, near Dreux, around fifty miles west of Paris, where Paul's grandparents were farmers. Mathurin moved to Paris, and married Marie Pauline Godier in 1854. Her parents were Parisians, and her father was well-off enough to be living on a private income on a road just north of the Arc de Triomphe. Mathurin and Marie were both in their 20s, and already had at least one daughter by the time Paul was born in August 1857. They were pâtissiers, living and working on the Rue de Caumartin, running a shop on the ground floor and living in an apartment on one of the floors above. At the time, pâtissiers translated loosely to the English pastry chef, a specialist occupation that was part baker, part confectioner, and whose fare included pies, pastries and breakfast goods, as well as gateaux, cakes and sugarwork, but which did not encompass bread (which was made by a boulanger or baker) or dessert items such as ice creams and bonbons (confiseur or confectioner). The address was a good one, and about to get better, as the impact of Baron Haussmann's enormous building programme began to be felt.

Nineteenth-century Paris was a city of revolutions: the big one in 1789, with the added impact of the Europe-wide wars that followed, another in 1830, and yet another in 1848, known as the 'year of revolutions', as monarchs across Europe were toppled (most of them ending up in

Britain). Louis-Napoleon Bonaparte, Napoleon's nephew, became president of the French republic after the fall
of the then king, but ended the republic, which consti-
tutionally barred him from being president for more
than one term, by declaring himself emperor in 1852. He
immediately set about reforming the economy and
schooling (especially with regards women's education),
and modernising France's infrastructure. However, his
most notable legacy lay in his ambitious – and mainly
realised – rebuilding of Paris. Under the direction of
Georges-Eugène Haussmann, normally known as Baron
Haussmann, the city was redrawn. The overall aims
were multiple, but centred around hygiene, that great
nineteenth-century obsession, and security. The arch-
bishop of Paris summed up the former, writing to
Haussmann that 'in broad straight streets that are bathed
in light, people do not behave in the same slovenly
fashion as in streets that are narrow, twisted and dark. To
bring air, light and water to the pauper's hovel not only
restores physical health, it promotes good housekeeping
and cleanliness, and thus improves morality.'[2] Broad,
straight and very wide streets also stopped – or at least
made more difficult – the building of barricades, and
facilitated troop movements in the case of civil unrest, a
lesson learned from 1848 that would prove very useful in
later years.

The Haussmannian reforms saw street after street of
cramped Parisian housing demolished, making way for
wide-open boulevards and squares. Works were also
underway to delineate and restructure working and
leisure spaces: open spaces, used by street traders,

tramps and impromptu gatherings (sometimes of a politically sinister nature from a governmental point of view) were replaced with enclosed parks, open markets were covered to alleviate pollution, laundry barges along the Seine were replaced with purpose-built structures, and the water supply and sewerage systems were completely overhauled.[3] For over thirty years, and all of Paul's childhood, Paris was a construction site, and a very physical one: the building programme was carried out with pick and shovel, and Paul would not have been able to wander far from home before encountering a building site. Haussmann wasn't the only person instigating building either, and in 1865, when Paul was 8 years old, the construction of the department store Printemps started, at the top end of the Rue de Caumartin, where it met the new Boulevard Haussmann.

The upheavals that the fabric and people of Paris experienced as their housing changed and the arrondissements in which they lived were renumbered went on for years. The Landemares, unlike many families who had to move to make way for new streets, remained at 37 Rue de Caumartin throughout the rebuilding. In addition to Paul, Mathurin and Pauline also had a daughter, Léonie, seventeen months older than Paul.[4] In September 1860, Marie gave birth to another son, Henri. Less than a month later, presumably of complications related to his delivery, she died. According to her death certificate, she was 29 years and two months old. Paul was only 3, Léonie was 4, Ernest just a year, and the baby was six weeks old. With so many children and of such a young age as well as a business to run, which now lacked one of its partners, it's not surprising that Mathurin married again, and quickly. In March 1861, five months after Pauline's death, he married a dressmaker, Eugenie Angelique Vitry, who, like his first wife, was Parisian-born. She was already on the edges of the culinary scene in Paris, for her uncle was a cook. It was a close-knit world, and all of the official documents relating to the family include witnesses – friends, relatives and neighbours – drawn from across the world of food and cooking. Paul would barely have remembered his mother as he grew up, and he was clearly close to his stepmother, naming two of his daughters (Eugenie and Angelique) after her in later life.

The Landemare pâtisserie was successful, and was listed in the *Annuaire-Almanach du Commerce*, the directory of businesses in Paris, until Mathurin's retirement in the 1880s.[5] Its offerings were many and varied, and Mathurin would have been producing both staple shop goods and items made to order, which could take many days to prepare. Sweetened breads and brioches were popular breakfast foods, and needed to be ready for the morning. Professional pâtisserie manuals of the time give recipes for snacks, such as flavoured biscuits designed to go with tea; macaroons; madeleines; the gorgeous-sounding 'batons au chocolat', which were chocolate- and vanilla-flavoured almond pastry biscuits, dipped in meringue and chopped pistachios; and various garnished brioche and choux buns, often filled with cream flavoured with coffee, chocolate or fruit. Then there were small entremets, slightly more serious pastries that could be eaten alone but also form part of a meal: éclairs, nougats (also sometimes filled) and an endless procession of little tartlets, including the 'hérisson' – hedgehog – which was topped with meringue studded with slivers of almond. Larger, and even more serious, were the pastries intended for lunches and dinners, which habitually involved layers of cake or puff pastry, filled, iced and decorated. Pâtissiers were advised that they should acquire the skills to make their own wooden moulds so that they could produce marzipan fruit and pastillage decoration to order.[6]

Like Georgina, Paul's background was affluent working class. With Marie dead, and Eugenie untrained in the ways of sugarcraft, it's likely that Mathurin employed both apprentices and junior pâtissiers learning their trade and living in the surrounding streets. Paul would certainly have worked there, learning the very specialist skills of the trade from his father. Sugarwork was an especially valued skill, and although the towering, delicate pièce montées beloved of the generation before were declining on the tables of the rich, the ability to mould pastillage and pipe intricate royal icing designs onto cakes was still important, and in both France and Britain confectioners were regarded as a species apart from general cooks and bakers. He would also have learned skills in pastry and dessert making, as well as learning the discipline involved in the culinary arts, getting up early, keeping the premises clean and, of course, the delicate interplay of recipe and experience that marked the culinary expert from the enthusiastic amateur.

The Rue de Caumartin was a thoroughfare, and a

typically mixed street, in a Paris that, despite the rebuilding programme, still contained almost every imaginable
trade. Number 37 alone housed a civil servant's office, a
butcher, an architect and a mason in addition to the
pâtisserie, as well as living apartments on every floor. If,
in the mid-1860s, Paul had walked from the bottom of
the road, starting at the Boulevard des Capucines, he
would have passed shops selling carpets, corsets, dresses,
boots, general edible goods, toiletries, the intriguingly
categorised 'curiosities', jewellery, shirts and wine. At
number 9 was a limonadier – a lemonade maker and
seller – which was a trade that in Paris went back over
200 years, to the itinerant street-sellers of the seventeenth century, roaming the roads with their lemonade
strapped to their backs. There was another pâtissier at
number 10, and a picture-frame gilder at number 21.
Messier or noisier trades included a paper-maker, piano-
maker and a fabric dyer, none of which stopped a baron,
a count and a countess having apartments scattered
throughout the buildings. As he approached the family
shop, the scent of perfume would have mingled with
spice and chocolate from the shops on either side, with
freshly baked bread coming in just before the smells of
sugar and sweet dough coming from his father's premises. There were hotels, too, providing ready customers
for the shops, and in the late 1860s the building next door
added to the general drift of cement dust and noise of
building when it was converted into the upmarket Hôtel
St Petersbourg. From 1862, he could have stood outside
his parents' shop and looked up the Rue Boudreau to see
the Paris Opéra being built, its construction notorious

for flooding and financial issues, which stalled building work several times.

Almost anything the family wanted could have been obtained within a short walk, and if Paul had continued on, heading north, he'd have passed furriers and pharmacies, opticians and bookbinders, clock-makers, hatters, dentists, furniture-makers, shoe shops and an enticing array of yet more food shops, from dairies to chocolatiers, often several of each. Above these shops, the offices of lawyers and bankers opened onto landings they shared with painters and engineers, army officers and language teachers. There were theatres, schools and furnished apartments for short-term rentals, often by British or Americans, who found Paris cheap and ever-so glamorous. Winston Churchill's mother, Jennie Jerome, spent most of her childhood in Paris during the 1860s, as part of the shifting population of the English-speaking *bon ton*. Paul's road ended in another building site, and the Boulevard Haussmann, where, unlike the Rue de Caumartin, many of the bourgeois apartment blocks didn't have shops underneath, and which was a shining example of the attempt to separate business from domesticity that Haussmann was promoting.[7]

Parisian life was based on multi-storey apartment blocks, although actual living space encompassed everything from a dilapidated room in a slum area to the high ceilings and elegantly proportioned spaces of the new developments of the Bois de Boulogne. Most buildings had concierges, who in areas of mixed income and use such as the Rue de Caumartin, played the dual role of security guard and supervisor for children. Just as

Georgina played on the streets of London in the 1880s and 1890s, Paul's life was lived as much on the streets as it was in often crowded private homes:

> in the poorer quarters, a great number of domestic occupations and maternal cares are transferred to the street in front of the dwelling; in fact, the fondness of the French for out-of-doors is one of their most striking characteristics. The women and young girls will sit sewing or knitting in the streets or the public parks, and the men at the open-air tables of the cafés, on the wettest and rawest of days.[8]

Again, just as Georgina and her siblings used parks and open spaces for play, so too did Parisians – but in Paris this was actively encouraged by the city authorities. Sundays were particularly notable:

> on this day Paris disgorges its population upon the Boulevards, the Champs-Élysées, Bois de Boulogne, public gardens, and museums. The throng is interminable, but a more orderly, happier looking and better dressed crowd is nowhere to be seen. The working faubourgs send their population outside the barrier. In fine weather the Champs-Élysées present the appearance of a fair. Every species of jugglery, Punch and Judy, concerts and dog shows, booths, games, and mountebank tricks are in full blast, and each becomes the centre of a curious circle.[9]

Commentators from America and Britain were especially intrigued by the emphasis on eating out, even among the (more affluent) working classes, and, on sunny days, as he grew older, Paul would have joined the flock, sitting in teahouses in the various parks, drinking lemonade or fruit waters, or perhaps a glass of cheap wine or beer, while watching the crowds around them. Many were incomers, and only around a third of the population by the end of the century had been born in the city.[10] It was exciting and bewildering, and the opportunities – especially in the food industry – were expanding fast under the reformist regime.

In 1870, Paul was 13, the age when boys were usually apprenticed out. For whatever reason, he decided not to stay in the pâtisserie business, which left the family when his father retired, and he set off to become a more generalised cook or cuisinier. Reading the memoirs of French-trained chefs from the 1850s to as late as the 1950s, it is remarkable how similar their experiences were across the decades. Paul's next few years looked set to follow exactly the same pattern. Firstly, he had to get a formal apprenticeship, of three years' duration, probably to a family member working in a restaurant, perhaps Eugenie's uncle. She had already added two more children to the Landemare household (her first child, a son, was stillborn in 1863), with two more to come, and the family must have been doing reasonably well for Paul to take up an apprenticeship – apprentices weren't paid, and indeed, usually the apprentice's family had to pay the would-be employer. It was a very hard life, and even with a relative in charge there was no slack for boys, as they experienced kitchen life for what in most cases was the first time.

Restaurant kitchens were frequently described as awe-inspiring, but also hellish, with coal-fired ovens belting out heat all day. They were also dangerous, with fire, knives and boiling water, fat and sugar all potentially lethal hazards, and the profession as a whole was held in pretty low regard. Auguste Escoffier, who was a saucier (sauce chef) at one of Paris's most prestigious restaurants at the point when Paul started his apprenticeship, commented bitterly that the world saw cooks as mere servants, not seeing that cookery was both an art and a science, and that he who put his all into such a thing deserved to be recognised.[11] As an apprentice, Paul would have been right at the bottom of the kitchen hierarchy, the butt of practical jokes, and, at 13, quite probably too short to properly function in the kitchen. Jacques Pépin, who trained in the early 1950s, remembered his face being permanently red from being so close to the heat of the stove, and having to stand in the door of the oven to reach the plates from the warming racks above.[12] Paul's experience didn't advance that far, however, for in July 1870 the French declared war on Prussia. It proved to be calamitous: by September, Louis-Napoleon had been toppled, and the Siege of Paris had begun.

The five-month-long siege of Paris is best known today, perhaps, for the ingenious use of balloons, which carried both post and pigeons out of Paris (the pigeons then took messages back in). The minister of war, Léon Gambetta, also escaped the city in a balloon, following the bulk of the bourgeoisie, who had largely fled to the countryside as the Prussian armies approached. The blockade was total, with the usual siege aim of starving the city – and through them the government – into submission. It worked. Existing supplies, especially of fresh produce, were quickly exhausted, although while stocks lasted the food shops all made money. Inevitably, the rich (those few who were left) fared better than the poor, and early panic-buying and hoarding benefitted them the most. When the live cattle stocks and preserved meats ran out, it was time for the working animals: mules, donkeys and the many thousands of horses. By October, after one month of siege, supplies were running low but it wasn't yet too awful, at least for those who could afford restaurants, and the teenage Paul may well have still had a job.

Henri Labouchère, a journalist who sent missives to the English paper the *Daily News* by balloon throughout the siege (he stayed because he found it 'interesting'), recorded that

> want may come, but as yet never has a large city enjoyed greater abundance of bread and meat. The poor are nourished by the State. The rich have, perhaps, some difficulty in getting their supply of meat, but this is the fault of a defective organization; in reality they are only deprived of those luxuries the habitual use of which has impaired the digestions of half of them. It is surely possible to exist for a few weeks on beef, mutton, flour, preserved vegetables, wine, milk, eggs, and every

species of sauce that cook ever contrived. At about
seven, provisions at the restaurants sometimes run
short. I dined to-day at a bouillon at six o'clock for
about half-a-crown. I had soup, salt cod, beef (toler-
able, but perhaps a shade horsey), rabbit, French
beans, apple fritters, grapes, and coffee. This bill of
fare is a very long way from starvation.[13]

By November he was mildly worried, as rationing and
requisitioning had now come in, and cats were selling at
20 francs apiece. He continued to eat in restaurants,
paying well for the privilege of salamis of rat (the pro-
prietor opted to call it game, which in some ways it was).
He also noted the continued presence of cakes and pastries in shops, so the Landemare pâtisserie was almost
certainly doing its bit. The poor, however, were beginning to starve: Labouchère lightly discussed the relative
merits of spaniel versus poodle in a letter in December,
but the price of even the much-disliked rats was rising,
and dog cost even more. By this point the rich were
starting to consume the contents of the Paris zoos,
which were on the outskirts of the city, rather close to
the fighting, and temptingly full of potential protein for
those who could afford the prices. Much of the meat
was bought by restaurants, keeping up pretences with a
certain style of black humour. For Christmas Day, 1870,
Le Café Voisin, one of the most famous restaurants in
Paris, published a menu that included stuffed donkey
head, roast camel, kangaroo civet, roast bear with
pepper sauce, wolf cooked as venison, antelope with
truffles, cat with rat, peas in butter and a cress salad. The

presence of vegetables at this juncture was almost as surprising as the meats.[14]

Christmas coincided with one of the coldest weeks of the siege. The Seine froze that winter, and disease ravaged a population already made weak through starvation. Smallpox and typhoid killed 203 people in a week in January.[15] Even Henri Labouchère noticed that the poor were suffering – the price of wine had risen beyond their reach. Finally, the restaurants closed their doors as the final sources of flesh in the city were exhausted. Castor and Pollux, two of the elephants from the zoo, were slaughtered and sold by the Boucherie Anglaise on the Boulevard Haussmann:

> it was tough, coarse, and oily, and I do not recommend English families to eat elephant as long as they can get beef or mutton. Many of the restaurants are closed owing to want of fuel. They are recommended to use lamps; but although French cooks can do wonders with very poor materials, when they are called upon to cook an elephant with a spirit lamp the thing is almost beyond their ingenuity.[16]

It got worse: the Prussians finally decided to bomb the city, leading to yet more misery:

> I went yesterday into the house of a friend of mine, in the Avenue de l'Impératrice, which is left in charge of a servant, and found three families, driven out of their homes by the bombardment, installed

in it – one family, consisting of a father, a mother, and three children, were boiling a piece of horse meat, about four inches square, in a bucket full of water. This exceedingly thin soup was to last them for three days. The day before they had each had a carrot.[17]

Eventually, after 130 days of siege, and around 12,000 deaths, the government gave in and admitted defeat: the Franco-Prussian War was over, and Paris was free.

Except that it didn't end there. Food supplies poured into the starving city, but before it was fully recovered, civil war broke out between the government and the National Guard. The short-lived Commune of Paris culminated in *la semaine sanglante* (bloody week), during which the French army retook the city from its defenders, among whom were thousands of Parisians, men and women, who had risen in support of the Commune's utopian aims. Recriminatory executions were rumoured to have included anyone who even looked suspicious, especially if they had gunpowder traces on their hands. Several official buildings, including the Tuileries Palace, were deliberately destroyed by the Communards, with explosives and fire, and, in the weeks that followed, the city continued to reverberate with gunfire from court martials. Around 8–10,000 people are thought to have died, from disease, death in battle and execution, and as Zola wrote, 'when the echoes of the last shots have ceased, it will take a great deal of gentleness to heal the million people suffering nightmares, those who have emerged, shivering from the fire and massacre'.[18]

The people did recover, however, despite the death, destruction and the deportation of tens of thousands of undesirables in the aftermath. France from 1871 to 1914 entered what became known in retrospect as La Belle Époque, and restaurants, theatres and other places of leisure flourished. Eating out was part of Parisian life, with a huge range of eating places catering to everyone, from the bouillons for tired workers wanting a restorative meal, through middle-class cafés, to the high-end restaurants beloved of the British Prince of Wales, later Edward VII, whose love of France, and French food, drew him to Paris to eat on every possible occasion.

The first restaurant in Paris had opened in 1766, the culmination of decades of shifting food patterns in the French capital. It was a restaurant in the true sense, intended to literally restore, both health and jaded palates, by serving nutritious broths to those whose delicate constitutions were embattled by the rich foods of the eighteenth century. Very much versed in pre-Revolutionary ideas of establishing (or re-establishing) balance, it, and the copycat restaurants that rapidly opened in its wake, were vaguely Rousseau-esque in their promotion of natural, yet scientific, remedies for whatever was wrong (be that in the body politic or the actual body). Unsurprisingly, the broths, which took hours to make, weren't cheap, and the accoutrements that surrounded them had a tendency toward equally simple-seeming, but decidedly upmarket, porcelain and silver cutlery. They became fashionable among Enlightenment gentlemen, for this was not the coarse soup of the worker, but the elevated bouillon of the person of wealth.

This version of the restaurant survived into the nineteenth century, though it was eclipsed before the Revolution by something more akin to the modern concept. The most famous of the late eighteenth century's next wave of restaurants was the Grande Taverne de Londres, founded by pâtissier Antoine Beauvilliers in 1782, and vaguely modelled on a slightly misplaced idea of the British inn. It was rapidly followed by others, especially once the upheavals of the Revolutionary Wars were over, and well-known venues of the nineteenth century included the Véry, Le Grand Véfour, Café Foy and Adolphe Dugléré's Café Anglais. These establishments served soup – and also fish, poultry, game, beef, vegetables and towering sweet entremets – all the dishes their clientele were used to at home. The latter in particular was reputed to be the birthplace of a number of iconic dishes, including pommes Anna (slender slices of potato packed tightly into a mould with oodles of butter and seasoning, pressed down, and cooked to form a flattish cake that is both crispy and melty), and sole Dugléré (sole poached with onions and tomatoes, and served with a sauce based on a reduction of the cooking liquid). They were defined by the existence of their menu à la carte, which provided a choice of dishes, rather than the existing model common in inns in both France and the UK, where food was served, but there was no choice and a simple fixed fee was paid.

Over the course of the nineteenth century, restaurants boomed in France, not just in Paris, but in every urban centre.[19] By the 1880s, prestigious, highly regarded restaurants existed in all the major cities, especially those that attracted an international clientele of very wealthy socialites, which included royalty, aristocrats and the self-made men of the American upper class. By the late nineteenth century, restaurants had completely changed the way in which cooking operated as a profession in France.

Traditionally in France, as in Britain, the most upmarket cooking took place in private homes. Would-be chefs such as Paul in the 1820s still started mainly as scullery boys in upmarket houses or, as was the case with Antonin Carême, one of France's most hallowed culinary figures, they trained in sugar confectionery or similar specific areas, and then went into private service in the middle ranks of the staff, gaining experience across the board and working their way up to head chef. By the 1860s, however, fashionable and wealthy individuals were as likely, if not more so, to host dinners in restaurants as they were in-house. They still employed chefs, universally male, but those who aspired to be at the top of the profession now headed for restaurant kitchens, and not those of mere dukes or princes.[20]

Once in, and on the all-important formal apprenticeship, the process was arduous. The British journal *Hotel World* described training in France as a 'lengthy and tedious process', as the aspiring chef worked his way both up and around the kitchen, spending time in each of the various divisions – fish, meat, sauces, vegetables, sweet dishes, pastry and so on. Paul's official apprenticeship, which would have given him a solid grounding in all of these areas, ended after three years, leaving him by 1874 free to move around, gaining experience in as many kitchens as possible. Chefs were encouraged to move jobs frequently: Henri Charpentier, a chef who started his training at the very end of the nineteenth century (and later claimed to have invented Crêpes Suzette), recalled that his mentor 'encouraged me, because he was so sure that in each restaurant that was new to me I would learn something of value'.[21]

Many of them worked according to the movements of the international jet set: the Riviera in the winter, Paris in the summer and perhaps a jaunt to the Normandy coast, where the casinos and wide, sandy beaches attracted a slightly less wealthy but still significant playboy clientele. There were others too, decidedly less wealthy, but still connected, who found France congenial to both their budgets and the way they wished to live. Clementine Churchill (then Hozier), along with her mother Blanche and sister Kitty, lived in Dieppe from 1899 to 1900, hiding from Clementine's violent father. Blanche gained a reputation for fine cuisine and slightly eccentric behaviour. She was the daughter of an earl, but impoverished, addicted to gambling at the local casino, and something of an elegant bohemian. Clementine ate brioche and learned about the price of fish, and returned to England a committed Francophile, like her future husband.

One of the most significant figures in French cuisine, Auguste Escoffier, followed exactly this pattern, moving from his natal village of Villeneuve-Loubet, near Nice, to Nice itself and then, after his apprenticeship, working in Paris, Switzerland and the Riviera. He would go on to head up a veritable empire of restaurants, incidentally causing a quiet revolution in professional cookery on the way, and his books remain part of the training for class-ical chefs today. At the time Paul finished his own apprenticeship, Escoffier was several years ahead of him, working as head chef at the Restaurant du Petit Moulin Rouge, where he was devising menus for the Prince of Wales (he later asserted that he was at least partly responsible for the entente cordiale, as some of the pre-liminary meetings between Bertie and various French ministers took place across his *pommes noisettes* and *hari-cots verts à l'anglaises*).

There's no record of where Paul worked in 1874, but in later years his family thought he may have trained under Escoffier at some stage, and, if true, it's most likely it was in these early years, when he would have been very junior, rather than later on, when they were both senior chefs working in London.[22] He may also have worked at Café Voisin, of elephant-cooking fame, run by Alexandre Choron, for a copper pan marked with that name was among Georgina's own batterie de cuisine at her death. If so, he was doing well. Choron was known for sauce Choron (Béarnaise enriched with tomato), and Café Voisin was extremely well-reputed.

By 1877, true to the pattern, Paul had left Paris and was following the fashionable set. When, aged 20, he became eligible for military service, his registered address was with his retired father, now in Tournon in the countryside outside Paris, from where he went off to carry out his first set of military exercises. He was described on his record as measuring 1m 65, having chestnut eyes, a high forehead, medium-sized nose and mouth, and a round chin and oval face. Apparently, he had his own hair. Service was by lottery, and, like most young men, he was never called upon for active service, just being sent on exercises for a few months at a time every few years. It didn't interfere with his career, which included a stint in Cannes.

On his return to Paris he lived first, on Rue Neuve-St-Merri, near both Les Halles, the major Parisian market, and the upmarket restaurants of the Rue de Rivoli, and then, by 1882 as one of very few residents of the tiny Rue Babille near the Halle aux Blés (later demolished, in yet another phase of Parisian rebuilding).[23] He was now living with a fellow cook, one of the lower ranks of French cuisiniers, because she was a woman. Ann Chabrier would have had no chance at working in the kind of upmarket restaurant so sought after by career chefs, but was probably either working for a private bourgeois family, or in a café or middle-ranking public eating house. She was from Riom, in the Puy de Dôme, near the very industrial Clermont-Ferrand. Born illegitimately herself, she gave birth to Paul's first child, a daughter they named Marie Louise, in 1881, and she and Paul were married the following year, formally recognising and legitimising Marie at the same time. Eugenie, their second child, was born in 1883. By this point, Paul's career had diverged from the path of the successful French chef, however. On Eugenie's birth certificate, he and Anne are listed as fruitiers – fruit-sellers – on the Rue La Condamine, near Montmartre Cemetery in the 17th arrondissement.[24] On the face of it, things seem to have gone wrong, but not long afterwards, he decamped to the small rural town of Amblainville, in the Oise, about thirty-five miles north of Paris, almost certainly to work as a domestic chef. The local Château de Sandricourt was owned by the Marquis de Beauvoir, who was spending vast amounts of money having the gardens revamped at the time.

Still highly peripatetic, he was back in Paris by 1884, spending the next two years living on Rue des Dames, the next street down from his previous home, though he moved apartments within that. His constant moves don't necessarily mean that things weren't going as planned, but they certainly hint at it. He was struggling to find permanent work, and his growing family must have increased pressure financially. Finally, in 1886, like so many French chefs at the time, Paul decided that if things weren't working as planned in Paris, he'd try his luck in a new country, one that had a mania for all things French, especially the food, and where there was already a thriving community of French people, especially chefs. He initially only moved to London for a few months, but in June 1886, he returned to Paris, collected Ann, Marie and Eugenie, and the family left France for England. It proved to be a permanent move.[25]

Like Georgina, Paul's London lay south of Hyde Park. In 1891, he moved from Cadogan Street, just west of Sloane Square, to 80 Redesdale Street, both of which, like the Youngs' home over in Ashburn Mews, were listed by Booth on his poverty map as 'fairly comfortable; good ordinary earnings'. A few houses further up from number 80 and Paul would have been strolling into a middle-class area, the houses looking onto the grounds of Chelsea Royal Hospital with, beyond that, the upper-class roads round Sloane Square itself. The houses were those built by speculators in the 1830s: solid, bay-fronted and tall. They were ideal for division into flats, and Paul's family occupied only four of the nine rooms in the house, still the largest of the subdivisions, for elsewhere in the house was a one-room lodging, and two two-roomed flats.

Like Paul, the inhabitants were not native London-ers: they came, like him, from France, as well as Austria and Ireland. Most of the street's residents were in service, including a full house of butler, cook and house-maid next door, possibly related to the manor house just a few doors down. There were carvers, cabinet makers, coachmen, gardeners and, reflecting the growth of the hotel and shopping trades in London at the time, a number of cashiers, hotel staff and shop workers.

London, like Paris, was in the grip of a massive expansion of leisure provision: theatres, hotels and res-taurants. Unlike Paris, it did not yet have anything grand enough to attract the international set, and the norm was still to entertain privately, while gentlemen of means joined clubs and ate there. The leading chefs of London tended to cook at these clubs (particularly the Reform Club and Crockford's, renowned for the quality of their food) or work for the aristocracy. There were restaurants, including some very upmarket examples such as the Café Royal and Kettner's, both established in the 1860s by Frenchmen, both serving French food. There were other options, including Rules, and Birch's turtle restaurant, both pretty expensive and frequented by those with money to burn – but hardly the venue for a gentle bit of princely seduction, or a sophisticated ducal dinner.[26]

Establishments such as Willis's Rooms in St James's fitted in somewhere between the two, with a French-ish menu and the ability to cater for private dinners, but also featuring roast beef rather prominently.[27] The pubs of London – and there were over 7,000 by the 1890s – catered for a largely working-class clientele, mainly there for the drink, and while chophouses, 'ordinaries' and other eating options abounded, the range of choices, especially at the upper end, was a very pale reflection of the Parisian culinary scene. One American journalist summed it up succinctly, saying simply 'I do not find many places to dine.'[28]

When Paul arrived in London, he was riding a wave of French gastronomic migration. The 1880s saw the opening of the French *chambre de commerce* in London, and there were around 13,000 French people living in London by 1891. The vast majority – possibly as many as 5,000 – worked in food.[29] The elite of England wanted French chefs, universally, like Paul, men who had worked their way up in the continental restaurant trade, and who could turn their hands to anything from private dinners, to catered events, to starting up, and working in, the establishments London was desperate for: restaurants that could cater for the super-rich, and bring the fashionable world flocking to London, putting it properly on the culinary world map.

The key date for London finally having an establishment to compete with Monte Carlo, Paris, Lausanne and

Nice was 1889, when Richard D'Oyley Carte opened the Savoy Hotel, conveniently situated next door to his theatre of the same name, with rooms overlooking the Thames, and all the most modern of mod cons. The chef was one of the Carpentier brothers, who had worked together for the Rothschilds at Gunnersbury Park, before transferring to White's, one of the leading gentleman's clubs of the time. The grand opening brought forth a glittering set of attendees, including Jennie Churchill, very much part of the set D'Oyley Carte sought to attract. Her enjoyment of the Savoy was one she would pass to her son, and Winston later became such a devotee of the establishment that he founded a dining club there.

The initial buzz foundered though, and it wasn't until César Ritz, along with Escoffier, took over the running of the hotel and its kitchens, that the Savoy really did what it was intended to do. Between them, the two men caused a quiet revolution in London dining, forcing a law change to allow dining out on a Sunday, promoting women dining alone, unchaperoned and unhidden, and ushering in new systems of organising kitchen hierarchies and food production based on cooking in hotels, rather than in private homes. They were so successful that they also sparked off a hotel-opening boom, with a string of grand hotels, aimed at the same wealthy, international clientele as the Savoy. Openings included the Grand, the Metropole, the Victoria, First Avenue, Claridge's, Coburg (later the Connaught) and others. Existing hotels also moved upmarket, including Bailey's, the hotel at the end of Ashburn Mews, childhood home of Georgina Young and her family.

In 1898, Ritz and Escoffier were sacked from the Savoy, ostensibly for fraud, though the affair was much murkier than it appeared, and gave way to much salacious bickering in the papers.[30] They then went on to mastermind the Carlton and the Ritz. All of these establishments had excellent restaurants as part of their appeal. All were staffed exclusively by men, most of whom were French. Paul therefore found himself in a new world of opportunity, fast-changing and prestigious. It was said of London by the end of the century that there was not one 'first rate London restaurant in which the cooks were not all Frenchmen'.[31]

There's no record of where Paul worked in his first decade in London, but until 1901 he was listed in official records as a chef de cuisine, a term generally attached to chefs working in public establishments (or private clubs). Georgina later wrote down several recipes marked as coming from, or named for, London hotels, so it's very probable he was working in that environment. Family lore puts him at the top of the Ritz, but there's no evidence he rose quite that high. He was at the top of the kitchen hierarchy, but by no means at the pinnacle of the profession, and he was almost certainly a cook for hire, working in various places but not attached to any one long enough to make a name for himself as the resident chef.[32]

Henri Charpentier, who was working in London at a similar time, records a story full of ups and downs: he was front of house in a boarding house, then he worked in the lower ranks of the Savoy cooking staff, and, when sacked because he fell out with his immediate superior, he starved under London Bridge. Just as junior chefs moved around frequently, so too in many cases did fully qualified chefs, at least in London, with its insatiable appetite for French food. French food had been fashionable at the top of society for nearly 200 years, but at the end of the nineteenth century it took over the middling ranks as well.

Georgina, working her way steadily up to head cook within the domestic sphere at the time, was picking up both English and French cooking skills, but she was not French, and, in the late nineteenth century, this meant she could never be regarded in the same light as a true French chef. The slightly bastardised version of French food often grouped under the heading of 'recherché' in English-authored cookery books for the upper middle classes was not at all the same kind of thing being promoted under the same heading by male French chefs at the same time. For example, both Agnes Marshall and Charles Herman Senn published recipes for 'potatoes', to be served as a trompe d'œil sweet entremets. (Potatoes seem to have been a favourite for such visual jokes – the witty dinner-giver could also buy ice cream garnishing moulds designed to look like potatoes.) Senn, a Swiss chef working in a classical French tradition, simply used Genoese sponge put into oval moulds, hollowed out, filled with confectioner's custard, with two half-ovals then stuck together with icing, rolled in egg white and then chocolate, and with the eye marked out with a skewer. He assumed the reader would know what a Genoese was (or could look it up): in professional kitchens boys learned the basics before progressing upwards, and this idea is implicit within his writing.

Marshall's version was also essentially a Genoese, but she didn't call it that, merely described the process, with chocolate mixed into the batter for colour. She then crumbs the cake, mixes it with sieved jam and vanilla essence, before rolling it into potato shapes filled with cherries. Then each potato is covered with marzipan, rolled in egg and chocolate, and she further suggested exactly how to present them on the plate. The added level of faff does not necessarily make for a better dish.[33]

Those who aspired to be part of really fashionable society were well aware of the differences, and that the rigorous training of French chefs in restaurants meant that the food they produced was, if not better, at least more desirable. But French chefs charged French chef prices, and many of those aspiring to be fashionable simply didn't have the money. Then there were the other costs: one of Ritz's trademarks was vast quantities of flowers, and décor that matched each specific dinner, as long as the booker was prepared to pay enough. For one banquet, in 1905, the inner courtyard was turned into a lake, and guests dined on a gondola. After dinner, a small elephant was ushered in bearing a cake.[34]

At home, costs could spiral for the unwary middle-class hostess trying to follow high-end recipes. A typical lament, published in the *Englishwoman's Domestic Magazine*, came from a woman who complained that the cost of French food, and the expectations of society, meant that 'little dinners' of the type she wanted to put on were just not possible for the 16 shillings a head she had in her dinner-giving budget. Books such as *Party-giving on Every Scale* tried to help out, suggesting tips and tricks for the wannabe culinary fashionistas, including such gems as

> in providing entremets, a great deal or very little may be spent; here, again, the ultra-fashionable and the wealthy are prodigal in this direction, while less wealthy and economical ball-givers content themselves and endeavour to content their guests with a few modest jellies and creams interspersed with inexpensive pâtisseries; but every menu comprises jelly ... allow sufficient for two-thirds of the guests present, jelly being very popular with ladies.[35]

Ultimately, though, 16 shillings per head got diners a very good meal in a restaurant, and increasingly the upper middle classes, too, turned to restaurants for entertaining: the resulting need for slightly less upmarket, but still satisfyingly French, eating houses meant yet more opportunities for men such as Paul. It also put pressure on cooks like Georgina, trying to balance the desires of her employers for French food, with the versions of dishes published in English cookery books, and the skills that she'd already learned (or hadn't).

Restaurants weren't the only booming area of employment in this French-focused environment. One of Escoffier's previous establishments, the Maison Chevet in Paris, had specialised in outside catering, sending out prepared dishes, along with a team of chefs to finish them off and prepare any last-minute extras such as soufflés and canapés. They sent carefully packed dishes across France – and even to England. Gunters, the London equivalent, had started off as a confectioners' shop, but by the 1890s was a high-class caterer (and restaurant), supplying hampers for house parties – and the occasional schoolboy.

Winston Churchill sent a plaintive letter to his mother when he started at Harrow in 1888 requesting a chicken, three pots of jam and a plum cake.[36] Jennie Churchill's erratic lifestyle meant that her own entertaining was frequently done at restaurants, but she was a typical example of someone who regularly employed outside caterers. Her aims were generally higher than her finances would allow, hence reaching out beyond her in-house cooks for special occasions – and given the circles she moved in, there were quite a few. One, notable, example was a cook called Rosa Lewis. Rosa was unique in Britain at that time: she was a woman, but by the 1890s she nevertheless held her own in the upper ranks of the culinary profession, despite the gender prejudice. By the late nineteenth century, there were a growing number of well-regarded and recognised women in cooking. Apart from Rosa, however, they did not work in the male-dominated environment of very high-end restaurants, though some ran or cooked in smaller hotels of impeccable quality, often in provincial towns. Most were, like Agnes Marshall, cookery teachers, a recognised route by which a woman could make a living in cookery. Some did outside catering, or specialised in specific areas, generally with an English bent (cakes, for example). There were a very small number of female cooks who were employed by the lower ranks of the aristocracy: there was an agricultural depression in the 1880s, and those with suddenly reduced incomes from their land found that the savings involved in employing a woman outweighed the loss of potential prestige in not keeping a man, but it was still rare to have a woman heading up the kitchen for those above the level of a baron.

Rosa, who had trained in a resolutely French environment in the kitchens of various exiled French royals, took advantage of the craze for the cuisine in which she was practised, along with the straitened circumstances of many would-be socialites in London, and found a niche as a jobbing cook and caterer in the mid-1880s, cooking authentically recherché food with her impeccable credentials. She would probably not have made the leap to the next level without Jennie Churchill, whose cooks varied with her level of debt, and was one of Rosa's clients.

Rosa was already earning a great deal, and she charged up to 3 guineas a day – more than the going rate for men like Paul, who was probably being paid 1–2 guineas a meal, but she did not have the prestige of a leading restaurant to her name. It was at one of Jennie's dinners that Rosa caught the eye of the then Prince of Wales, later Edward VII, of whom was said that 'there is probably no man in England who has mastered the art of dining so completely as the Prince of Wales. To a man of less method and restraint than the prince, 35 years of public dinners might have been fatal.'[37] Her cooking was reputedly excellent, and he was a man who valued food – and female beauty – a lot.

The prince's patronage was absolutely key to her later success, as hostesses eager to attract him to their own dinner parties found employing her as a cook almost guaranteed his presence. Later, she married, entirely for the sake of social form, and bought the Cavendish Hotel, becoming the first woman to join the ranks of the truly first-rate hoteliers. Her reputation for providing stunning food and a discreet atmosphere for illicit aristocratic sexual liaisons were her selling points. She was also an early influence on Winston, who wandered into the kitchen during one of her early stints with Jennie, to be greeted with the sight of five cooks working on lunch – far more than Jennie's budget usually stretched to. Rosa, in her well-worn telling of the story, claimed she was unaware that he was the son of the house, and told him to clear off, adding as an explanation for the number of cooks that they were 'one for each course, Copper Top' (he had red hair, and the nickname stuck for quite a while).[38]

Back at home, the Landemare family was expanding. In 1889, Ann gave birth to the couple's first son, also called Paul, followed by Annette in 1891. On the official documents connected with the family in the UK, Ann was now frequently calling herself Annette Landemare, while Marie was listed as Louise, her second name. She followed Paul's stepmother into the dressmaking trade, as did her sister Eugenie. Paul, meanwhile, was increasingly working for private clients on short-term contracts, rather than as a one-off jobbing cook, and the whole family moved up to Nottinghamshire in 1892, living in Hardwick, the village attached to the Clumber Park estate.

Paul was now working for the 7th Duke of Newcastle, Henry Pelham-Clinton, very much of the rank to employ a French male chef and pay the appropriate wage of around £120–150 p.a. He was on the payroll until 18 August 1899, when he left, his final payment a respectable £6.4.6d.[39] He moved back to London, to 8 Eardley Crescent, as a man of some substance. Eardley Crescent was firmly in Booth's second-highest category: 'middle class, well-to-do', and Paul and his family had the entire four-storey house to themselves.

They were running it as a small boarding house, presumably with Paul cooking, although he was also still working for more general clients, and employing a woman named Frances Russell as a waitress and general domestic servant. Books of the time recommend an income of around £150 p.a. for the keeping of one servant, which is in line with the expected wages of a good French chef (and the same wage Churchill was busy moaning about as he set off for India in the 1890s). The street was full of boarding houses, recommended in *Baedeker's Guide*, since 'the visitor will generally find it more economical to live in a boarding house than at a hotel. For a sum of 30–40s per week or upwards he will receive lodging, breakfast, luncheon, dinner and tea, taking his meals and sharing the sitting rooms with the other guests.' They were generally advised as more suitable for those making long stays, and occupied by boarders for weeks or months, rather than days.[40]

The culinary world of London was changing still, and English cooks – and indeed, English cookery (and sometimes even women) – were being increasingly recognised as a valuable part of the gastronomic world. Alfred Suzanne, one of Paul's countrymen, who had also made a career in Britain, wrote a book in 1904 specifically aiming at French chefs wishing to work in Britain and America. While being rather rude about pork pies, he admitted that 'cuisine has made enormous progress in England over the last 50 years, and today in London there are English cooks who can even rival with their talent the best of French chefs'.[41]

Suzanne was a member of the Universal Cookery and Food Association (UC&FA), a culinary institute founded in the 1880s both to organise culinary exhibitions in London and to promote best practice in teaching cooking. It also acted as a forum for chefs, men and women, and provided health insurance. It was not the only club in town, and in 1891 Paul was listed as a member of the more niche Club Culinaire Français, which, as the name suggests, mainly had a membership of French chefs (though there was a lot of crossover, and by no means were all of the members French). Juste Alphonse Menager, the Prince of Wales' chef, was a member, as were several men from Queen Victoria's kitchens. It held an annual banquet, showcasing the best of French cuisine with a menu that was typical of the kind of thing members would have been preparing for their clients.

In 1897, the banquet was held at the Hotel Cecil, and comprised *croûte-au-pot à l'ancienne* (clear consommé with croutons), followed by *filets de sole Florentine* (sole with spinach and cheese), then *civet de lièvre Bourguignonne* (hare with red wine and onion sauce), *gigot de mouton Bretonne* (mutton leg with butter and flageolet beans), *faisan en casserole* with *salade de chicorée* (casseroled pheasant with a chicory lettuce salad), then *spaghetti au gratin* and, for sweets, a choice of *poires bourdalouse* (a very delicate pear tart with almonds) or *parfait moka* (coffee mousse), followed by dessert (understood always to be fruit, nuts and ices) and *café noir*.[42] The menu, written in French, would not just have been comprehensible to the native French speakers present, but was part of a universal culinary language, understood by diners (or at least, the right kind of diners) and chefs alike.

Another of Escoffier's reforms was to write down a codified repertoire of French culinary terms, such that anyone who read his book(s) and learned the lists within would immediately know what they were getting. To the modern diner, Edwardian menus are relatively impenetrable, but armed with a copy of Escoffier's *Guide Culinaire*, or *L'Aide-Mémoire Culinaire* or the later (and still very influential) *Le Répertoire de la Cuisine*, penned by one of his pupils, anyone present in 1897 would have been able to reel off, not just a list of key ingredients, but also the garnish and presentational style for each course. Paul was immersed in this world and, later, would pass this knowledge and reverence for Escoffier to Georgina, who carefully copied out lists of terms into her own, handwritten recipe book when she was working as a cook in the 1930s.

The UC&FA was a bigger organisation than the Club Culinaire, and in 1900 Paul joined this as well. In addition to the potential networking and insurance benefits, he received their regular journal, which meant he would have been able to read lengthy reports on their culinary exhibitions. These were prestigious events, part of the efforts of the culinary societies to showcase cookery as a profession, and to try to increase the standing of its practitioners at the time. They comprised show tables and competitions, which were open to men and women, although the editors admitted that the dishes presented by women (all of whom were cookery teachers) 'were probably more severely criticised by chefs than others, and several prominent authorities admitted freely the general improvement in the high-class work produced by ladies, which, in several instances, ran very close to that of French chefs'.[43]

The association fought hard to stop the exhibitions being taken over by big manufacturers, like Borwick's or Bird's, the very companies producing the products that cooks like Georgina would have relied on to produce dishes that better-paid cooks in more prestigious environments would have made entirely by hand. Household brands did sponsor several prizes, though, including, in 1897, the best dish of curry made using 'Empress' curry powder, and the best dish of pastry using 'Eureka' flour. There were stands showcasing industrial products ranged around the edges of the exhibition hall, rubbing shoulders with the likes of Mr Lusty's display of fine turtles and turtle preparation and, within the hall proper, the tables of the exhibitors themselves. There, you could worship the most excessive examples of the marriage of French culinary artistry, technological innovation and the Edwardian love for the truly over the top.

Leading chefs (all members of the UC&FA) presented utterly insane visual masterpieces, usually displayed on stands carved from lard and wax, which bewildered the average visitor. One review of the 1906 exhibition described the crowds as being a mixture of disdainful French apprentices and serious and overawed young female cooks (whose mistresses had paid for their entry), along with mature British housewives muttering darkly such things as

> if you ask me, I say things ought to look just what they are, and not be made to imitate something else. All this glazing and sauce-making and fiddle-faddling can only be done by people who have nothing better to do. I wanted to find a new pudding for Sunday's dinner, and can't; if I'd wanted to lay out a ball supper, it would have been a different matter.[44]

The association was also keen to encourage students of cookery, and to defend its many (and increasing) British members. In 1901, a furore broke out over an obnoxious and deliberately inflammatory *Daily Mail* article slating English cooks, to which the UC&FA responded in outraged tones:

> people whose puny minds are unable to comprehend the causes of an effect have proclaimed their solemn belief that English folk can never make good cooks. This is the view taken by the immature journalists who conduct the *Daily Mail*. As a matter of fact, the Council of the UC&FA have always

maintained that English boys and girls are as capable of acquiring, in time, a deservedly honoured position at the top of the arduous profession of cookery as are Continental youngsters.

The author went on to commend the efforts of cookery schools, and to call for more regulation and a recognised apprenticeship system, as in France.[45] This was laudable, but also a tad unrealistic: girls like Georgina would not have been able to afford the fees for cookery schools, or face the lack of wages when her family needed her earnings. She was not a member. In addition to staunch defences of the culinary profession, as a subscriber to *Food and Cookery* (the rather uninspired title of the UC&FA's journal), Paul would also have been able to read a long-running series on 'Table Serviettes and How to Fold Them', and articles covering such thorny topics as 'Various Ways of Preparing Lettuce', 'Test Experiments in Preserving Eggs' and 'The History of the Pâté de Foie Gras'.

There were further articles (and recipes) on 'West Indian Cookery', 'Diet in Diabetes', 'The Art of Salad Dressing', an exciting set of answers to correspondents' culinary questions and a section of recherché recipes mainly taken from the books of Charles Herman Senn, who was the instigator of the UC&FA and very much led from the front. Clearly, it wasn't fascinating enough to convince Paul he needed it, and by 1907 he was no longer a member.

Paul's family circumstances were changing as his older children married and moved away: Eugenie in 1903 and Marie Louise in 1904. Marie stayed close, in Pimlico, as the family moved yet again, this time to Redcliffe Road, less than a mile from their previous address, to yet another variant on the Georgian terrace. Paul junior was now 18, and may also have left home, while Annette, Angelique and Henri (born in 1893) were all of working age.

Family lore, coming from Paul's children, suggests that there was a dark side to Paul and Ann's relationship, one that might explain, even more than the usual vagaries of working as a chef, some of the family history of constant moves and financial ups and downs. Ann is rumoured to have suffered from mental illness, culminating, at some point in the early 1900s, in a 'fight with knives' in a kitchen where Paul was working. If this is true, it might also explain his forays into fruit-selling and boarding-house keeping, both trades that would have enabled him to work from home.

It's also been suggested that he was having an affair with Georgina, and that this may have precipitated the fight. Paul probably met Georgina when he was catering an event given by one of her employers, or they may simply have come into contact through the culinary network in London. Whether or not he was having an affair, their romance was not long-drawn-out. Ann died on 15 September 1909, but had been ill for some time, and with various symptoms. The doctor called upon to give the cause of death hedged his bets, listing liver cancer, exhaustion and heart failure. The death was notified by Marie. Paul was named as next of kin, but, given he did not notify the death, he may well not have been present.

Unlike his own father, he had no reason to rush into a second marriage, for his children were old enough to work, and he didn't need a partner in his business. It's unlikely that a potential illegitimate child would have pushed him into a sudden marriage – Marie had been born out of wedlock, and it was certainly not infrequent for children to be born to unmarried parents among the working class. He was probably, quite simply, in love. Just over two months after his first wife's death, he married Georgina, and a new phase began in both of their lives.

4

Married Life

'Angelica macaroons', from Georgina Landemare's 1930s hand-written recipe book. Nicely sticky macaroons in the traditional continental and British style, with the added benefit of surprising flecks of green.

> *8 oz almonds, one white of egg, add 10 oz of sugar, 3 whites, put the paste in a stewpan & stir. Remove from fire, mix in 3 oz of angelica.*[1]

Georgina now found herself in a very different situation. In less than an hour, in the modern confines of Chelsea Register Office (finished the year before), she had gone from being Georgina Young, spinster, to Georgina Landemare, a married woman with a ready-made family of six. Admittedly, Marie Louise was a year older than she was, and even Henri, the youngest, was 13, and therefore almost old enough to work, but it was still a significant change of circumstance.

The marriage was witnessed by Marie Louise's husband, Alfred Diesch, and one Arthur Mellier, a hint that the wedding may have been somewhat rushed, or not entirely to the approval of the Youngs, as normally one of the bride's relatives acted as a witness. Paul was a Catholic, and she was Church of England, so the choice of the register office was probably because it was neutral ground. Paul was listed as a chef, and Georgina as a cook, a reminder of the differing statuses of men and women in the Edwardian culinary field.

The newlyweds moved initially to Paul's address at 6 Redcliffe Road, near Brompton Cemetery, but within two years, they'd moved further north, to Stratford Road. There, they had rooms in a squat, three-floored terrace. As with so many of the houses Georgina would live in, whether in Kensington, Chelsea or Pimlico, it had been built as a middle-class dwelling, and was now subdivided into much smaller units. It was something of a come-down for Paul, though, from his Eardley Crescent house with its boarders and servant: now he and Georgina shared their front door with Charles Kilchey, a farrier, and his wife Lucy; Meta Berry, a dressmaker; and two lodgers.

The street was typical of the areas inhabited by the affluent, urban working class, and the Landemares' neighbours included a butler, a bootmaker, a carpenter and a clerk. There were a number of women on their own, both widowed and single, working in dressmaking and millinery and, if Paul had wanted to speak his native language and talk to a fellow Parisian, Mademoiselle Frankein was a few doors away, along with a Bordelaise couturier and her small son. They weren't the only immigrants: Heinrich Dohmeyer, a German, ran a boarding house that, on census night in 1911, was positively overflowing with Swedes.

It was a time of change for the whole Young clan: in 1905, Frederick Bower, for whom Mark Young had worked since the late 1880s, died. His wife Sarah had predeceased him, so the household was broken up. Mark, Mary, Archie and Eve moved back to London (Algy had already left and was now working). Whether Mark, now aged 49, was feeling unable to carry out the highly physical duties of a coachman, sitting out on an exposed box in all weathers, or whether, as he once predicted, he was unable to find work with his beloved horses, in an age where the rich were increasingly turning to motor cars, he now took on work as a bank messenger. Messengers were typically slightly older men, like Mark, who could provide impeccable references proving their honesty, and who knew how to handle themselves. They were charged with collecting money from traders and returning it to the bank, and were therefore not only often handling significant sums of money themselves but, in their bank uniforms, were obvious targets for thieves. It was a responsible position but, in working for an institution and no longer a private individual, Mark joined the rest of his family in not working in service. Only Georgina was left, and she would remain in service until she retired.

The other siblings had gone in very different directions, taking full advantage of the burgeoning service sector, and exhibiting what Georgina called the 'Messider artistry' from her mother's side of the family. Her uncle James, a railway signalman in Northamptonshire, painted in his spare time, but that was the generation above when, as Georgina tersely put it, 'in those days you got nowhere'. By 1900 though, opportunities had opened out, and both Algy and Archie became designers. Algy went to work as a fabric designer for Liberty, staying in London and lodging with one of Mark's coachman colleagues in Ashburn Mews when his parents and younger siblings moved out to Egham. He moved back in with his parents when they returned to London, saving money to contribute to the family pot.

Archie, meanwhile, went on to design tiles and mosaics for Turner, Lord & Co. off Grosvenor Square. Maud, awesomely naughty in Georgina's memory, applied for the post office, but failed the exams. However, she had the same streak of willpower that Georgina had, so she took Pitman courses at night school, and secured a job at Harrods – very sought-after and with more than a touch of glamour. In August 1909, three months before Georgina's own wedding, she married Thomas Moss, moving out to Far Cotton in Northamptonshire, where Thomas was, like her uncle James, a railway signalman. Indeed, she had met Thomas through James, for he was James's nephew by marriage, and had been brought up by him and his wife, Eliza. Unsurprisingly, Maud and Thomas lived next door to Uncle James (who still had one of Thomas's brothers living with him), keeping the family and community links alive. They had a son, Reginald, in 1910.

The family links that had been so important to Georgina's mother in the 1880s remained a key part of Georgina's life in London in the 1910s. She and Paul lived about an hour's walk away from Mark and Mary, who were at Claverton Street in Pimlico, and there were both

Youngs and Messiders in various suburbs of London, forming a network of connections upon which to draw in times of need. Algy married in 1911 and moved to Harbledown Road in Fulham. His wedding breakfast was catered by the same confectioners where he and Georgie had discovered the joys of slightly stale pastries when they were children.

Paul's family was scattering: his parents were both dead, and while he still had siblings in Paris, whom he and Georgina visited regularly, his children in London were striking out on their own. Eugenie had married in 1903, to an electrical engineer named Stephen Dingle. In 1910, they emigrated to America, settling in New Jersey. A year later, Paul junior joined them, giving his occupation as an advertising man. He promptly married Cecilia Long and set up business with Stephen. They invented a 'self-restoring hook', and threw themselves into life in their new country. In 1919, Henri also emigrated, again to New Jersey; Angelique followed in 1920.[2] Both were naturalised in the 1930s. From France, to England, and now America: it was a brave new world, full of exciting opportunities, and the younger Landemares clearly felt no need to stay close to their father now that he was remarried.

Children certainly weren't a priority for Paul and Georgina. In stark contrast to Annette's regular pregnancies, Georgina gave birth only twice. Paul may have stopped being quite so virile, or Georgina may have been lucky. They may also have chosen to use contraception, though this was relatively rare before 1920, especially in working-class families, or have fallen back

on the tried and tested methods of preventing concep-
tion: coitus interruptus and simple abstinence.[3] Paul had
nothing to prove in the child department, and both he
and Georgina remained very career-focused. His endless
moving about had largely come to an end, and his second
marriage seems to have stabilised him. He and Georgina
stayed at Stratford Road, almost certainly both still
working, until in 1913 she gave birth to her first child.

Marcel Emile Landemare was born on 17 January 1913
and died on 30 January. His life was so short that the
same registrar dealt with both his birth and his death,
signing both certificates the day after he died. Cause of
death was given as influenza and bronchopneumonia.
Influenza accounted for around thirty deaths in 100,000
at the time, mainly affecting the very young or the very
old. Infant mortality, while gradually declining, was still
relatively high, and in 1911 you were as likely to die before
your first birthday as you were to die after your 65th.
Marcel fits neatly, but sadly, into statistics that provide a
stark reminder that, even as the Edwardian age came to
an end, in many ways society was still very much Victorian.[4] In the wake of his death, the family moved house,
and by 1915 they were living on Winchester Street in
Pimlico. They were now only five minutes on foot to
Mark and Mary Young, who had also moved, a half mile
up the road, to 29 Denbigh Place, close to what is now
Churchill Gardens.

Pimlico at the time remained very mixed, and rather
unfashionable. It mainly comprised streets of Georgian
and early Victorian terraces, built by speculators and
converted to flats or boarding houses. Both Denbigh

Place and Winchester Street had predominantly three-storey houses with additional basements and attics, but where some of Denbigh Place's housing was fairly mixed, and frontages narrow, Winchester Street's houses were only a few steps down from the sweeping façades of Gloucester and Sussex Squares. There were a few areas in Pimlico with even larger houses, which had escaped conversion and remained desirable, but because it was largely unfashionable were satisfyingly cheap for those in need of handsome accommodation on limited means.

Winston Churchill, who had married Clementine Hozier in 1908, was a five-minute walk in the opposite direction to Mark and Mary, at 33 Eccleston Square. He was paying £200 p.a. for the house, rather more than Paul and Georgina would have been earning combined, and managing – just – to keep the kind of establishment that would have attracted Georgina, though he would not have been able to afford Paul. It's not entirely clear how many servants he employed, but he had insurance for seven full-time (i.e. live-in) servants at Eccleston Square, plus a governess. The seven probably included three men, since he had a licence for that number (male servants required a licence, essentially a canny way of extracting taxes from those wealthy enough to afford them without using the actual dreaded word 'tax', which tended to send the upper classes into hysterics). He employed a female cook, and probably one kitchen maid.

Clementine was the almost-certainly illegitimate daughter of Lady Blanche Ogilvy and her husband, the profligate, autocratic and at times violent Henry Hozier. She had been brought up with the shadow of an ongoing custody battle looming over her (her parents had divorced in 1891), and spent much of her childhood in Dieppe. She had an abiding dislike of debt based on her experiences living with a mother who was incapable of living within her means, and an equally abiding sense of elegance and taste, also influenced by Lady Blanche. Marriage to Winston unfortunately meant living constantly with the former, but he did very much value and encourage her in the latter. Later renowned as a hostess, in the Eccleston Square years – and indeed beyond – one of her key habits was to employ pretty basic cooks, often girls with very little experience, and to train them up herself. Her mother had been a good, if erratic, cook, and the family had done their own shopping in Dieppe, so she knew what good ingredients looked and smelt like.

Clementine had been working as a French teacher when Churchill met her, so was by no means as disconnected as many ladies of her class, and knew her way around a kitchen well.[5] Later in life she was proud to declare that 'I have all my life had a taste for cooking, having inherited this interest from my mother and grandmother'.[6]

When Winston became First Lord of the Admiralty, in 1911, they moved to Admiralty House, which came with the position for a minimal rent, but kept Eccleston Square, subletting it while they enjoyed their new home. Ever unable to afford to live quite as they desired, the move was not only delayed by eighteen months, but eventually involved shutting up a whole floor of Admiralty House because they simply couldn't afford the twelve servants necessary to keep it all maintained.[7]

However, they still needed to entertain: Winston, like Ian Hamilton, had long understood the importance of a good networking lunch or dinner, and as tensions in Europe increased, he had a whole flotilla of naval officials with whom he needed to maintain relations, as well as his fellow politicians, journalists, publishers and anyone else who could potentially either keep him informed or pay him money, preferably both. He did a lot of his schmoozing on board the Admiralty yacht HMS *Enchantress*, and his accounts include regular payments to the Treasury for private entertainments on board. He also made much use of hotels, especially the Carlton, which billed him for three luncheons in 1912 – the diners enjoyed caviar, oysters, liqueurs and cigars as part of it, and it came to £26, roughly the annual wage of one of his housemaids at the time.

Large-scale light teas were hosted by the House of Commons, which laid on basic sandwiches, cakes and pastries as well as ginger beer, whisky, cider and tea. At Admiralty House, by necessity, things were more lavish, and Clemmie's barely trained cooks could not cope with the kind of function they were expected to cater. The Churchills called in extra help, relying on agencies to supply extra staff, as well as bringing back maids who had left when they married. They also made use of high-end caterers, hiring extra tableware as well as buying in food.

On 14 June 1912, Kingston, Miller & Co., who had a

royal warrant for confectionery but also advertised themselves as 'private caterers and ball furnishers', billed £106.10.0d for catering a dinner for sixty persons. This included all the food (to a menu approved by Clementine), dessert fruit, copious amounts of alcohol, including Pol Roger and Perrier-Jouët champagnes, flowers, tableware, waiters 'and others'. It also included the hire of chairs, a subject on which Churchill was particularly demanding, once dashing off a several-page rant to Clemmie, who replied, thanking him for his 'dissertation on dining chairs'.[8]

It was a good time to be working in catering: demand for cooks was high, and wealthy Edwardians vied with each other to put on a show through their dinners. Food was one of the best means of grandiose display, whether it was through the kind of primped, preened and ubermoulded creations Georgina was used to in her nouveaux-riches milieu, or the prolific use of truffles, turned (artfully shaped and carved) vegetables and time-consuming sauces of the fashionable French style in which Paul cooked.

In many ways, and especially visually, British food reached its most dizzying heights of silliness in the three or four decades before the First World War. However, while the upper middle classes wallowed in aspic and eschewed anything too natural-looking upon the table, among some, at least, of the upper class, reaction was starting to set in. Seasonal ingredients, for example, were being revalued by the rich, as market gardens and tinned food took some of the cachet out of eating peaches in March and peas in December: Clementine wrote to Winston in 1913, describing a meal of 'all the delicacies of the season – plovers' eggs ... salmon, lamb, asparagus and rhubarb'.[9]

Hotels and restaurants were booming, and both the Churchills regularly recorded dining with friends at the leading eateries of the day, instead of entertaining at home. In Britain as well as France, this was the height of the retrospectively named 'belle époque' (the Americans preferred the term 'gilded age'). Even those of Georgina's social standing would later look back with nostalgia and sadness, and it became difficult to think of life in the 1910s without seeing it through the lens of what came next. Dot Barnes, a 20-year-old cook in Nottingham in 1914, remarked, much later, to her granddaughter, that 'what people say about the summer before the war is true. It was the most beautiful summer I've ever seen.'[10]

In June 1914, Franz Ferdinand, the archduke of Austria-Hungary, was shot dead in Sarajevo, triggering a sequence of declarations and invasions that led, on 4 August, to Britain declaring war on Germany. It was, for those not following European politics closely, rather sudden. D. H. Parker, a country house footman at Lansdowne House, was in the middle of counting silver teaspoons after a garden party when, as he recounted, the butler rushed in and told him to 'get your motor coat and cap on quickly to go to London; there's going to be a B***** War'.[11]

The four years that followed had an indelible impact on British society, culture and food, driving forward understanding of the needs of the population, both nutritionally and in terms of maintaining morale and a sense of togetherness. The lessons learned would under-pin official policy in the 1939–45 conflict, but at the start of the war, very few people, in government or in the country at large, thought the war would last long enough to require anything other than the usual laissez-faire approach. A sugar commission was appointed, reacting to the fact that two-thirds of British sugar was imported from Austria-Hungary, and wheat, which mainly came in from the States and Canada, was stockpiled – recogni-tion that the British diet was still heavily dependent on bread, especially among the working classes.[12]

But there was no immediate worry over such minor concerns as the country's reliance on imported goods – at least half, and in some cases more, of even such staples such as cheese, ham, bacon and butter were shipped from overseas, and, of course, that bastion of British life, tea, was hardly a home-grown product. It wasn't until German submarines started sinking shipping at a signifi-cant rate in 1915–16 that the problems inherent in this approach started to become clear.

For Georgina and Paul, 1915 was significant for another reason. On 20 June, their daughter Yvonne was born, delivered by Georgina's paternal aunt, Lydia. Lydia had married a building contractor of some means, but had been widowed and moved to Harrow. Whether she worked officially or simply helped out family members, she was experienced in gynaecological prac-tices and nursing (not least because she'd had seven children herself).

In the 1911 census, Lydia was given the official title of 'monthly nurse', a term used for nurses who helped out mothers in the first month after giving birth. (She was, however, performing these services for her daughter, with the newborn listed, rather endearingly, as 'baby Smith'.) *Mrs Beeton's Book of Household Management* gave a lengthy description of a monthly nurse's supposed duties and preferred temperament: 'she should be scrupulously clean and tidy in her person; honest, sober and noiseless in her movements; should possess a natural love for children, and have a strong nerve in case of emergencies'.[13] Cleanliness was doubly important for midwives, present at the delivery itself, and who were notorious for spreading infection due to poor understanding of hygiene: the sharpened fingernail used to induce one birth often carried with it the fluids from another, and infections carried from one woman to another were one reason childbirth remained the biggest killer of women at the time.

For Georgina, this time all was well, and her daughter was baptised Yvonne Pauline (sharing her second name with Paul's late mother), at St Gabriel's, Pimlico on 25 July. St Gabriel's was officially Anglo-Catholic, a compromise position between Yvonne's parents' differing beliefs, and the liturgical practices she'd witness attending St Gabriel's would be closer to those Paul was used to than those of other, more traditionally Anglican churches. When she eventually married it would be as a Catholic, though, and her daughters would be brought up in that faith. She shared her baptism with Algy and Rosina's son Geoffrey, born just four days before her.

Paul was listed on Yvonne's birth certificate as a professed cook, something of an insult, given his training.

However, the war had, unsurprisingly, somewhat affected his employment potential already. The aristocrats for whom he worked were, of course, still about – their sons often joined up in the first few weeks of war, eager for adventure and glory – but the country houses at which he'd presided over balls and elegant dinners were now increasingly shut up for the duration. Some were requisitioned and, as the war stretched from months to years, and the toll of dead and wounded steadily increased, many became hospitals and convalescent homes. Their owners flocked to London, to stay in the comfort of their clubs and hotels if they did not already possess London townhouses or apartments (the price of the latter rocketed in line with demand).

Attitudes toward staff varied hugely, from those who, like Julius Drewe at Castle Drogo, refused to employ anyone of military age, to those who nobly hung on to their servants, declaring that they were showing their patriotism by paying out wages and keeping the job market fluid.[14] In 1916 conscription was brought in, extended quickly to all men between 18 and 51. The impact on large, staffed estates and wealthy townhouses with plenty of manservants was immediate, compounded by, in many cases, the death in service of heirs and/or incumbents, which threw administration into disarray and impacted financially through death duties, then at 20 per cent. Reactions differed. Some families retrenched, reducing staff and relying on restaurants for entertaining more than ever, now that their chefs and footmen were at the front, while others, more daringly, kitted their parlourmaids out in livery – corsets and gowns, naturally, with never a whiff of a trouser – and called them footgirls.

The Times grimly reported that 'if things go on, the domestic servant will become as rare as breakfast bacon in Germany'.[15] (Actually, sausages were in shorter supply, because cows' intestines were needed for making zeppelins, and so sausages, which made use of intestines for their casings, were banned.[16]) Paul, aged 59 and well over the age of conscription, and Georgina, who as a woman was not included anyway, were in good positions to pick up the slack, except that, as the full horrors of trench warfare became apparent, and what was to be a quickly won war became a lethal deadlock, the scope for lavish entertaining became ever dimmer.

By 1916, the jolly policy of wait and see that the government had been pursuing with regards food was faltering. With Yvonne in tow, Georgina would have been well used to waiting in endless bread queues, and food shortages became a fact of life. There were rumblings of discontent among both the populace at home and, more importantly in view of the enterprise as a whole, among men at the front, who, not unreasonably, felt that the least that could be done was to ensure their dependants had enough to eat. The government response was to appoint a committee, a time-honoured way of shelving the problem, and when it reported back that in theory things were fine – the civilian population should have been able to access 3,900 calories a day, and the theory held that they only needed 3,400 – the president of the Board of Trade felt quite happy reporting that 'we want to avoid any rationing of our people in food'.[17]

Others felt a little differently, and over at Buckingham Palace what passed for rationing was brought in
internally early on: meals were cut to three courses, and
wine was banned. Queen Mary felt strongly that palace
policy should reflect the wider situation of the people,
and so meat was also limited, throwing the cooks into
blind panic, and causing much resentment, for from
their point of view 'meat was not scarce'.[18] George V
issued an official proclamation, to be read from churches,
exhorting people to limit their bread consumption and
to cut down on pastry. Restaurants were ordered to
serve only two courses at lunchtime and three in the
evenings (though nothing was said about quality, price
or quantity, providing further impetus for those who
could afford it to just eat out instead of trying to find
food in shops). Communal canteens were set up to feed
the workers – a venture to which Clementine Churchill
dedicated herself wholeheartedly, persuading Prime
Minister Lloyd George himself to come and open that
of Ponders Green.[19]

Finally, in November 1916, the Food Department was
established, and by the spring of the next year, with the
depredations of German submarines on shipping at their
peak, rationing started to be considered. By now, there
were reportedly queues of 3,000 people at one London
grocer, and outrage over the very visible gap between
what the rich could eat in restaurants and the poor pickings available to everyone else started to lead to violence
– window-breaking and stone-throwing initially, but it
was enough to provoke government action. In 1917,
ration cards were issued, after a last-minute muddle as to

how the system would actually work, and on 1 January 1918 sugar became the first foodstuff to go on the ration. Meat, margarine and butter followed, extending to other foods, including tea and jam in the summer.[20]

Despite government fears, rationing went down well, because it was fair. It applied not only to individuals but to restaurants, and, together with the shortage of labour in Britain, which meant that, for the first time, unemployment was virtually at zero and that everyone had a wage, it ultimately increased the standard of living for the majority of people. It also meant that Georgina and Paul gained experience of working in catering during rationing, experience that would prove vital for Georgina two decades later, when the system came in again.

The Churchills were rather less badly affected: although Churchill was sacked from the Admiralty in the wake of the Gallipoli landings in 1915, he still felt able to write to Clemmie, now living in Cromwell Road with Gwendoline (Goonie), his brother's wife, and nine (female) servants, 'keep a good table: keep sufficient servants & yr maid: entertain with discrimination, have a little amusement from time to time. I don't see any reason for undue scrimping.'[21]

Out of a Cabinet job, he joined up, heading to France and the trenches. Like many men, he wrote back from the front when he arrived there later that year requesting extra provisions, in this case 'sardines, chocolate, potted meats, and other things which may strike your fancy'. Later he added 'large slabs of corned beef; stilton cheeses; cream; hams; sardines – dried fruits; you might almost try a big beef steak pie; but not tinned grouse or fancy tinned things. The simpler the better; & substantial too; for our ration meat is tough and tasteless; & here we cannot use a fire by daylight.'[22]

He was well aware that with a wealthy family back home, he had access to better provisions than the men he commanded, advising his fellow officers, 'live well, but do not flaunt it'.[23] For men in the ranks, chocolate was a frequent request, adding a small bit of pleasure to an unending diet of stew, potatoes, high-extraction bread and dry biscuit. Service rations were, at least, adequate, and for the first time more men died through enemy action than disease, usually related to a bad diet and poor hygiene.

Georgina's brother Archie Young joined up before conscription was brought in, in December 1915, entering the 5th Rifle Brigade before being transferred to the Labour Corps in 1917. Like many others, when the war ended, he did not immediately return home, finally being demobilised in February 1919.[24] Like Paul's son Henri (who joined up around the same time, but instead of staying a private, ended the war as a corporal, this time in the Royal Field Artillery), Archie duly received his basic service medals in 1920 and returned to his family and pre-war job.

Georgie and Paul were lucky: although around a sixth of those who fought died, none of their immediate family were included, and none were permanently disfigured. None suffered so badly from shell shock that they could no longer settle, and swell the ranks of the homeless. Out in rural Norfolk, Mollie Moran remembered the post-war 'tramps', 'trudging from village to village for lodgings and food. They all wore the same haunted expression and often had missing hands or feet … others had faces that were a patchwork of scars.'[25] There were still 65,000 men in mental hospitals in 1929 – and they were the lucky ones, with families able both to recognise the need and pay for the care.[26]

A sort of collective shock set in as fathers and sons returned as strangers, if they returned at all – although not all the consequences were gloomy. In East Lancashire, what remained of the Accrington Pals Brigade had spent the previous few months kicking their heels in Fécamp waiting to be demobbed. There, the herbal liqueur Bénédictine was produced and marketed heavily as a health drink, with the usual invented claim to monastic origins lost in the mists, etc. The men of East Lancs picked up the taste for it, and brought it back with them. It's still the drink of choice at Burnley United Football Club, and Burnley Miners' Club is the single biggest consumer outside France.[27]

In the wake of the war, men and women picked up the threads of their previous lives, only to find that in many cases, going back was now unthinkable or undoable. Women who had worked during the war in jobs previously reserved for men, especially those with pay parity such as bus drivers, now found themselves pushed or persuaded out of them, told that hanging onto them was unpatriotic now that the men were back, but that did not mean that they would meekly return to lower-paid jobs, especially in service. Post-war, life in service had neither the inevitability nor the draw that it had had for Georgina. Especially at the lower levels, it was stigmatised, and a largely invisible, but nevertheless bitter battle was fought between servant-keepers (which generally included the press) and working-class women.

The government, unsurprisingly given that its members were definitely of the former category, sided against the working women (who, despite the extension of the franchise in 1918, still couldn't vote, for the vote had both wealth and age restrictions). When unemployment benefit was introduced in 1920, it excluded servants, for, as the *Daily Mail* put it, 'houses are shut up in every direction, housewives are being endlessly inconvenienced and social life is being hopelessly dislocated, just because the government will not do the one perfectly obvious thing and make it illegal for women to draw the dole when they are capable of domestic service'.[28] *Time and Tide*, a suffragette magazine, interviewed one housemaid, who simply stated that 'the whole atmosphere is so awful', that it was no wonder girls weren't flocking to shore up the lifestyle of the desperate middle classes.[29]

One solution was to favour jobs that enabled the servant to live at home, rather than being subject to the restrictions of living-in, despite the disadvantages of having to pay rent and household bills, and by 1929 around a third of servants were employed in this way. Most were 'dailies' or 'chars', and regarded as rather low class. The model worked, though, not just for those doing it, but for their potential employers, who found the flexibility a boon: not having to provide rooms or all their meals meant they could save on rent and have a smaller house. The Churchills inevitably fell into this category, and Winston called charring 'an honourable profession'.[30] Paul, of course, had already established a career doing just this, at the upper end of the servant scale, and with the growing acceptance of live-out servants, he and Georgina were now able to forge a partnership based on exactly this model.

It's not known where the couple worked, or whether they always worked together or took separate jobs, and the years between 1918 and 1932 remain indistinct. Georgina would easily have been able to obtain jobs in the kind of households she'd always worked in, and, post-war, in more prestigious households as well, for male chefs in domestic households were becoming something of a rarity in more straitened times (although upper-class catering remained dominated by them). Marrying Paul was a canny move, for she now gained access to her own personal teacher, as well as to his networks of fellow chefs and potential employers. In an interview given in the late 1950s, Georgina said that she had 'worked with and learned from, her husband, who was a distinguished chef', elevating her own skills to a new level.[31]

Through him, she became part of the network of career chefs, and Paul introduced Georgina to many of his culinary connections in both Britain and France, including, on a visit to Paris just after the war, the chef to the English ambassador to France, Lord Derby.[32] Yvonne later recalled a life spent shuttling from house to house, following her parents' jobs, and she was frequently sent down the road to stay with Mark and Mary. Mark died in 1922, with Algy in attendance. He was still working as a bank messenger, and had contracted pneumonia. Mary now moved in with Algy and Rosina in Fulham, and Paul and Georgie took over the lease of their rooms in Denbigh Place. This was to be Paul's final move, and it was the Landemare base from 1922 until 1939.

One, somewhat tantalising, photograph of the Landemare partnership at work exists in the family archive. (Sadly the original has been lost and the photocopied reproduction is not good enough quality to include here.) Taken in the early to mid-1920s, in an unidentified private kitchen, Paul stands at the front of the central worktable, resplendent in his whites and sporting an excellent moustache, his hair still dark brown. Behind the table, Georgina looks steadfastly at the photographer, her hair neatly tied back, with the same calm and rather steely gaze as in her earlier studio photograph, taken before her wedding in 1909. Next to her is another maid, face downcast, and a jaunty young man in toque and tie completes the picture.

The table, as was standard in kitchens of the era, is covered with a white linen cloth, and has a pot of tools, a spice box and a heavy wooden work board upon it. Why was the picture taken? When? Where? The kitchen is probably late eighteenth or early nineteenth century, with a late-nineteenth- or early-twentieth-century extension. It has electricity and, given their base in Denbigh Place, it's probably in London or within easy reach of it. Working with her husband, Georgina would have been in a junior position again – something she'd not experienced since her promotion to cook in 1907 when she was 25 – but presumably she felt it was worth it. She had another studio picture taken at around the same time, wearing a natty floral blouse and with an endearing half-smile. (She later wrote a shopping list on the back of the photo.) She gives every impression of being in the prime of life, working hard, but happy.

The inter-war era has traditionally been seen as one where the old aristocracy declined, where country houses were sold or left to crumble, and where domestic service fell in importance. With the top rate for death duties at 40 per cent in 1919, the Duke of Marlborough, Charles 'Sunny' Spencer-Churchill, Winston's cousin, melodramatically lamented that 'the old order is doomed'. He went on, 'are these historic houses, the abiding memorials of events which live in the hearts of Englishmen, to be converted into museums, bare relics of a dead past?'[33]

He was rather premature. Although around a quarter of the land in England was put on the market between 1918 and 1921, this was as much large landowners consolidating their estates as it was smaller ones going bust, and it is indicative of a buoyant and healthy market. Country houses were in demand, especially those within easy reach of London, to be used particularly for entertaining (including shooting). The land with them was less desirable in many cases, and sold separately to farmers. The country gentry outside the draw of urban centres probably saw the largest level of decline, as agricultural rents fell, and society continued to shift toward a more urban outlook.[34] There were certainly some, again rural, landowners who fell deeper and deeper into debt, and either didn't have land or assets they could sell, or nobody wanted them. (One example is Sutton Scarsdale, the shell of which is still visible on the skyline to motorists on the M1, sandwiched between Hardwick Hall and Bolsover Castle on the opposite side of the road. The owner sold the land for over £100,000 in 1919, but the house itself failed to sell, eventually being asset-stripped and left to rot.)[35]

Maintaining servants in such circumstances was challenging (or foolish, depending on the point of view). Jean Rennie was a kitchen maid at one house in 1925 where the footman was asked to return the sixpence from the Christmas pudding. Outraged, he simply threw it on the dining room floor and walked out. In a sign of changing times, and the difficulty of country living, she commented that, 'he nearly got the sack, but good footmen who would live in the country were scarce'.[36] The majority of landowners, titled or not, regardless of location, simply got on with it, and expected their servants to do the same.

It was easier to get on with it if you were rich and your house was well-located: Charles Dean, who went to work at Badminton House as a second footman in the 1920s, explained that the house

> had been allowed to run down as a result of the war and it was to be my job to help to get it back to its former glory and that meant a lot of hard work; employers had a habit of expecting things to return to what they considered as normal very quickly, and couldn't seem to understand that in service as in anything else it wasn't easy to get a good team working together.

He continued, highlighting the tension between post-war working-class views of service, and the determination of employers not to recognise them: 'attitudes had changed; there was a smell of socialism in the air, and it took some time for most of us to realise that the upper classes were determined that things should be as they had been, and to understand that with high unemployment we would be forced to dance to their tune'.[37]

For all those who cut back on expenses for a while, or sold off far-flung bits of their holdings, there were others who flourished off the back of wise previous investments – and there were also new landowners, often outsiders such as Philip Sassoon, who commissioned or wholly renovated country pads, explicitly aiming for comfort and ease of living, from their tiled swimming pools to their modernist bathrooms (and lifts, electric dumb waiters, hot and cold running water and snazzy cocktail cabinets). In 1922, the Churchills joined their ranks, having previously dabbled in country house ownership with Lullenden, and bought Chartwell in Kent. This meant that in addition to the three housemaids, two parlourmaids, cook, kitchen maid and scullery maid in London (since 1920 in the more upmarket confines of Sussex Square), they now had to find the means to pay for an additional two housemaids, a kitchen maid and a varying number of gardeners.

It was now quite common to employ cheaper and more readily available parlourmaids over footmen, and no longer necessary to pass them off as footgirls. At Chartwell they wore a uniform of black alpaca dresses with stiff white collars and cuffs and a goffered cap (ironed in tight creases with a goffering iron), tied with a black velvet ribbon at the back of the head, and largely ornamental white, well-starched and goffered aprons tied with a large bow. The housemaids had more practical, larger aprons, with a bibbed front. When Winston was at II Downing Street as Chancellor of the Exchequer from 1924 to 1929, he replaced the parlourmaids with footmen – his position demanded it – who wore dark suits with wine-coloured waistcoats.[38] Gertrude, the under parlourmaid from Sussex Square, was promoted to head housemaid down at Chartwell, in recognition that it was hard to recruit good staff, and worth keeping them if possible.

The determination to get back to some kind of normal also encompassed food, which on the surface seemed not to have been affected at all by the war. The memoirs of 1920s and 1930s cooks in gentry houses dwell almost universally on the fiddly nature of moulded foods, the repetitiveness of pushing soups through sieves and the sheer physical labour involved in working in spaces that remained unchanged from fifty or even a hundred years before.[39] The pressure was enormous, for, as one regular house-partygoer in the period remembered,

> the food was always frightfully good. It was no effort at all for the hostess – she just told the cook how many there were. At that time, English cooking, generally, was frightful, except country house cooking, which was very good of its kind.[40]

Most country houses still relied on coal, with the occasional gas range and, unsurprisingly, given that their owners were largely of the Edwardian or Victorian generation, their owners wanted the food they were used to. But change was happening, especially among those for whom money was not a worry, and who were, by virtue of working in business or politics, connected to the fashionable, urban set centred, in England, on London.

Technology was changing, including electricity, which was gathering pace as a way of lighting houses and powering equipment. It wasn't a serious competitor for solid fuel and gas for fuelling cooking ranges until the 1930s, and the invention of the automatic oven control, but it was very useful for an increasingly large range of other kitchen equipment, most notably fridges. Improved domestic fridges (and freezers) started coming onto the market in the 1920s and, although they didn't hold as much as traditional slate-shelved cold larders, and certainly couldn't compete with gauze-lined game stores, they were convenient and modern. The Churchills bought a refrigerator from Harrods before the First World War for their house in Bolton Street, but this was almost certainly the older version, which was simply filled with ice (and sometimes salt, depending on the desired temperature inside).[41]

Technology, and its adoption, was hugely varied and very haphazard, and the main buyers of the various gadgets that were invented (or improved) in the 1920s were the middle classes, who were increasingly struggling to find subservient, cheap servants, and were also caught up in tensions over the desirability of live-in servants, or even servants at all, in the midst of a growing emphasis on privacy, and on the home as some form of sacred family space. Women trying to balance the need for housemaids and cooking staff with the moral and social pressures of the modern age could seek solace, from 1922, in the pages of *Good Housekeeping* magazine, founded with the bold cry that Britain was on 'the threshold of a great feminine awakening', and that labour-saving devices should be embraced for allowing 'the educated classes to be independent of domestic help'.[42]

This was a deliberate stand against the profligate monied classes, but one that still enabled the middle-class wife to forge an identity apart from the dreaded working sorts. Education, scientific understanding and embracing feminine agency were together the underlying thrust (to a large extent, they had also underpinned Victorian domestic advice, but this was conveniently ignored, as the Victorians weren't modern). Of course, *Good Housekeeping* wasn't suggesting that the modern mistress should do everything herself – at the very least, she would need help with the 'rough', the very physical tasks that included most of the housework – but its words of encouragement were eagerly lapped up by women such as Virginia Woolf, always a servant-keeper, but in the 1920s a very conflicted one, who dreamed of a house 'entirely controlled by one woman, a vacuum cleaner, & electric fridges'.[43]

Middle-class food underwent the most significant changes in the inter-war era, driven partly by the lack of trained servants, partly by a reaction against the lengthy, often rich meals still consumed by many of the upper classes, and partly by a new fashion for dieting, which went hand in hand with changing dress fashion and its new emphasis on boyish figures and limited corsetry. Ideal menus, still a feature of 1920s and 1930s cookery books, were now shorter and simpler, and were often written in English (although Nancy Lake's *Menus Made Easy: How to Order Dinner and Give the Dishes their French Names*, which did exactly as the title suggested, continued to be reprinted until at least 1954).[44]

Dish presentation was also simplified, especially in the realm of the aspirational wealthy urbanite, with a marked decrease in the amount of aspic and novelty moulds, and a corresponding increase in fresh produce cooked and served fairly simply. Post-war presentation suggestions in cookery books eschewed such silliness as miniature snooker cues, moulded out of spinach and rabbit forcemeat with the details picked out in coloured aspic,[45] but instead erred on the side of unctuous sauces poured over at the last minute.

Lady Sysonby, whose *Cook Book* was published in 1935, went as far as to include an illustration of a dish of lamb cutlets, ends covered with paper frills, captioned 'this has been drawn as a warning. Don't ever use paper frills.' Clementine Churchill had a copy.[46] Pared-back presentation did not mean that professional cookery became less skilled, however: indeed, for those trained in the ways of the Edwardians, it was often a case of *un*learning previous habits.

Virginia Woolf sent her cooks, first Nellie Boxall and

later Mabel Haskins, to train with Marcel Boulestin at Fortnum & Mason. Boulestin had been a writer, an interior decorator and a lampshade maker en route to becoming a cookery book writer. He had no actual experience of cooking, but explained airily that 'like all Frenchmen from the South-West of France I instinctively knew how to cook', and wrote of his style that,

> there are many ... who, disappointed at seeing that many famous French dishes are simple, complicate them purposely, probably adding other flavours detrimental to the taste. This is also where 'daintiness' is to be feared; frills and arrangements, artistic effects carefully prepared (the dish meanwhile gets cold and loses freshness), colour schemes, parsley all round (and not enough in the sauce), little decorations made of gelatine, all the horrors of a third-rate table d'hôte – such is, unfortunately often the ideal pursued and, more unfortunately still, too often attained.[47]

French food was still very fashionable, but Boulestin's version was taken from bourgeois tradition, and was therefore more economical and more seasonal than the Escoffier-derived French dishes of the rich – although, ever-abreast of changing times, Escoffier rewrote the *Guide Culinaire* in the 1920s with pared-down versions of his earlier dishes, ensuring that his books remained the go-to guides for professional cooks working at the upper end of cookery, such as Georgina and Paul. Boulestin, meanwhile, a popularist who in 1937 would become the first TV chef, ran courses for both cooks and their mistresses. Cookery became something that a middle- or upper-class woman could be interested in, and even take an active part in, without social censure. Jean Rennie summed it up from her point of view, in conversation with her immediate superior, the cook:

> 'Lady' cook! It means somebody who can make you a wonderful soufflé, or a marvellous vol-au-vent, but they couldn't skin a rabbit, or wash a saucepan clean, nor show anybody else how to do it. 'Lady' cook! Don't you worry about them, and their 'Schools of Cookery'!'. Neither she nor I knew what a menace and positive danger these 'lady cooks' and their 'schools of cookery', and their 'certificates' were going to be to our livelihood in the days to come. It was something new – cooking, considered 'low', was even then making its first tentative advances to the 'upper classes', and soon the secrets of great chefs were to be put up in packets and tins – just add hot water.[48]

It was the start of a slippery slope: in an article of 1932, cookery writer Elizabeth Craig felt quite happy advising her readers to put away the annoyingly tarnished silver, and to rely on tinned and bottled substitutes for elaborate preparations. Not so Georgina, who, in later years, would explicitly state her dislike of 'gadgetty kitchens', quite deliberately staking her claim to be a proper cook, trained in the old ways, with never a tin or an electric plug-point in sight.[49]

By the late 1920s, Paul was in his 70s. His children were regular visitors to the UK, now travelling second class, having emigrated in third. He still listed his profession as chef, whenever called upon to do so, but he was slowing down. In August 1929 he made his first (and only) trip to the States to visit Henri, Paul and their wives, Helen and Leona, spending time in New York and Boston. He probably bought his first camera to take with him, and from this date onwards, he and Georgina come to life in photographs. She didn't go with him to America, having stayed behind to work, but she did caption most of the photographs he took, tongue firmly stuck in cheek and with an evident affection for a husband she calls 'the sheik', 'his lordship' and, on a picture of Paul resolutely in a three-piece suit in a deck-chair on a beach in Long Island, 'the governor and his three maids, Leona, Queenie and Helen' (the women, more sensibly, are all in bathing suits).

His hair was now grey, but he was still trim, and, although he is vaguely using a walking stick in some of the pictures, he is just as likely to be sporting a cigarette. He posed, with and without the rest of the family, in all of the tourist hotspots: the boardwalk at Bay Shore on Long Island, Atlantic City, Belmont Park race course, Manhattan and Coney Island, where Paul donned a Mardi Gras mask and lounged nonchalantly against a pole, watch chain glinting in the sun (the overall effect is mildly terrifying). He stayed with Henri, who was living in a typical nineteenth-century New Jersey house, clad in weatherboarding with a large covered porch and striped sun-awnings over the windows.

They also posed outside the clubhouse of the Orange County Elks, an American organisation more or less along the lines of the Freemasons and to which, presumably, Henri belonged. (Georgina's captions for these run along the lines of 'the chief elk'.) He took a plane from Boston to Newark ('Newark airport a very distinguished person in the foreground') and they toured the Hudson River on a pleasure boat, taking pictures of the 'millionaires' yachts'. It was a thoroughly American middle-class experience and, with his comfortable house and gleaming motor car, Henri exemplified the new America as Americans wanted to be seen: a salesman, an immigrant and doing well. This belied the reality of life for a lot of people: 71 per cent of the American population lived on less than $2,500 a year, which was the generally accepted minimum for a reasonable standard of living. Some 42 per cent were below the poverty line, and most of these were first-generation immigrants, especially Italians and Chinese. America at the time welcomed certain types of immigration, mainly western European, and in 1924 President Coolidge had passed the National Origins Act, to try to stop Asian and southeastern European (and Jewish) immigrants arriving in large numbers, declaring that 'America must be kept American'.[50]

Paul saw mainly the good bits, although it's unlikely he embraced prohibition, which had come in nine years previously, creating all sorts of new opportunities for criminal gangs, and affording alcohol a rather romantic air of danger that didn't exactly help efforts to enforce the ban. Wealthy Americans flocked to London to drink; less wealthy ones risked moonshine (side effects, depending on which type of backstreet booze the drinker chose, ranged from paranoia and hallucinations to violence, internal bleeding and death), or smuggled alcohol from speakeasies. One enforcement agent reckoned that, from the time a would-be lawbreaker arrived in any given city, it took about half an hour to get a drink.[51] In extremis, it was possible to obtain a prescription for a drink, generally taken to be whisky, and more whisky was prescribed by doctors in the years of prohibition than was legally bought in the years before it. This was Winston Churchill's solution on his trips to the States during these years. In 1932, Winston was recovering from an unfortunate incident when he was hit by a car. He was, as ever, running late and rushed across a street in New York, forgetting that Americans drive on the right, and he failed to look the right way when crossing. Invalided out to the countryside, his accompanying doctor's note stated that his convalescence 'necessitates the use of alcoholic spirits especially at meal times. The quantity is naturally indefinite but the minimum requirements would be 250 cubic centimetres.'[52]

Paul's trip ended on 24 September 1929, and he sailed back to Southampton second class on the Cunard line's *Berengaria*. Almost exactly a month later, Winston Churchill made the same journey, returning from a trip around Canada and the States, during which he'd discovered the stockmarkets of both countries, and invested happily as he travelled (he was also a keen investor back in the UK). On 25 October he wrote to Clementine that he'd witnessed a suicide from his hotel window, brought on by a deepening financial crisis in New York. Four days later, as he travelled back to England, the stockmarket plummeted, wiping out $75,000 of his capital (around £800,000 in modern prices). The Wall Street Crash heralded a new phase in post-war life, as what later became known as the Great Depression began.

The Depression didn't affect everyone equally: those who had jobs and didn't lose them carried on regardless, although the pressure on the job market increased. Georgina's photograph album shows no sign that the Landemares were impacted: she and Yvonne went to Littlehampton with Paul's daughter Annette, and took a holiday with her and her family in Weymouth in 1930. Georgina, by now, was growing stout, a contrast to Yvonne, who at 15 was every inch the gawky teenager, fashionably skinny and a tad morose in the face of Georgina's beaming holiday face. (Georgina seems to have shared with Paul a determination to wear woollen suits on the beach, while everyone else is in light summer dresses.)

The same year, Henri and Leona came across to the UK, picking up Paul and Georgina and going on to Paris, where they caught up with Léonie, Paul's sister, and visited Paul's mother's grave. Henri and Leona raised their glasses (of beer and wine) happily for the camera outside a Parisian *tabac*. Georgina may have been working at the time for Richard, Lord Onslow, at Clandon Park, for there's a photograph of her and Paul there, taken in April of that year. Yvonne had started captioning some of the photographs now, including a rare one of her grinning, arms around Mary Young, now a white-haired old lady, stick-thin and wearing widow's black. Yvonne was 17, and at the left-leaning Morley College in Lambeth, the first of her family to stay at school beyond the statutory leaving age. Paul was 75, and starting to show it.

In June, Henri travelled across from America. He came first class, whether through choice or because it was all he could get at short notice, and stayed at the Carlton (suggesting he could choose first class: the Carlton wasn't cheap). Paul had lung cancer, and was dying. Henri stayed for just over two months, until 12 August, and returned home. Paul survived another three months, dying of cancer and bronchitis at home in Denbigh Place on 24 November. Proudly defined by his profession, his occupation was still given as a chef (not retired in any way).

He left the contents of his bank accounts, at the post office and the Crédit Lyonnais, to Georgina, which amounted to £235.6.4d (the equivalent of about £10,000 now).[53] It wasn't much, but she must always have known Paul would predecease her and, aged 50, she was in a better position than she might have been. She had the lease of the rooms in Denbigh Place, her daughter was an adult and could look after herself, and she had had twenty-three years of what seems to have been a very happy marriage behind her.

More importantly for her future, she had also had twenty-three years of working alongside a chef who, despite some possible early hiccups in his career, had latterly been working for very prestigious clients, keeping abreast of modern trends, and who had passed on his rigorous training and culinary knowledge to his wife. He also passed on several recipes for macaroons, which he claimed to have invented – or possibly Georgina claimed he'd invented. (He hadn't.) By 1932, the very grandest of households (mainly royal or ducal) still tried to retain male cooks, and still privileged French food. For the vast majority, however, women cooks were the norm, and it was largely accepted that they could be as skilled and as brilliant as men – but importantly they were still significantly cheaper. The newly widowed Georgina had no choice as to whether she continued working, but, as she assessed her options, they must have looked good. The next phase of her life would see her move from sidekick to solicited society chef, as she took charge of her future and made the Landemare name known for her skills, instead of and no longer just those of her husband.

5

Chef for Hire

'Boodle's orange fool', from Georgina Landemare's 1930s hand-written recipe book. A stunning cross between a (nice) trifle and a traditional fool.

> *4 oranges, 2 lemons, 1pt cream, sponge cakes. Take the juice of 4 oranges and 2 lemons, and the rind of one lemon and 2 oranges, fill a bowl with sponge cake, cut in four pieces each, mix cream & juices, sugar to taste, pour the mixture over the cake, this dish should be made some hours before serving.*[1]

The year after Paul's death, 1933, was the first that Georgina worked for Winston and Clementine Churchill, although they'd known her since the 1920s and eaten her food on a number of occasions. At 50 years old, she was in a strong position, with nearly forty years of experience in upper-class kitchens, half of those at the side of a French chef of some renown. She was used to commanding staff, ordering provisions and working at the top of a team, as well as accommodating a wide range of expectations and desires.

She was by no means the only jobbing cook around, but she was very well liked and respected, and had an edge over many other women in that she had worked for so long as a team with Paul. He had opened up for her a world to which she would have struggled to gain access otherwise, and she had an impressive range of connections and experience, far beyond that of many of her peers. She did not remarry, and made her work the focus of her life.

She did not, however, look for a permanent position with a steady wage now that she was on her own. Perhaps she had come to enjoy the flexibility of temporary work, which sometimes meant stints 'living in', but still enabled her to keep a fixed home address of her own, where her daughter could live while Georgina was off catering in the country. Unlike others, who flitted between jobs through necessity, she must also have appreciated that, if, like her, a cook was in demand, the potential was there to dictate her fees, earning more than a permanent live-in staff member and without having to be constantly on call.

Life as a cook for hire could be intense. One of Georgina's contemporaries, Lily MacLeod, described how 'when a jobbing cook was engaged for a very big dinner, she would walk into the kitchen on the stroke of nine, and from then until eight o'clock at night it was full steam ahead. How tense the atmosphere became as serving-time drew near. Timing was so terribly important.' In 1964, ten years after Georgina retired, Lily would become the Churchills' cook herself – Winston's last.

Working in a rhythm, with the permanent kitchen maid or other hired staff on hand, the early part of the day would be spent preparing cold dishes such as galantines, pies and jellies, as well as making aspic, stuffings and garnishes. Once dinner started, the food would disappear up to the dining room in the gloved hands of the footmen (often also hired for the night), coming back to be peered at by the cook, trying to ascertain exactly how it had been received. MacLeod commented that 'all that blooming work and it's eaten in a jiffy' was the invariable response from the kitchen maid, as she 'transferred from their silver dishes the resplendent mêlée, that only minutes before had been haute cuisine'.[2] There was very little respite, other than on days off, for cooks like Georgina weren't hired to look after day-to-day dining: all of their meals had to be glorious, for every one of their dishes would be served to guests whom their employers wished to woo or impress.

One important source of work was 'coming out' parties, following a well-connected girl's first presentation at court. The girls were known as debutantes, and Georgina prepared ball suppers for 'some of our most famous debs'.[3]

The equivalent for men was their 21st birthday party: these could be huge events, and very costly. Winston and Clemmie characteristically decided to hold their son Randolph's coming of age at Claridge's in 1932, at a cost of £135.16.8d (around £6,200 in today's terms – but well over a year's wages for the average skilled worker in 1932).[4] Winston, never one to miss a networking opportunity, used the occasion as an excuse to invite many of his political colleagues, receiving fulsome letters of thanks in return.

For girls, the fun didn't stop with one party, and parents were expected to host glittering soirées, to which mothers would accompany their daughters with a mixture of delight, boredom and fear at the mounting costs. The aim, of course, was to capture a suitable husband, although this was less important than it had been in the nineteenth century, for inter-war girls were somewhat freer to socialise and meet potential partners than their mothers and grandmothers had been. Both of the Churchills' older daughters married men who didn't exactly thrill their family: Diana married John Bailey in 1932 (a heavy drinker, in love with Barbara Cartland), and Sarah married Vic Oliver in 1936 (an actor, described by Winston as 'common as dirt', who had a mistress in New York and one failed marriage already behind him). Both ended in divorce.

Clementine's engagement diaries for the relevant years are full of the parties her daughters were going to, where she would sit on the sidelines trying to ignore the 'back-biting' talk of the other mothers. She wrote to one of her former secretaries, Margery Street, that 'I'm thinking of taking a cookery book to Balls. I could be hunting up tasty dishes for Margaret and Elizabeth to try, instead of listening to their gossip.'[5] Meanwhile Georgina was behind the scenes, catering the same parties, her status being stratospheric compared to the regular Churchill kitchen staff.

There were other society events, too, that provided regular employment for the jobbing cook. According to Clementine, when Paul died Georgina 'decided to do temporary work. She used to visit Scotland in the

Autumn, Newmarket during racing weeks, and in London she cooked the most delicious dinners and ball suppers.'⁶ Many jobs were one-offs, albeit often for repeat clients, but some were longer-term, and she worked on temporary contracts for weeks or months at a time.

It's impossible to track all of her employers, who must have counted into the tens, if not hundreds, in the seven years after Paul's death. Those who are identifiable present a consistent picture of the type of household in which she worked, which was a marked step up from those she'd started in, as wealthy as they'd been. Now her employers were often titled, very well-off, frequently politicians, and with a strong sideline in the racing fraternity. Very often, of course, the people who called upon her services fitted into more than one of these categories, since politicians tended to be from wealthy backgrounds – and a lot liked a flutter on the horses.

Quite a few of Georgina's clients also had a shared geography – three of them, the Hamiltons, the Islingtons and the Churchills, all lived at Hyde Park Gate at one point or another, and inevitably when the wealthy came to London, they clustered together, regardless of the location of their country houses. In working and socialising together, sometimes across party lines (especially in the case of the Churchills), they exchanged views, recommendations and staff. Key to Georgina's network, her former employers Ian and Jean Hamilton were well-established within this scene, and the fact that Georgina had remained in touch with Jean Hamilton, exchanging regular letters, doubtless helped her gain recommendations from a couple whom she had come to regard as friends – or as friendly as it was possible to be given such a huge social gap.

By the time Jean died, in 1941, Georgina had sufficient prestige – and Ian had sufficient regard for her – that her letter of condolence was published among a selection of others, from the rich and famous of the time, by Ian in a memorial volume. Georgie later gave a copy of the book to her granddaughter, Edwina, noting in the front that 'all these people's letters I knew them personally'. She added that 'I did many dinners in later life', confirming the importance of the couple to her career. At his own death, Sir Ian would leave her a gilded sunburst clock. She said he would always come to see her when he dined at No.10, and the affection they held for each other was evident.

Jean Hamilton's engagement diaries give details of the dinners she attended and gave throughout her life.[7] Even in the years when Georgina was working as a kitchen maid for them, names crop up of those who would later feature as employers, and throughout the 1930s the social circle in which they moved shows that they were regularly eating Georgina's food.

The Churchills continued to be frequent dinner companions, Jean's dubious initial impression of Winston having given way to firm friendship, and Jean and Clemmie also met up for lunches and teas in London. Winston's brother Jack and his wife Goonie were also regular visitors. Other key names that featured in the Hamiltons' dining set and also employed their former kitchen maid were Lord and Lady Islington, Violet

Bonham Carter and the Rallis (the same family for whom Mark Young had worked in the 1890s). There is solid evidence that they employed her through letters written to her, and to her family after her death, and by hints in her manuscript cookery book, but many of the Hamiltons' other friends must have done as well – people such as Philip Sassoon, the Asquiths, Lord Beaverbrook and Lord Londonderry, the owner of Londonderry House, to which the Churchills, the Hamiltons and the Bonham Carters were all regular visitors, despite their differing political views (especially on German rearmament).[8]

Lord Londonderry was a marquess but, in an indication of how much had changed for the status of women in kitchens between the wars, his permanent cook was a woman, Mrs Harris, who 'ruled her kitchen with a rod of iron'. Like Georgina, she gained widespread praise for her cooking, and was a recognisable name on the 1930s culinary scene.[9] George V and Queen Mary were regular attendees at Londonderry House dinner parties, and the names that appear on the guest lists there appear as well on the guest lists for dinner parties given by the royals in the same period. This includes the Churchills. The Queen's diaries somewhat undersell the whole thing, for she writes in similar tones to the average middle-class hostess. Her 'we gave a dinner party' in April 1927, for instance, doesn't even hint at the number of foreign ambassadors, dukes, earls and political figures, including Prime Minister Baldwin, who attended. The menu included Balmoral salmon, new season lamb, asparagus and cheese straws.[10]

It was a close-knit group, although plenty of others

came and went, for dinners, luncheons and overnight stays. Certain figures acted as hubs, and Sassoon in particular socialised on a huge scale. He was the owner of Trent Park near London, and the exuberant Port Lympne in Kent, described as both a fairy palace and a Spanish brothel (and featuring, briefly, an elephant mural so overpowering that even Sassoon was forced to admit it was 'monstrous'[11]). The Churchills were unable to keep away, not least as he had an endearing habit of picking his guests up in his private aeroplane.

Sassoon's parties were a heady mix of lavish hospitality and ferocious politicking, and his guests included both fellow politicians and celebrities such as Lawrence of Arabia and Charlie Chaplin (both of whom also dined at Chartwell with the Churchills). Keeping up, even on the somewhat smaller scale practised by the Churchill-Hamilton crew, wasn't easy, hence the need for skilled temporary cooks like Georgina to supplement the normal family provision. Even where cooks were capable and reliable, they had the annoying tendency to take leave.

Jean noted in her diary in July 1933, 'had a large lunch party here for which I had to get Mrs Brown to cook as Mrs Staramere and Blythe are away for a holiday'. (Blythe was the parlourmaid). Later, both threatened to give notice after a couple of dinners had to be rearranged at short notice, although matters seem to have been straightened out to Mrs Staramere's satisfaction, and she eventually stayed.[12]

Good cooks were hard to find, and worth retaining – something that needed impressing upon even young members of the household. Mary Soames (at the time Mary Churchill, Winston and Clementine's youngest child) remembered being banned from the kitchen, not just because of the dangers of the 'perpetual huge stock-pot, and large pans of boiling fat', but also because 'the prime reason was that the cook was a potentate, addressed always as "Mrs" – she who must be approached at all times with care; she who must not be ruffled (and cooks, I learned, were perennially prone to ruffledom)'.[13]

Political figures, whether MPs, wannabe MPs or simply influential from outside the official structures of power, were Georgina's mainstay. She favoured Conservatives and Liberals, of which, apart from Winston Churchill, Violet Bonham Carter was one of the more prestigious (at least of those definitely identifiable). At a time when women were rare in frontline politics, Violet headed up the Women's Liberal Federation, and, although she didn't stand for Parliament in the 1930s, despite several offers (she admitted being torn between politics and her family), she was at the forefront of the various debates over appeasement and the rise of the Nazis in the 1930s.

A great deal of politicking went on beyond the confines of the Houses of Parliament, and she was an important figure both for her speeches and as yet another key dinner-giver, enabling discussion and networking across the soups and chops. She was also Winston's closest female friend, and he once claimed he always sat next to her for the same reason he drank his favourite port – that both generated a 'special warmth'.[14] When he put together the Focus Club, a cross-party, but leftish-leaning, luncheon club, essentially a pressure group fighting appeasement, she had a leading role.[15]

Another political client of Georgina's was John Poynder-Dickson, Baron Islington, former Governor-General of New Zealand, former member of the House of Commons, now in the House of Lords. He and his wife Ann owned the enormous Rushbrooke Hall near Bury St Edmunds, which gave its name to 'Rushbrooke Gingerbread', written into Georgina's cookery book in spidery handwriting quite different to her own, probably by the regular cook, or perhaps a housekeeper or kitchen maid. It contains a 'few sultanas or fruit' in addition to the usual treacle (and demerara), flour, fat, eggs, milk and ginger, and is delightful, though extremely rich.[16]

She also worked at some stage for Alexander Spearman, who would become an MP in the 1940s, but who was descended from the Barings of Barings Bank, and at the time was a partner in a London stockbrokers. His wife, Diana, was also a political creature, standing unsuccessfully for election in 1935.[17] He later wrote to Georgina: 'I have very happy memories of all you used to do for us and so superbly.'[18]

Also in the world of finance and business was Sir Strati (Eustratius) Ralli, about whom Georgina said 'in my later years I came in touch with Sir Strati and Lady Ralli. I did a series of dinners and two Coming of Age Dance Parties.'[19] Ralli was described as a 'millionaire racehorse owner', in a headline case of 1958, when he was sued (aged 81) by a former mistress who felt unfairly bereft of the jewellery he had gifted her and then taken back at their split. Georgina's own love of horses had not abated, so cooking for the Newmarket Race season must have had an appeal on a number of levels, not least access to hot tips from the owners who enjoyed her food.

It's hard to tell how much Georgina was charging for her skills: in the 1900s a top-notch chef was charging 2–3 guineas for an event, which equates to around £4–6 in 1935.[20] The average cook's wages, based on contemporary classified adverts, were £50–60 a year for a woman working in a household of several servants. Even if she wasn't working every week, Georgina must have been earning a significant amount more than this – she may just about have approached the 1930s equivalent of the £150 that was probably Paul's salary at his peak in 1900.

She certainly knew her worth, writing of a potential client, a Kensington resident she'd encountered as a child, that, 'many years after I had the occasion to do a big weekend reception but the money wasn't enough'. She'd reached a stage where she could pick and choose jobs, dictating her own terms, before returning to a house (or rather, a set of rooms within a house) on which she was paying the rent independently: she was, in short, a leading society chef, breaking through the limits she had experienced in previous decades, imposed on her by her gender.

Domestic service itself was still fraught with tension, mainly around individual liberty and the role of the state versus the employer. One former servant gave, as her reason for leaving, the fact that 'I wanted to live my own life – not a life through someone else'.[21] The status that

Georgina now commanded was a world away from where she had started – and from the position that most of her peers were in (including the writers of the various later memoirs charting life below stairs at this time). Skill, training and sheer hard graft had got her there, along with the ability to keep pace with the changing culinary world of the 1930s, which encompassed both Victorian tradition and the latest in technology and flavour trends at the time.

In 1936, Georgina started a new book of recipes. She had undoubtedly been keeping one since her first forays into the kitchen as a 15-year-old scullery maid, but by now she inhabited a very different world. She bought a black, hardback exercise book with a dark-red spine and lined paper, and copied out all of the recipes, and other information, that she still valued. She wrote in the front, in her characteristically flowing and confident copper-plate, 'Georgina E. Landemare, 29 Denbigh Place, SW1. Recipe Book', and even set out her intended layout: soups, poissons, sauces, salades, meats, sweets and savouries.

As with so many such books, started with good intentions but at the same time intended as a work-in-progress, the order failed rapidly, and, although some of the recipes clearly fall into sections, others are more haphazard. There are no soups, quite possibly because the pages are now loose, and they have been lost.

The recipes reflect her forty-odd years of experience, including slightly creaky-sounding dishes such as 'Kidney Cake' (lots of pounding with ham and tarragon, shaped into balls deep-fried and served on sticks) and 'Canapés

Edouard 7th' (fried bread fingers topped with bacon, mushrooms and devilled herring roe), as well as a lengthy section of definitions for French soups and sauces.

Lists of this type ('Crétois <u>soup</u> – tomatoes and pumpkins' ... 'Doira – cucumber, Dubarry – cauliflower') are famously found in both Louis Saulnier's *Le Répertoire de la Cuisine*, first published in 1914, and described as 'the bible of the professional kitchen' (it still is, for classically trained chefs), and Escoffier's *L'Aide-Mémoire Culinaire*.[22] Both are designed to do exactly what they advertise, and also what Georgina's lists do: define dishes by name and key ingredients and/or garnishes, so that the cook can know, at a glance, what the diner expects.

She always referred to her own copy of Escoffier as 'her bible', and her much-thumbed copy of the 1914 version of Saulnier, translated into English, was bought the same year that she started her own book from D. Mangeolles, on Old Compton Street.[23]

Georgina's lists aren't, however, taken directly from either Saulnier or Escoffier, though many of the same dishes appear, and she was précising like mad – after all, the lists were only for her use, with no need for superfluous prose. There are several dishes that aren't in either book, for example 'Chicago Soup' ('cream of chicken, rice, bisque d'écrevisses [prawns]') and 'Jockey Club Soup' ('chicken broth with celeriac, carrots and peas').

Escoffier himself declared that cuisine was always changing, and that the task of the chef was to accept and embrace change, rather than decry modernity and hanker after the past. He repeatedly edited *Le Guide Culinaire*, his seminal work, simplifying existing recipes and replacing others, to facilitate the task of professional chefs. In the introduction to the 1921 edition, he simply wrote, 'since the publication of the last edition of the *Guide Culinaire* (May 1912), cookery, like every profession and industry, has undergone a grave crisis of which it still feels the effect. However, it has resisted victoriously, and we believe that the time is near when this painful post-war period will end, and cookery will once more march forward.'

In many ways, Georgina's recipes exemplified Escoffier's own principles: she took recipes, both old and new, and made them the best they could be, by reducing them to their underlying form, simplifying, lightening and doing away with all of the complicated garnishes, moulds and fluff of inferior cooks. That's not to say that they aren't complicated and intricate at times, nor that any cook could prepare them to perfection – it's hard to hide when a recipe is simple.

Georgie's book showcases both 1930s food and her own personal influences. There's a section of American recipes, doubtless influenced by her stepchildren, and perhaps contributed by Paul on his return from his 1929 trip. 'Southern Gumbo', 'Clam Chowder' and 'Waldorf Salad' all feature, as does the intriguingly named 'Playa Salad', which includes grapefruit, oranges and bananas with walnuts and mayonnaise dressing on a bed of lettuce (her food was delicious, but it isn't always entirely to twenty-first-century tastes – food does, indeed, constantly change).[24]

Foreign flavours were fashionable in the 1930s,

especially those of America, driven by society figures such as the American Nancy Astor at Cliveden (a frequent employer of jobbing chefs, and very possibly another Landemare connection), and given a further boost by the self-exiled American drinkers hanging around London cocktail bars. Composite salads such as this one were typical.

The vogue for exotica went beyond America, however, and authors of the time extolled the virtues of a bewildering range of cuisines. A number of books were published that explicitly threw out the old, heavy and meat-laden dishes of the traditional country house, and embraced lighter, frothier cooking. Some, such as Agnes Jekyll's *Kitchen Essays* (1922) and Catherine Ives' *When the Cook is Away* (1928), hinted at audiences of dispossessed young gentlewomen, making do without a cook. These were the living embodiment of the bohemian Bright Young Things (though reality suggests the real Bright Young Things employed at least a cook-general or a daily help).[25]

As with any cookery book, aspiration is key, and many of their purchasers were probably permanently without cooks, or at least only had somewhat inferior ones, and were a couple of titled relatives away from the projection the books put across. The decidedly more modest (and comprehensive) *Cookery Illustrated and Household Management* by Elizabeth Craig (1936) also included a section on entertaining without a maid, but was rather less upbeat about the whole thing (and included many more traditional dishes, along with the inevitable bananas and American-style salads).

Georgie's manuscript contains among its pages a cutting from a newspaper with recipes by Countess Morphy, without a doubt the most exciting proponent of exotic cuisine. Not actually a countess, but an American immigrant called Marcelle Azra Hincks, who'd grown up surrounded by servants near Georgina's old haunts in Kensington, she published a series of books with Selfridges, for whom she worked as a demonstrator.

The culmination was her 1935 *Recipes of All Nations*, which contained sections with recipes from across the world (albeit with a bias toward Europe and America, and with a whole section on the Creole cooking of her natal town, New Orleans). She explicitly wished to show both the 'unbridgeable gulf' that existed between nations, as evidenced by their food, and yet also to demonstrate to the middle-class housewife 'how, in quite simple ways, she can vary her menu and ring constant changes in the daily round of meals ... I hope my book will dispel this bugbear about "foreign cookery" and prove that it is often plainer and simpler, less "rich" in many cases, and far more economical than English cookery.'[26]

Recipes for 'Shark Fins' (Chinese, wherein she was helped by Mr S. K. Cheng of the Shanghai Emporium and Restaurant on London's Greek Street), 'Blackbirds or Thrushes in a Sack' (Sardinia), and fricasee of iguana (Guinea, via Mr Moritz, apparently not an expert, but a well-travelled gourmet), may just possibly not quite have fitted that bill, but in the main her recipes are excellent, and stand the test of time.

Georgina herself does not go that far, but she does include *kaiserschmarrn* and *kipfel*, different recipes for which are in the Austrian section of Countess Morphy's book, as well as quite a few other recipes with German titles (again, almost certainly Austrian) – examples include *kirchentorte* (cherries), *maudletorte* (nuts), *kastanientorte* (chestnuts) and *sachertorte* (chocolate, named for the Hotel Sacher in Vienna). There are also several recipes for *kougelhopf*, a couple of Creole dishes and the (not as exotic as it sounds) *peches thais* (peaches, strawberry purée, fresh almonds and vanilla ice cream).

In the main, though, Georgie's recipes are solidly Franco-English. Although she writes in English, many of the dishes have French titles, or a scattering of French words in them (in the 'Playa Salad' recipe cited above, she writes strawberries as *fraise*, though the rest is all in English). Her French was phonetic, with very few accents, and it's obvious she had learned it – and learned it well – from speaking and hearing it with Paul and his French friends and family.

It's especially evident when she writes recipes named for French cultural figures – *caneton harsène housaye* (stuffed cold duck covered with orange jelly fillets and very thinly cut tangerines and served with an orange salad) turns out to be named for Arsène Houssaye, a nineteenth-century French writer. She includes recipes drawn straight from the repertoire of the classically trained French chef (as Paul was): *tournedos Baltimore* (fried, and served with sweetcorn, tomato and pimento), 'Poulet Marengo' (supposedly invented for Napoleon), *pommes normande, moscovite de pruneaux à la Française* (a very rich moulded jelly of prunes, claret, plums and brandy) and various iced bombes and soufflés.

Then there are firmly Anglo-French dishes, invented largely by French chefs working in Britain, such as Crêpes Suzette (Escoffier or Charpentier, depending on the version of the story), *cotelettes reform* (Alexis Soyer, in the mid-nineteenth century) and a large number of what the French called *poudings*, classically British, but with a veneer of sophistication afforded by the change of spelling.

The quintessentially Edwardian *duck à la presse* is in there, starting with the alarming words 'roast the duckling strangled ...'. This recipe, which used a specialist duck press designed only for that purpose, was a classic hotel dish, and may have come from Paul's stint in grand hotel restaurants. Other hints at the hotel connection come through recipes for *cervelles à la Connaught* (curried brains with mango chutney), and *truite reine Marie*, by the side of which she wrote 'Ritz Hotel'. A *partridge chaudfroid* (boned, stuffed, poached, masked with white sauce and garnished with a great deal of care) was a classic of the cold buffet from the mid-nineteenth century onwards, and is annotated 'Hotel Grand'.

The cakes and biscuits section of the book is written largely in English, unsurprisingly, for it was an area at which the British excelled. The fancy pastry-work of the French sweet tradition was reserved for the dinner table, where gateaux and such like, once called sweet entremêts, were now increasingly just called 'sweets'. Afternoon tea, however, was firmly in the British tradition, having been practised since the late eighteenth century, and named for good in the late nineteenth century. The French called it 'le five o'clock', although they tended to be mildly horrified at the hefty British buns that came with it.

It's in this section that indications of other clients of Georgina are most in evidence – in addition to the Rushbrooke gingerbread mentioned above, there's a seed cake given by Lady Helen McCalmont (of Mount Juliet, in Ireland; she and her husband were keen horse breeders, and his horses were frequent winners on the flat).

Other inclusions are a 'bombe Chesterfield' (the 13th earl was in the Cabinet from 1936), 'mousse of café Wellesbourne' (potentially relating to the Fairfax Baronets) and a 'gateau Worplesdon'. However, the names appended to recipes don't necessarily indicate a connection – the 'soufflé Rothschild', for example, which she also includes, was invented by Antonin Carême in the early nineteenth century, and was a standard part of the French repertoire.

Then there are the unidentifiable Mrs Gibbs and Mrs Wyatt, quite possibly fellow cooks, but equally possibly employers. Mrs Fellowes, who is responsible for a 'Good Fruit Cake', was probably Daisy Fellowes, a regular house guest at Chartwell, married to Winston's cousin Reginald (Reggie), and a minor celebrity for her beauty, Gallic charm and habit of taking interesting lovers. Georgina's family also features, with mention of Louise (Paul's daughter), Maud (Georgina's sister) and Yvonne, the latter giving her name to a simple, slightly bland, chocolate cake.

Overall, the recipes are a mixture of modernised

French classics from the late nineteenth century, solid British baking and sweets, and some rather left-field examples of the latest in culinary fashion. Although the 1930s has a reputation for simplifying nineteenth-century recipes to the point of ruining them, while continuing the (undeserved) emphasis on stodge and suet, it certainly wasn't true of upmarket cookery, and the book very much reflects the milieu for which Georgina was catering: often Victorian-born, with an understanding of, and liking for, the rich flavours and complex presentation of the Edwardian era, but in general cosmopolitan and forward-looking, and eager to show that on their table.

The impression that Landemare catering meant meals involving copious amounts of cream is unavoidable, but there's also a decided bent toward zingy fruit flavours, from her ginger fruit cocktail (peaches, pineapple, orange, strawberries, sugar, preserved ginger, lemon and ginger ale on ice) to a selection of banana recipes. Her achingly fashionable 'poulet Madrid' has a fried apple and banana garnish, and there's even a recipe for stuffed olives (cayenne, cheese, cream). She also includes the frankly stunning 'Boodle's orange' (Boodle's orange fool), a popular dish at the gentleman's club of the same name, one of many clubs of which Winston Churchill was a member. It was not only one of her favourite recipes, but also a favourite of Winston and Clementine.

By the time she compiled her recipe book, Georgina had already done some work for the Churchills. She first cooked for them in April 1933, and mainly cooked on occasional weekends for particular house parties, but she also covered longer periods, working on three occasions for two weeks at a time.[27]

However, she doesn't appear in the archival record until 1936 (mainly due to the lack of any documents covering their domestic life in detail before that date). Winston was 62 that November, and Clementine was 51. They'd married the year before Georgina, in 1908, and had four children (a fifth, Marigold, had died at the age of 2). Randolph, the eldest, had already embarked on a career as an also-ran politician, philanderer and alcoholic, Diana had just divorced her first husband, and Sarah was about to elope with her first. The youngest child, Mary, who would eventually prove to be the most stable and accomplished of the brood, was just 14, born the same year that Winston had purchased – against Clementine's wishes and without entirely telling her – Chartwell, their country house.

Winston had been born at Blenheim, seat of the dukes of Marlborough (his grandfather was the 7th duke) and was firmly entrenched in the British social and political elite. After several years both fighting and writing about fighting in India and Africa, he'd returned to Britain to follow the time-honoured path for untitled relations of the aristocracy, and became a Conservative MP.

Georgina had made cook at 25: Winston entered Parliament at the same age. For the next few years, he steadily worked his way up the ranks, swapping sides to become a Liberal on the way, and was made First Lord of the Admiralty in 1911. He was effectively sacked after

the disaster of the Gallipoli campaign, which he supported, and Ian Hamilton led, in 1915. After a brief stint
on the western front, he returned to become Minister
for Munitions, lost his seat in 1922, gained another in
1924, and returned to the Conservative Party, becoming
Chancellor in 1924.

.After the crash of 1929, and defeat of the Tories in the
election of that year, he was out again, widely criticised
for his decisions while Chancellor, which exacerbated
the consequences of the crash. He didn't hold a ministerial position – although he remained an MP – until 1939.
Although he owned or rented various houses in London,
throughout the 1920s and 1930s, Chartwell was the
Churchill home, and, for Winston particularly, a focus of
time and money, spent lavishly if not wisely, in the
pursuit of luxury.

After its purchase, Winston, one of whose major fail-
ings was his acute inability to live within his means,
decided to rebuild most of the house, leading to years of
financial wrangles and an inevitable falling out with the
architect, Philip Tilden, the result being that the job was
somewhat fudged, with leaking ceilings, a kitchen at
one point described as being in a 'lamentable condition'
and both parties left feeling entirely hard-done-by.[28]

By the 1930s, works behind him (apart from endless
pottering about with the lakes, the swimming pool,
various walls and earthworks), Chartwell was a modern,
well-appointed manor house, with stunning views over
the Kent landscape and a menagerie of animals whose
adventures in living, dying, escaping and weeing on the
landing carpet form a comfortably domestic background

to the hard politics that also fill the couple's letters to each other at this time. Winston wrote cheerfully to Clementine when she was away, 'I drink champagne at all meals & buckets of claret & soda in between, & the cuisine tho' simple is excellent'.[29]

Churchill had the reputation of loving food and was well-known as a gourmand. However, he loved the rituals around eating as much as, if not more than, the food itself, and he thrived most when surrounded by people at the dinner table.[30] That said, he ate and drank energetically, and suffered from indigestion. He sought medical advice in the mid-1930s.

Dr Beckett-Overy sent him a dietary, advising a minimum of red meat, underdone, with chicken or bird breast or white fish instead. He allowed green vegetables and salad, some potatoes and fresh fruit, supplemented with Ryvita or Vita-wheat (proprietary brands of savoury cracker, marketed at the time as digestive aids). Eggs, bacon and ham were to be eaten 'very sparingly', no sweets allowed except jellies, no soups except clear consommé, and forbidden absolutely were 'liver, sweetbreads, kidneys, high game, pies and pork', along with sauces, pickles and mushrooms.

This wasn't entirely to Winston's liking, and he sought a second opinion. This time Dr Thomas Hunt, his longer-term doctor, wrote to him saying that 'the stomach is a very active one – too active in fact – and I have no doubt the indigestion is due to nothing more than this, as the wind will get held up at times and the stomach will contract too energetically and secrete too much acid'. He advised that smoking was part of the problem, but also suggested 'the most important thing is to keep meals fairly small and frequent – not going longer than about 3 hours without taking something to eat', and prescribed an anti-indigestion medicine.

He also gave a full list of dishes to be avoided: 'highly seasoned food – cooked cheese – high game – strong coffee – marmalade peel – coarse vegetables e.g. celery, watercress stalks, radish, cucumber, raw apples, pineapple, rich pastries, new bread'. He went on, advising the use of a cigar holder, and cutting down on alcohol: 'Port – one glass after dinner. Brandy will suit better than port' and stated that vegetable soups were better than meat soups or broth.

Winston replied, relatively demurely, that eating sandwiches before bed was helping, and that

> I note what you wish me to avoid. I presume as I get stronger I can get bolder. I do not like vegetable soups and always have chicken broth, or some variant of it, made for me. I hope you do not attach too much importance to this … port – noted. I must not drink brandy before the end of the year, as I have a wager. I will endeavour to eat a few sandwiches for tea, and have a little soup and sandwiches before I go to bed about midnight. As I do not breakfast until 8.30 and lunch at 1.15 there is no need to eat anything between whiles.[31]

The brandy wager was with Lord Rothermere, and won him £600. He had refused to give up all alcohol 'as I think life would not be worth living'. Over half of his yearly expenditure on alcohol was on champagne, mainly Pol Roger, but he also enjoyed wine, rarely touching beer.[32] He prided himself on having a good cellar, and on putting on a good show at dinner. On occasion, he even exerted himself to obtain particularly interesting recipes, requesting, and receiving, a recipe for a 'consommé Madrilène' from the Paris Ritz in 1934. It appeared on one of Georgina's menus for the family in May 1937 (it was also served sometimes at court).[33]

Despite Winston's lack of official position, he was not without power or influence. While there were many who regarded his obsession with German rearmament as tiresome (and his habit of leaving Parliament after his own speeches were done as rude), he was still highly regarded, both for his oration and his skills at bringing people together.[34]

Meals had always been a favourite forum for Winston to network, convinced as he was of the importance of face-to-face contact. He wrote to Clementine in 1916, 'I much prefer people coming to dine with me than dining out with them', and throughout his life, he treated the dining room as a stage, and dinner as a performance.[35]

Yet it was Clementine's excellence at stage management that enabled him to put in his storming turns, her brilliance as a planner that backed him up, and it was as a team that they worked best. He recognised this, writing to her in the 1920s, 'we must gather colleagues and MPs together a little at luncheon & dinner. Also I have now a few business people who are of importance. We ought to be able to have luncheons of 10 often & dinners of the same size about twice a week.'[36]

As the mistress of the house she had charge of the servants, hiring, firing and taking on extras, and it was also her task to plan suitable menus, order flowers and ensure the dining room was dressed appropriately, and arrange, with Winston, the table plan to best facilitate whatever conversations he wished to happen. Winston could, and at times did, monopolise the table, and could sometimes be a trying companion: Austen Chamberlain reported from a weekend at Chartwell in 1933 that 'only the family here, with a guest or two at most meals – very pleasant but on the tiring side, for both Winston and Randolph roar when excited in argument'.[37]

However, in the main he was a consummate host, solicitous of his guests' comfort and dietary requirements, and enormously entertaining, discoursing on any subject he got onto with knowledge and wit, and on occasion re-enacting battles of the past, 'making barking noises in imitation of gunfire and blowing cigar smoke across the table in imitation of gun smoke'.[38] By 1936, the tone tended to be more sober, as his influence grew, and Chartwell became the hub for a wide-ranging group of politicians, influencers and experts, all convinced of the German threat, and intent upon readying Britain despite the best efforts of its government at the time.

Food was obviously key to the success of these proceedings: a bad dinner would not have encouraged repeat visitors, despite the prestige of the company and the importance of the discussions. In London, hotels and restaurants continued to provide venues for lunches and dinners, even after the couple acquired the lease to 11 Morpeth Mansions in 1931.[39]

The top two floors of a late-nineteenth-century apartment block, the flat had a tiny kitchen, and, although Winston did entertain there on occasion, it mainly served as a base in which to sleep and have private meals. The anticipated yearly wage bill in 1937 was £75 (as opposed to that at Chartwell, for which was allowed £450), and the food bill was set at £180. This was Winston in a characteristically hopeful mode, trying to cut down on costs, for the real bills were somewhat higher, albeit with significant monthly differences – £9.13s.6d in January, £17.0s.3d in February and £20.13s.1d in March, for instance.

However, this probably meant that they kept a permanent staff at the flat of three; a cook-housekeeper, a parlourmaid and a tweeny (who would help out with both) would have been usual. Winston and Clementine both had personal servants – a butler-valet and a lady's maid, but they would have travelled with them and been included in the Chartwell wage bill.

The Morpeth Mansions cook was almost certainly Margaret Hancock, the same Margaret to whom Clementine referred in her letter about wishing to take recipe books to Sarah's balls. In 1935 the (unknown) Chartwell cook gave notice, with Winston writing, 'the cook is going. She sent in her spoon and her ladle on her own account. I am very glad. She had the knack to the highest degree of making all the food taste the same, and that not particularly good. I subsist on soup which Margaret makes for me secretly in London and is delicious.'[40]

Margaret Hancock appears on the electoral registers for Morpeth Mansions from 1933 to 1939, having previously worked for William Belcher, a lawyer, in Newbury, in a household with only one other servant. She'd been born the same year as Georgina, but widowed in her 20s, and was, like Georgina, working to support herself and her daughter Doris, born in 1908.[41]

She wasn't cooking particularly gourmet food, but it was substantial: the Army and Navy Stores, who supplied provisions to Morpeth Mansions in 1938, sent over seven pounds of potatoes, one pound of sprouts and 1.14 pounds of scrag end of lamb on 19 December, along with six oranges, two lemons and two pounds of apples, one pound of pork sausages and a Clementine favourite: a Dundee cake. Two days later they had a Dover sole, one pound of lard, plus parsley, apples and pears. A week's worth of food came to 18s 10½d, but this is only fresh produce, not including dairy. It's broadly in line with the upper-class budget for the time.[42]

It's rare to be able to identify the Churchills' servants, outside the heady confines of the more personal attendants – bodyguards, secretaries and the occasional housekeeper. There was a Chartwell kitchen maid called Lily in 1924, another called Jessie Cameron, who started in 1935, and cooks called Mrs Logan and Mrs Phillip in 1937 and 1938.[43] They were fleeting presences in the Churchills' lives. Generally, neither Winston nor Clemmie paid much attention to the names of their servants, dismissing them as 'cook', or 'my maid' or 'the tall housemaid'.[44]

Typically, when servants appear in the letters between the two, they are as figures of mild fun or exaggerated woe: Clemmie's maid Annie was engaged to a seaman in 1911, who turned out to be a 'faithless swain', and now

'Annie is drenched in tears and Cook's heart-broken'.[45] This was probably the same cook who tearfully but steadfastly advised drowning some of an overly large brood of kittens, and indeed, 'the final decision was made by the Cook'.[46]

If she was still there in 1913, further drama followed, for Clemmie reported that 'the new kitchen maid is mad ... she ... chased the cook round the kitchen threatening her with a carving knife'.[47] It's not surprising that staff didn't last long: in addition to fecund cats and suicidal maids, neither Winston nor Clementine were easy employers. While both could – and did – inspire immense loyalty and admiration in their staff, they could also incite exasperation and intense dislike.

Winston, described by Neville Chamberlain as 'mercurial', could be short-tempered, pugnacious and egotistical, shouting at his staff (and then apologising), and was infamously oblivious to any needs they might have for sleep (especially his secretaries, but this also applies to his maids and kitchen staff). He may have suffered from some form of Asperger's, and could be extraordinarily self-centred.[48]

Clementine, who lived on her nerves and was a perfectionist, could be snappy and rude, and had exacting standards that were bound to be disappointed given the household budget for wages.[49] One of her later secretaries said 'everyone writes about her beauty and brains and how she was a calming influence in the hurly burly of [Winston's] life, but ... she was reserved and often shy and very highly strung and ... so often the effort was exhausting'.[50]

Georgina Landemare, about to be married in *c.* 1909, and a wife, mother and cook-for hire in the early 1920s. The latter photograph has a shopping list written on the back.

Contrasting beginnings: Aldbury, late nineteenth century,
showing the village green. The Young house, where
Georgina was born, was up the hill to the right.

Rue Caumartin, Paris, 1866. No. 37, which included the
Landemare patisserie and home, is the first building with
the awning on the left hand side of the street.

Yvonne, Paul and Georgina, 1932. Paul, as ever, is clutching a cigar.

Through the generations:
Paul and his son Henri
in New York in 1929.

Yvonne with her grandmother,
(Georgina's mother),
Mary Young, in 1932

The dining room at Chartwell, 1927. Winston Churchill is at the
front, and Clementine second left. Many of the others would
be familiar faces when Georgina started working there from
1933. (*clockwise from front:* Winston Churchill, Therese Sickert,
Diana Mitford, Edward Marsh, Prof. Lindemann, Randolph
Churchill, Diana Churchill, Clementine and Walter Sickert.)

Cooking for the Prime Minister: The kitchen at Downing Street, early 1930s.

Spread from Georgina's manuscript recipe book. The mousseline pudding at the top was the dish she was preparing on the night she nearly died during the Blitz in 1940.

Mousseline Pudding

Take 2 oz of Butter and the grated rind of two lemons. work together to a cream. Then add 2 oz of sugar and work again and by degrees, add 2 oz of flour 5 raw yolks the juice of a lemon mise well again for 10 minutes. Then add the 5 whites whipped   steam 80 minutes

Circassian Pudding

4 oz of Butter 4 oz of Sugar 4 eggs 4 oz of crumbled sponge cakes, 2 oz of chopped peel 4 oz of cherries, a wine glass of brandy proceed in the usual way a little caramel and a jill of cream. Steam 2 hours

Lemon Cream

4 eggs 6 oz of Sugar 3 lemons gelatine and cream, beat the yolks with the sugar for 15 minutes add the juice of 3 lemons and the grated rind of 2 beating well all the time snow the whites, and add the gelatine & whites

Paradise Pudding

On a war footing: Winston and Clementine inspecting bomb damage.

The tiny kitchen in the Cabinet War Rooms, complete with unexpected man.

The family: Algy, Yvonne, Georgina and Maud, mid 1930s.

Yvonne and Georgina.

Georgina's headshot for publicity around her recipe book, 1958.

Georgina, Elisabeth, Yvonne, Edwina and Ted, 1951.

Old friends: Clementine Churchill on her 80th birthday,
and Georgina Landemare on her 79th.

Winston was constantly overspending and having to cut back, a never-ending cause of tension with Clementine, who'd been left with a lifelong fear of debt after her rackety childhood. Money worries exacerbated the rifts sometimes apparent in their close relationship: there were rumours that the couple were near to divorce in 1933, and throughout much of the marriage Clementine took regular breaks from Winston, staying at health farms or departing happily with friends on holidays on the continent or on their yachts.[51]

There were sporadic and usually half-hearted economy drives: in 1926 Winston had declared that 'no more champagne is to be bought. Unless special directions are given only white or red wine, or whisky and soda will be offered at luncheon, or dinner. The Wine Book to be shown to me every week. No more port is to be opened without special instructions.'[52]

Staff were a big cost, and always at risk when economies were necessary. They usually consisted at Chartwell of five to nine female indoor staff (a lady's maid, parlourmaid, cook, kitchen maid and two housemaids, plus housekeeper and assorted other parlour- and housemaids depending on the yearly budget), plus six to nine male staff. Most would travel with them to London when they went, leaving three or four people back in Kent.

In 1937, Winston's licence for manservants included a butler (who doubled as a valet), three gardeners, chauffeur, odd man and an estate carpenter. There was sometimes a groom and there had been nannies and nursery maids, although by now they had gone, leaving only Mary's governess/companion Maryott Whyte (Clemmie's cousin), and there was also a varying cast of private secretaries and researchers for Winston's books. Of these, Grace Hamblin, who started in 1932 as a temporary assistant secretary was the most significant, though in general the secretaries tended to outlast the domestic staff below them. Laundry, with all those goffered aprons and starched collars, was sent out.[53]

The accounts for Chartwell and Morpeth Mansions in the 1930s show a constant procession of servants, especially maids, and the family seem to have haemorrhaged staff. Maryott Whyte, Chartwell's custodian in Clementine's absence, wrote to her in April 1935, apologising for burdening her with domestic details, but

> The kitchen staff at present consists of Mrs Moore temporary cook whom you know – fairly good and quite agreeable gets on well with the staff, and [an] excellent [temporary kitchen maid]. I simply could not get a permanent one from any of the offices or by advertisement. The very good little local girl who I engaged as between maid I have turned into scullery maid as the [kitchen] maid would not come without one. The point is this: we cannot go on with an expensive temp k[itchen] m[aid] & as we seem unable to get one without a scullery maid shall I get the latter or try to putting the little between maid back into the house? I shall hang onto the temporary km till you have seen her. I think if she would undertake it she is the kind of girl you might like to train as cook.[54]

Such concerns were typical and never-ending. Clementine's engagement diaries are full of both interviews for staff and details of when new maids started, and when they were to be picked up. They used extra help at weekends as a matter of course – a Mrs Alvey in 1937, probably a washer-upper and general char – and Winston's budgetary proposals for 1937 included registry fees of £15 to cover all of the temporary staff they used.

Cooks were frequently hired in, mainly from the usual agencies – Massey's, Hunt's and the Regina Agency, and on occasion whole dinners were purchased for the London flat.[55] In March 1938, the Chef Supply Company supplied consommé double, *poulet sauté chasseur*, smoked salmon and brie at a cost of £1.7s.6d.[56] Even at Chartwell caterers were used, including the pre-eminent London firm of Gunters, who catered a garden party in 1934 with items including foie gras sandwiches, caviar and a range of French pâtisserie, as well as the ice creams for which they were famed.[57] Winston may have relished the occasion as much as the food, but he had been brought up on expensive, quality ingredients, and had an appreciation of fine dining, along with definite tastes, mainly for consommé, foie gras, caviar and plovers' eggs.

Clementine, an avid dieter at times, shared his love of a well-prepared dish, writing from a convalescent home in 1928, 'I am thinking of all the delicious food I shall eat when I get home'.[58] Unlike her husband, who could barely cook an egg, she well knew how it was all created. Her early memories revolved around food, from the scones she ate in Scotland as a child, to the horrors of her school, which smelt of haddock, to the food that surrounded her as a teenager in Dieppe.

Her mother, Blanche, had contributed articles to the *Daily Express* on cookery, and according to Clemmie she 'was very much interested in food. She was in fact an excellent cook, but not a good housekeeper, because when we had food it was delicious, but sometimes when she was bored we had no food at all.'[59]

It was a lesson that left Clemmie determined to be both, which was why she enrolled in Marcel Boulestin's cookery classes, heading off for a month's work of lessons in October 1933.[60] She and Violet Bonham Carter both knew his restaurant already, and she may well have added his books to her collection.[61] They were very popular, based on his philosophy of cooking: 'I decided my work should be of the empiric kind and with as few technical terms as possible … cooking must be natural and exact science was of no help'.[62] In other words, he didn't include many weights and measures, and his recipes were short and to the point. Georgina's were the same.

Lessons with Boulestin, and her own sharp intelligence, meant that Clementine, who described herself as 'a theoretical, rather than a practical cook', was an exacting mistress for her culinary staff. She admitted that she took on 'eager but inexperienced young cooks', who were cheap, but also rarely lasted more than a year or so.

She armed herself with an array of cookery books, identifiable from the notes she scribbled in the daily menu books, and tutored her cooks not only in what to cook but also how to construct the perfect menu. Mary

Soames recalled that as a child she would hide under the desk, or burrow into the scented silkiness of her mother's underwear in the wardrobe, while a succession of visitors came through to talk to Clemmie, still in bed with a breakfast tray and her curlers in.

This included 'the daily conference with the cook, who, in spotless white overall and apron, bearing the menu book, would draw up a chair and seat herself at the bedside'.[63] The only surviving pre-war menu book, which is very much a working document, contains page after page of carefully written menus, with Clemmie's large, erratic pencilled notes across the pages. She crossed out some dishes, and wrote in others, sometimes adding whole menus in French, which she both spoke and wrote immaculately.

She also gave recipe references: 'swedish lamb cutlets G. F. page 103; veg chicory page 218, pommes à la frangipani 154 Lady Sysonby', on 24 October 1936, and 'goulash of beef 217, try meringues à la suisse page 241' on the 25th. From the pages of the book, a partial list of her recipe books emerges: *Good Food* by Ambrose Heath (1932, the cover was proudly proclaimed to be both 'WASHABLE' and 'WATERPROOF'); *More Good Food*, also by Ambrose Heath (1933); Lady Sysonby's *Cook Book* (1935, aimed at 'those, not necessarily rich, who want good food and mean to have it'), and *Scents and Dishes* by Dorothy Allhusen (1927).

Dorothy was Clemmie's first cousin once removed, and had collected her recipes from various titled or well-known ladies in France and England. Among the pages was a recipe for chocolate cake, given by Clemmie's mother, Blanche. Clemmie must have shared it with Georgina, for Georgie, having tweaked it slightly, wrote it into her own manuscript.[64] Clemmie almost certainly had another of Allhusen's books, *A Medley of Recipes* (1936), to which Clemmie contributed some of her own recipes, including one for 'parmesan fingers' and another for 'leeks à la Greque' (to be served cold, having been boiled in oil, water, lemon juice and seasonings).

Another cutting slipped into the pages of Georgina's manuscript book was a recipe from Ambrose Heath: she and Clementine shared very similar tastes. Georgina's 'Mousse of Café Wellesbourne' is almost word for word that published by Dorothy Allhusen in *A Medley of Recipes*, as is her 'Gateau Worplesdon', though the former is attributed by Allhusen to Mrs Allhusen, and the latter to Lady Celia Congreve (a poet and holder of the French *croix de guerre* for her work as a nurse during the 1914–18 conflict). Where the various recipes originated, and who borrowed what from whom, is impossible to say. Allhusen's book was partly sold on having contributions from her circle of well-known socialites and relatives, and a willing suspension of disbelief must have been required from her readers, to think that all of the recipes came directly from their often aristocratic pens, and not those of their cooks.

The Churchill menus were mainly written in English (except where Clemmie wrote dishes in), and were plain but varied. Lunch on 9 October 1936 involved eggs (Clemmie has added 'fried' and 'tomato sauce'), roast shoulder of lamb, onion sauce, roast potatoes, spinach (replacing the cook's suggestion of marrow), lettuce salad and apple fritters (with hot apricot sauce added). Dinner was soup, whiting au gratin, roast duck, chips, orange salad, green salad and (added by Clemmie) a charlotte as a sweet.

Pencilled notes on ordering show that four wild ducks and four partridge were required, the latter originally planned for the next day. On 15 October, lunch was cold boiled beef, cabbage, potatoes, salad and 'cinnamon apples cream', with dinner of chicken soup, grilled sole with 'sharp buttery sauce', roast pheasant, bread sauce, the glorious-sounding 'buttery crumbs', chip potatoes, 'spinache' [sic], salad and 'merengues' [sic]. Mary's nursery supper was liver and bacon, potatoes, 'salad' and more 'merengues'.

From this menu book comes the first detailed mention of Georgina at Chartwell. The Churchills had an established record of hiring temporary cooks, both to cover holidays and for specific occasions. While many were average agency cooks, they ranged up and down the culinary hierarchy. In July 1936, Winston was given a dispensation to use a French chef, Maurice Pierre Pinel. Was he too expensive? Not good value? Just dreadful? Whatever the problem was, he was not heard of again.

Instead, in November 1936, amid the pages of slightly dubiously spelt menus written by the anonymous everyday Chartwell cook, Georgina's flowing writing, nearly all in French, stands out a mile. The book, along with Clementine's engagement diaries, show that she was at Chartwell for the weekends of 21–22 November 1936, 5–6 December 1936 and 8–9 May 1937, and then that she arrived, departure unknown, on 1 and 8 April (both

Thursdays) and Saturday 15 October 1938. On the latter day, at least, she came down by train from London, arriving at Westerham, then the nearest station to Chartwell at 2½ miles away, at 8.58 a.m.

On the weekend of 21–22 November 1936, Winston and Clementine hosted Jack and Goonie Churchill, Winston's brother and sister-in-law; Edward (Eddie) Marsh, one of Winston's ex-private secretaries, now a civil servant in the colonial office and a very long-time collaborator; Pierre-Étienne Flandin, the ex-French prime minister, now foreign minister; and Professor Frederick Lindemann (later Viscount Cherwell), an Oxford University physicist and close advisor to Winston during the 1930s and 1940s.

The 'Prof', as he was known, was a challenge for the cook: virtually teetotal, vegetarian and fussy. His meals were listed separately: on 12 January 1938, he had onion soup, eggs in mayonnaise salad and macaroni cheese; on 30 January, it was tomato or pea soup, macaroni and mayonnaise and spinach; and on 24 April, it was pea soup, spaghetti cheese au gratin and egg mayonnaise plus lettuce. Mary Soames recalled that her mother 'took immense pains to see he was provided with delicious special dishes. He said he liked eggs, but Sarah [her sister] and I used to observe with astonishment how he would meticulously remove the yolk, consuming only the whites.'[65]

He had something of a propensity for white food – and his delicious special dishes involved a lot of pasta. He didn't arrive until the Sunday on this weekend, so the meals Georgina cooked on the Saturday were for everyone. Lunch started with *oeufs ecarlatte* – the recipe in Georgina's cookery book calls for hard-boiled eggs with finely chopped tongue and whipped raw egg to be steamed (probably in her beloved fancy moulds), and served on fried bread croutes; they then went on to *gigot d'agneau* (leg of lamb) with vegetables and *sauce soubise* (a velouté sauce made of a roux plus stock, with added onions) and *gateau de riz* (rice pudding) with apricot sauce and iced whipped cream.

Dinner comprised a consommé, *filets de sole meurat*, *faisans hongroise* (pheasant), *glace andalouse* (ice cream) and savoury canapés. The menus were in French, not in honour of Monsieur Flandin, but because that was what Georgina cooked and why she was employed. The pattern of soup-fish-main-sweet-savoury was a pared-down version of the old Edwardian soup-fish-entrée-roast-sweet-dessert-maybe-a-savoury-and-possibly-a-few-extra-courses-as-well dinners in which Georgina had had her earliest training. The nod to Hungary and Andalucía added a cosmopolitan touch without going too far down the composed salad or savoury banana route.

Clementine, who approved the menu, had only made two changes, substituting the leg of lamb for a planned shoulder, and the apricot sauce for Georgina's suggested apple (she also added the iced whipped cream, but dessert was often implied, rather than written, so this may not really have been an omission).

The next day was similar, and again all in French: eggs 'Victoria', sautéed chicken with sauce chasseur (a rich, dark sauce enriched with tomatoes) and vegetables, a biscuit cake and pear purée for lunch, and a thick soup, turbot 'indienne', stuffed partridge 'Italienne', praline ice cream and more savoury canapés. Diners weren't necessarily expected to eat everything, or even sample everything, and it's impossible to tell exactly who ate what, but it's hard to escape the impression that Winston's dietary advice hadn't completely taken hold.

It wasn't the first time Georgina had cooked at Chartwell, but she must have made a particularly good impression. There were no more flirtations with French male chefs, or indeed any cooks other than the Chartwell regular, and instead the Churchills brought Georgina back, this time in December, cooking for the leader of the Liberal Party, Archibald Sinclair, and his wife Marigold, as well as Harcourt Johnstone, a politician who was at that point out of Parliament but nevertheless a leading Liberal.[66]

At lunch they ate gnocchi, chateaubriand steak with a provençale sauce and a lemon soufflé, while for dinner it was chicken consommé, sole filets 'pompadour', roast duck with vegetables, vanilla-and-fig ice cream with cherry sauce and the usual savouries. Sunday's offerings included eggs with tripe, lamb with vegetables, peach or pear rice pudding for lunch, and for dinner, borscht to start, red mullet, sautéed chicken Stanley (onions, tomatoes, mushrooms, cream) with vegetables, pineapple ice cream and a matching compote, and a croque-monsieur to end.

Again, the menus were in French, and, while some of the recipes featured in her manuscript book (the chicken Stanley, borscht and the sole, for example), others did not. That weekend was a fraught one for Winston, who probably missed lunch, and possibly dinner as well, on the Saturday: that evening he was still in London, at the Churchills' flat in Morpeth Mansions, writing a desperately reassuring letter to Edward VIII, 'no pistol is to be held to the King's head. No doubt that this request will be granted. Therefore no final decision or Bill till after Christmas.'[67]

This was the Abdication Crisis, which was coming to a head: despite Winston's reassurances, on 11 December the king abdicated in order to marry Wallis Simpson, and Winston, whose support of the king had led to him being booed out of the House of Commons on Monday the 7th, reached what one biographer has called 'the lowest ebb of [his] career'.[68]

Lunch on 9 December, made by the usual cook, included one of Winston's favourites, Irish stew, along with carrots, onions, boiled potatoes, salad and sweet. Dinner was fried filets of sole, anchovy sauce, roast chicken with bread sauce, puréed potatoes, braised celery, salad, lemon curd tartlets and cream. The contrast with Georgina's menu just a few days before was stark. It was a low ebb indeed.

Supporting the (now ex) king was a terrible career move, however laudable the principles behind his stance may have been, at least to him. However, he was far from ended, and, despite attempts to deselect him, Winston continued to host his dinners, as well as attend regular dinners at the 'Other Club', a political dining club he had co-founded in 1911, and he kept his power-base alive and well. His finances nosedived, however, even to the extent that he – briefly – put Chartwell on the market.

The Chartwell cooks were encouraged to learn from Georgina on her days with them, and she was generous with her knowledge: Clementine said that 'to them she would impart as much of her knowledge and skill as they were able to absorb'.[69] On 21 February 1937, the cook had a crack at borscht, and Boodle's orange fool makes five and a half appearances in the menu book (one is crossed out). The recipe was written down in *Scents and Dishes*, as well as being in Georgina's own book, and was an easy one to follow.

Meanwhile, the Churchills struggled to afford even temporary staff of the standard they so desired. In 1938, Winston proposed the drastic measure of cutting the Chartwell indoor servants down to three (with two more to be kept at the flat) – whether it happened is a moot point, although Clementine placed an advert in the *Irish Independent* in late September: 'Mrs Winston Churchill requires first class cook-housekeeper for house in Kent. Kitchen maid kept. Hard-working and economical manager, used to numbers and entertaining. Age 30–35. Wages £80–90.'

The kitchen maid's position had been advertised, with a salary of £40–45 and a desired age of 19–22, in the days just before, with 'Mrs Winston Churchill' a little less prominent – beady-eyed potential cooks might not have spotted that the family were clearly in mid-servant crisis and seeking cheaper staff, despite their apparent status.[70] That said, the adverts still mean that they were aiming for two staff in the kitchen, and so it's likely that there were four or five in total, for it would have been unthinkable not to have had at least one housemaid and a parlourmaid as well.

The butler had already gone, with Clementine writing in his reference that they were opting for a cheaper parlourmaid instead.[71] Irish servants had the reputation as being cheap and hard-working, hence the adverts for the kitchen staff being in the *Irish Independent* and not *The Times*. They were also looking through Hunts at the same time, paying 2s 6d for expenses to interview a potential cook-housekeeper on 4 September 1938 (presumably it didn't work out).[72]

Georgina doesn't appear in Clementine's engagement diaries between October 1938 and January 1940. She charged more than the Churchills could now afford, but it didn't matter to her, for she had plenty of work elsewhere.

In August 1939, the Churchills went on a family holiday to France, staying in Normandy with Consuelo Balsan, the ex-Duchess of Marlborough, since divorced and remarried. Winston went to inspect the Maginot Line, returning to join the rest of the family and assorted guests as they swam, played tennis and foraged for wild strawberries (he mainly spent the time painting).

However, it was impossible to ignore what he called 'the deep apprehension brooding over all', and as Germany and Russia signed their pact of mutual non-aggression, the family travelled home, passing through the Gare du Nord which, as Mary Soames noted, 'was teeming with soldiers: the French army was mobilising'.[73]

Georgina, meanwhile, was spending the summer near Newmarket, where the race season went from July to October. She was cooking for William Tatem, Baron Glanely, a significant racehorse owner, known as 'Sporting Bill' within the racing fraternity. He'd made his money in shipping, working his way up from a clerk's position, and been ennobled in 1918.[74] Widowed, his only son had died in infancy and he ploughed his considerable talent and money into houses and racing, owning La Grange Stables near Newmarket when they were at their peak. Exning House, one of two houses he owned near the town, was an imposing Georgian mansion that had been more than doubled in size in the 1890s with the addition of a somewhat incongruous, albeit stunning, Arts and Crafts extension.

The kitchen came complete with its own cook's room, generally built to house male chefs away from the shared rooms of the female staff in the Victorian era, so Georgina would have had her own room, which led both onto the kitchen and out to the service courtyard, with its game larder and larders, and the laundry block at the end. She had the services of a kitchen maid, Minnie (Camilla) Sargant, and a scullery maid, Edith Chapman, who at 18 was younger than Georgina's daughter Yvonne, now 24 and working.[75]

Tatem entertained on a grand scale, hence the house and its top-notch staff, brought in for the season (his housekeeper, Margaret Dunning, was permanent, and well-regarded in the area). It showed just how far Georgina had come.

However, war was looming. As the horses pounded

round the Newmarket flats, plans were already being put into place for the evacuation of mothers and children from London, to be sent to safe areas, which included both Chartwell and Exning, as well as Northampton, where Georgina's sister Maud took in two evacuated schoolboys.

On 1 September, Hitler invaded Poland; on the 2nd, Neville Chamberlain issued his ultimatum; and on the 3rd, Britain officially declared war on Germany. Georgina had already lived through one world war, and she was well aware of the potential impact on the people she cooked for, and the houses she cooked in.

In the first few weeks of war, decisions had to be made, and made quickly. William Tatem dropped everything and headed for Cardiff, where his business interests were, leaving Georgina and the rest of his servants in Exning. Margaret Hancock, the Churchills' cook at Morpeth Mansions, and at 57 the same age as Georgina, had already retired, and had moved to Reading to live with her daughter. The cook was now 35-year-old Minnie Brady.[76]

Meanwhile, Winston Churchill re-entered the Cabinet and was made First Lord of the Admiralty. His utter conviction that he was destined to make history seemed to be coming true. For an ageing cook in need of job security in a suddenly very insecure world, the Churchills, who couldn't afford her, but would definitely value her, must have looked like a very sound bet indeed.

6

The Wartime Cook

'Mousseline pudding', from Georgina Landemare's 1930s handwritten recipe book. A gorgeously light steamed sponge pudding.

> *Take 2 oz of butter and the grated rind of two lemons, work together to a cream, then add 2 oz of sugar and work again and by degrees, add 2 oz of flour, 3 raw yolks, the juice of a lemon. Mix well again for 10 minutes, then add the 5 whites whipped. Steam 80 minutes.*[1]

On 29 September 1939, a National Register was taken, detailing the population of England and Wales. It was less comprehensive than the various censuses had been, but nevertheless provides a comprehensive snapshot of the nation. In these early days of the war, schemes that had been hastily planned in the previous months were put into action: evacuation of mothers and children, full armed forces mobilisation, the issue of identity cards, the voluntary recruitment of women and the conscription of men. Less than a month after war was officially declared, the Register recorded a population that was confused, displaced and only half-prepared for war.

Exning House, where Georgina had been catering for William Tatem's horseracing parties, like so many homes in rural areas, was deemed safe for evacuees and selected for billeting. Three schoolteachers and twenty 13- and 14-year-old boys descended upon the house in early September, and were duly recorded there on the 29th. Tatem's eight-strong domestic staff were still resident, although with Tatem off in Wales they were probably deep in brown paper and boxes, packing up his belongings and safeguarding the furniture.

They were not alone in being swept up in evacuation: the *Cambridge Daily News* reported that 630 children and thirty mothers of children of pre-school age were now in the area, and that several locals had already contracted scarlet fever from them. Plans were afoot to deal with the evacuees' 'verminous bedding and clothing', for, as was not uncommon in children evacuated from the poor areas of London and other urban centres, many of which had not changed much from before the last war, many children had lice.[2]

Exacerbated by class differences, as well as the norms of rural life, complaints abounded among host families about their new charges' hygiene, behaviour and eating habits, particularly when it came to using – or not using – cutlery. It was a culture shock for the evacuees, too, who often found country life boring after the whirl of London – the two families who found themselves at Chartwell left after a week because it was 'too dull'.[3] Georgina and the other house staff weren't being paid to stay at Exning and look after the boys, though, and their dispersal was inevitable, whether through retirement, in the case of housekeeper Margaret Dunning, or by joining up, seen as a duty for single women even before the advent of female conscription in 1941.

At 57, Georgina was too old for conscription when it eventually arrived. Neither was she the retiring type. Her pension was limited to what the state would provide, and, unlike the Churchills' London cook, Margaret Hancock, who moved in with her daughter, the idea of living with Yvonne can't have held much joy, given their lacklustre relationship. At 24, Yvonne was now a shorthand typist for a chartered accountant, living with Eve in Brentford, and prone to depression. She was romantically involved with Horace (Ted) Higgins, then editor of the *Morley College Magazine* (she'd met him when she attended the college herself).

The college was left-leaning, with several prominent feminist figures on its staff, and Yvonne may well have chosen it deliberately for its liberal stance, so removed from Georgina's own, more right-wing, outlook. Ted was intelligent and charismatic, and devoted to the cause of education, becoming the secretary for the National Association of Boys Clubs in 1940. They would marry in 1941. At some point in the late autumn of 1939, therefore, Georgina wrote to Clementine Churchill, proposing herself as their wartime cook.

It was a very strange time in Britain that autumn. The Phoney War, as it became known, led to 4,000 deaths through accidents in the blackout, and only three deaths through enemy action. Mary (Churchill, better known by her married name, Mary Soames), Winston and Clementine's daughter, then aged 17, recalled spending hours sewing blackout curtains while her father energised the Admiralty, but Neville Chamberlain, the prime minister, took the weekends off.

Ration books were issued, in line with a scheme carefully drawn up based on learnings from the previous war, with bacon, butter and sugar due to be restricted by law from 8 January 1940. Chartwell, after the unsuccessful evacuation experiment, was mothballed. Kathleen Hill, Winston's personal private secretary, wrote letters, including to the regular coffee supplier, Captain Harry Jackson, instructing them to cease deliveries 'as this house is now closed'.[4]

Most of the staff were laid off, including the under-gardeners, and the lakes, which were so distinctive from the air, therefore making the house an obvious target for German bombers, were partially filled in. Those remaining were used for a more successful evacuation venture, when negotiations with Sidney Plater of the Harrods Live Stock department resulted in 1,000 valuable fish being deposited there (Churchill got to keep the prettiest ones in return).

Accounts of the occasional visits that the family made back to Chartwell throughout the war show that the fish were a definite hit, even after the lack of maintenance elsewhere started to show – Mary described the once 'limpid cool-glittering green' swimming pool as 'covered with brown splodges', and the tennis court as looking 'as though it's got eczema' in July 1941.[5] The kitchen garden was, however, maintained, and was able to keep up a steady supply of vegetables and fruit throughout the war – including Winston's favourite peaches, which were fan-trained against the garden walls, and which he was in the habit of munching on as he ambled around the gardens before the war.[6] There were also beehives, which were very productive, at least in the early days of the war, and honey was a permanent feature of the Churchill wartime family breakfasts. The wider estate was dug up for root crops, which suffered rabbit damage, before eventually being turned over to grazing.[7]

Three days before rationing started, on Friday 5 January 1940, Clementine's engagement diary records a meeting with Georgina. It was a fairly typical week for Clementine in 1940: an Admiralty dinner party on the Tuesday, a wool committee meeting on the Wednesday, a perm on the Thursday, with visits to Goonie and Chartwell, and a film showing on the Saturday. Whether this was a formal interview or merely a meeting to set out Georgina's terms of engagement, it proved satisfactory to all concerned. Clementine later recorded her delight in securing Georgina's full-time and permanent services, saying that 'I was enchanted because I knew she would make the best out of rations, and that everyone in the household would be happy and contented'.[8]

She joined the household as cook on 2 February 1940, initially at Admiralty House. Officially a French citizen (by dint of her marriage), she had to be naturalised as British. Admiralty House was connected to the Admiralty itself, and meals were frequently broken up by tidings coming through the connecting door between the Churchills' living quarters and the offices next door. Winston, who took personal control over as much as possible, would rush from the table, leaving his family to continue with the meal. Mary remembered that

> sometimes he would return before the meal was finished and, picking up the thread of conversation as best he might while his plate (carefully kept warm) was placed before him, excuse himself with the (obvious) explanation and apology for the necessity of urgent business – and one knew better than to enquire further.[9]

In May, disastrous action in Norway precipitated a vote of no confidence in the government, leading to the resignation of Chamberlain, and appointment of Churchill as prime minister. By 17 June that year, Clementine and Winston, along with Mary, had moved to No.10 Downing Street with their immediate domestic staff. Only two would prove to be permanent fixtures until 1945: Georgina and the valet, Frank Sawyers, 'a little, baldish Cumbrian with a round florid face, piercing blue eyes and a pronounced lisp'.

Sawyers was prone to practical jokes, but he was utterly devoted to Winston Churchill, and he was one of the few people who could successfully control him when he was ignoring his doctors' orders, or chivvy him along when he was running late. Both Frank Sawyers and Georgina were named as people to be evacuated with the Churchills in the event of London being invaded, the only two of his domestic staff to be included in a list of eleven (other support staff, not domestic, but secretarial, were Kathleen Hill and his official private secretaries, Eric Seal and Anthony Bevir – the rest were mainly family and close advisors).[10]

There were other servants around though, including a housemaid and a parlourmaid, Nellie Goble, who once came rushing in screaming that the Germans were coming, because she'd seen a parachutist standing on the roof of Admiralty House – which turned out to be the statue on top of Nelson's Column seen over the roof from Horse Guards Parade. There was at least one kitchen maid or, more likely, one of the other staff doubled as kitchen help when required. Elizabeth Nel, another of the secretaries, recalled that 'labour was naturally a very difficult problem in those days, especially as much official entertaining had to be done, and these people were hard-worked. However, though well aware of their responsibilities, they were a cheerful crew and often made us laugh.' She described Georgina as 'a round body who could tell one in detail the intricacies of marriage and divorce among the aristocracy'. She was certainly rotund by 1940: Charles Thompson, Winston's personal assistant, said she was 'short and very stout', but also reiterated that 'she produced superb meals, often under most difficult conditions'.[11]

All of the staff were subject to security vetting, although they could come and go as they pleased once they were known. With St James's Park directly opposite Downing Street, it became a haven for employer and employee alike, with Elizabeth Nel's recollections of pelicans and ducks reflecting Mary Soames's wistful musings on the flowers and the sense of freedom from war when walking in the park.

The kitchen at Downing Street, predictably, given it was a Georgian terrace, was in the basement, but it had the advantage of a huge glass window at the back, only the lowest panes of which were below ground level. The kitchen occupied a full slice across the building, and there was another, only slightly smaller, window opposite, but it also had electric lighting above the central table and working areas.

Photographs from the 1920s show a whole wall of gas burners as well as gas ovens, but there is also a coal-burning closed range and a large, separate, warming cupboard. Hot water was provided by a boiler with a huge tank fitted to one side of the chimney, and there would have been a separate scullery and the usual larders and store rooms. The photographs also show a slightly ramshackle selection of dressers and cupboards holding copper pans and lids, as well as graded jugs and other vessels. The presence of spit racks on one wall, as well as redundant spit fittings over the range, provide evidence of years of use and physical change, which were not over, for the kitchen was further modernised in 1937, including the addition of a service lift to transport the food up to the dining room on the floor above.[12] Churchill himself would, on occasion, pop past to tell the kitchen staff 'we are ready', or to warn them there were extra guests.[13]

There was a picture of the bombers heading out on the wall of the nearby servants' hall, and Georgina remembered Churchill looking at it with tears in his eyes, saying 'I saw them all go out ... and very few came back'.[14] She was well used to cooking in kitchens with a mixture of old and new technology, including that of Chartwell, with its coal-fuelled range and electric refrigerators, and was entirely unfazed by her new working environment.

She was also provided with a bedroom at Downing Street, along with a place in the air raid shelter, built in the gardens and soon to be in frequent use. She gave up the lease on the rooms in Denbigh Place at some stage during the war: Yvonne was living with Eve when she married Ted in 1941, so there would have been little point in continuing to pay for them – especially with the risk that they might be flattened in a bombing raid, with all of the hassle that would incur.

Another official residence was Chequers, given to the nation in 1921 on the grounds that not all future prime minsters might have their own country houses, and that the peace and antiquity of the place might 'suggest some saving virtues in the continuity of English history, and exercise a check upon too hasty upheavals'. It came with its own staff, under the housekeeper Mrs Lamont, and expenses were to be met by a combination of the Chequers Trust, the government (official entertaining) and the incumbent (personal expenses).

Churchill used it, like Chartwell, both for entertaining and for political discussions and policymaking away from the formal structures of power. People were invited for luncheons, or to 'dine and sleep', and it would become a key part of the pattern of unofficial, but vital, diplomacy that he liked to practise. Displaced monarchs and other statesmen, such as Charles de Gaulle, were regular visitors, along with ambassadors, advisors and – occasionally – friends. Outsiders – 'fringe' friends – were carefully excluded in case of security issues. Security, along with the difficulty of recruiting and retaining staff, also led to changes in the household personnel. Civilians were phased out, and members of the ATS and WAAF brought in to replace them (in keeping with so much early women's war work, which had a tendency to reflect notions of what women should be doing, according to ideas of the time).

A staged photograph of the kitchens shows four fortuitously young and lovely female service personnel at work in the kitchen, which had been built as a new wing in 1910, and subsequently modernised to provide space not only for the ministerial cooks but also for a canteen for security and support staff.[15] The house had its own farm to provide extra vegetables and fruit, but it was surrounded by troops, both temporarily billeted in nearby fields and permanently there for official protection, and they made for dangers of their own. Doris Miles, one of the nurses looking after Winston when he was recuperating from an illness there in 1943, felt sufficiently unsettled by one of her encounters with them that she noted, 'next time if I see any soldiers I shall go the other way'.[16]

Over the course of the war, the Churchills spent most weekends at Chequers – except when the moon was full, and the house deemed too obvious from the air, at which point the family decamped to Dytchley House, to stay with Conservative politician Ronald Tree and his American wife, interior designer Nancy Tree, whose own cook then took charge, complete with extra rations to cope with the influx. Georgina initially seems not to have cooked at Chequers, presumably because there was an in-house cook until the staff reorganisation.

In December 1940, Mary gave details in her diary of a dinner without Clementine, who had gone to bed with a sore throat: 'Papa in very bad mood over food and of course I couldn't control him & he was very naughty & rushed out & complained to the cook about the soup which he (truthfully) said was tasteless. I fear the domestic apple-cart may have been upset! Oh dear!' He returned, in a foul mood, to 'give a disquisition on the inadequacy of the food at Chequers and the fact that the ability to make a good soup is the test of a cook'.[17] Soup remained a true Churchill obsession, and Georgina later recalled that 'Mr Churchill liked clear soup, he was very, he always liked consommé, you see ... at night time, cold, he used to have sometimes, you see, and she liked, she liked thick soups but she liked clear too.'

The bits of his doctors' dietary advice from the mid-1930s that he liked had stuck, notably the suggestion that he snack: in Yalta in 1945 he was supplied with chicken soup in a thermos in breaks from meetings, and the pre-bed jellied soup habit continued well after the war. Georgina would make batches and keep it ready for him, so that he could have it every night – even when travelling, when it would go with him, to be served last thing by his valet (or, on one occasion when the valet was late back, the King of Denmark, who found it hilarious).[18] His personal accounts from his trips abroad inevitably include payments for soup – in America in 1942, Magruder Inc. in Washington DC presented him with a bill that included sherry, lemon juice, phenomenally expensive imported sardines, and both clear sherry soup and royal consommé.[19] It's entirely possible therefore that this tasteless soup incident was a contributory factor to the change of staff, for later in the war Georgina would be driven over to Chequers, to cook in lieu of the barely trained ATS provision.

Downing Street and Chequers would be only two of the kitchens in which Georgina would operate during the war, however. Even before the official declaration of war in September 1939, it had been recognised that in the case of air raids, better protection was necessary than the underground stations that formed the mainstay of early wartime provision. The London Passenger Transport Board itself took up residence at the former Down Street station (between Hyde Park Corner and Green Park stations, and out of use by 1932), and their dining room garnered quite a reputation among those eligible to eat there.

Jock Colville, whose diaries form an acerbic and detailed commentary on life at Downing Street during the war, ate there as much as he could, and he was by no means the only senior figure to seek culinary solace underground. In November 1940, he and Winston enjoyed 'caviar (almost unobtainable in these days of restricted imports), Perrier Jouet 1928, 1865 brandy and excellent cigars'.[20]

Meanwhile at Storey's Gate, the next building over from Downing Street, feverish work was afoot to build a

Central War Rooms (also known as the Cabinet War Rooms, or CWR), which would eventually encompass the majority of the large basement area under the New Public Office (now Treasury) building, and house hundreds of personnel. Rooms were set aside for Clementine and Winston as bedrooms, and there was also a dining room and (by 1941) a kitchen.

The kitchen was tiny, intended for occasional and emergency use, but it was still fully functional. It had two standard-sized domestic electric ovens with grills, electric plate warmers, hot running water from a boiler and a huge extractor fan. Ingenious use was made of pull-down worktops and shelves, but it was thoroughly utilitarian: even the pans were enamelware or aluminium, and, like the rest of the bunker, it had the air of something thrown together at the last minute. Oddly, the only photograph of it shows a man posing as if taking something out of the oven, but this was never a man's domain: it was Georgina's. That said, although Clementine and, indeed, Mary, slept in the bunker on a number of occasions, Winston hated it, believing his role was to remain visible and above ground (often literally, since he had a habit of nipping up to the roof to watch the bombs fall over the rest of London).

It wasn't just him, either, and he wrote to Randolph in 1941, 'The Annexe is now becoming a very strong place, but we have only once been below during a raid. Your Mother is now insisting upon becoming a fire watcher on the roof, so it will look very odd if I take advantage of the securities provided.'[21] How many times Georgina actually used the CWR kitchen is moot – it was probably used mainly for boiling water for tea. Separate provision was made for those working down there, and, although Colville dismissed it as 'endless soup and sausages', it was fairly typical of mainstream mess-room provision. Upstairs in the offices there was yet another mess, specifically for the staff from No.10, under the command of a Mrs Norgren, a Swedish cook supplied by Brendan Bracken, a long-time supporter of Churchill, appointed Minister of Information in 1941.

One of the reasons for the constant attempts to better bomb-proof the bunker, as well as the addition of the kitchen, was the London Blitz of September 1940 to May 1941. Eight months of daily and nightly air raids left over 40,000 people dead, and much of London in ruins. Londoners grew used to going to bed half-dressed, hastening to shelters when the sirens went, or, for those without cellars or private provision, to spend the night bunked down in tube stations.

Bombsite tourism drew crowds to the worst-hit areas, especially when they were well-known streets. Vere Hodgson, an office worker who kept a diary to send to her relatives, was typical:

we took a bus to Marble Arch, passed Whiteleys and saw the mess. Only fourteen people were killed … but it was bad enough … walked along Bond Street – a lot of damage. In Piccadilly found St James' Church – it is just standing, nothing more … then I took a bus to St Paul's. Found the place where the Time Bomb was … scarcely a business premises that is habitable, though a few more than in Holborn.[22]

Clementine and Winston were conspicuous and welcome visitors to bombed-out streets, and the former was also very active in organising compensation schemes, as well as food and lavatory provision in temporary accommodation. Photographs of the couple, either jointly or alone, with officials and civilians and a background of devastation, helped to form their public image, and as the raids spread across Britain in the months that followed, Winston and his cigar, and Clementine and her bright turbans, one of which had Winston's speeches printed upon it, became iconic. Back at Downing Street, he would hustle Georgina down to the shelter, admonishing that, 'I always have to be out after you. If Mr Hitler gets you, I won't get my soup!'[23]

On 14 October, Vere Hodgson wrote, 'what an awful night we had. They never ceased until after 5am. We could not count the bombs we heard.' Several fell very close to No.10, where the sirens had just started wailing. Georgina's recollection of events is typically underplayed:

> I didn't think they were overhead, which they were, you see ... I'd got a mousseline pudding on you see, and it was – I don't know – it was half past seven or eight o clock at night – and he was late for dinner and of course this is a pudding you can't turn out, you see. If it had been an ordinary sort of sweet I'd've had it ready for him but the raid came on, as it did come on quick, you see.

Winston's own version is a tad more grandiose:

'Suddenly I had a providential impulse ... I became aware of the big window (25ft high plate-glass in the kitchen) behind which Mrs Landemare, the cook, and the kitchen maid, never turning a hair, were at work.' Georgina admitted that she was always one of the last to go to the shelter, and that he always had to check on her. 'I got up abruptly, went into the kitchen ... and ordered the cook and the other servants into the shelter.' She argued: 'I'm alright, really sir,' worried about her pudding ('if I'd've turned it out, it'd've been no more – it was so light, you see'), but he insisted, and they duly left. Moments later the window exploded into shards and the back wall partially collapsed, leaving 'the table – ooh, the rubble, terrible'. She was quite clear on the debt: 'he saved my life, I'm sure I wouldn't have been no more'.

Like so many kitchens in Britain, the rubble was cleared, the windows patched up, and it was back in use as soon as it could be.[24] Meanwhile, the Churchills camped out upstairs. Clementine wrote to Violet Bonham Carter that

> we have been 'blown' out of Downing Street and are living in two rooms – one of them your former sitting room looking out onto the garden. We have no gas or hot water and are cooking on an oil stove. But as a man called out to Winston out of the darkness the other night, 'it's a grand life if we don't weaken!'[25]

However, in the wake of the near-miss, work started on an alternative home for the Churchills and their immediate domestic staff. On the first floor of the New Public Office building (it's really the ground floor, but like most Victorian official buildings, it was raised up by half a floor with steps to access the main doors from ground level), immediately above the CWR kitchen, a set of rooms was converted into a Downing Street Annexe.

Winston and Clementine moved in immediately, accompanied by the sound of hammering and drilling both from the conversion itself and from the continuous efforts to better bomb-proof the War Rooms: successive layers of concrete that became known as the 'never-ending slab'. He showed his new apartment off 'like a small boy showing his new toy and all that it could do!' There were separate bedrooms for both, plus a study, sitting room, dining room and kitchen, scullery and bathroom.

Like a normal apartment, there was a front door, next to which were the stairs, guarded by a Royal Marine, which led to the War Rooms underneath.[26] Unlike a normal apartment, the front door was armour-plated. No trace of the Annexe now exists, though the kitchen was almost certainly where the ladies' loos are now, with a window looking out onto a central courtyard. Like the War Rooms kitchen below, it was almost certainly fully electric.

The Annexe was the main residence for the Churchills themselves from the end of 1940 although the whole place was still in disarray, with Colville remarking that 'to call it a madhouse would be an insult to lunatics'.[27] Georgina, Frank Sawyers and the rest of the domestic staff, along with the secretaries on duty, still slept over at No.10 for another two or so years – indeed, the bedrooms remained in occasional use by various members of staff or family who couldn't face returning to homes or clubs in the blackout throughout the war. Even the kitchen remained in use, once restored to working order.

Churchill hated the thought of leaving Downing Street completely, and so had a set of former offices in the basement, which were under the garden, strengthened with iron bars, and converted into a new dining room. Clementine worked her usual design magic, and the result was less like a bunker than it might have been: Harold Nicolson commented that 'they have made it very pretty with chintz and flowers and excellent French pictures'. He was there for lunch, at 1.15 p.m., with the inevitable lack of Winston, who was late.

'We go into luncheon: sea kale, jugged hare and cherry tart. Not well done.'[28] Serving the Churchillian version of rationing fare was fraught, and on occasion things did fall down. Winston was usually the cause, constantly changing his mind as to where he was dining, right up to the last possible minute. Elizabeth Nel found that

one of our most urgent duties each morning was to find out where meals and appointments for the day were to be kept. Much of our time was spent trotting between the two offices, and confusion was frequently caused when visitors failed to make sure of the rendezvous. The kitchen staff would wail in despair when dinner turned out to be 'at the other side' and a hurried exit with dishes and baskets of food would take place.

Mary Soames elaborated: 'darling Mrs Landemare would have to transfer from one kitchen to the other, sometimes at a rather late stage, and be driven round in the duty car, with the covered dishes, wrapped in shawls to keep them warm, clasped tightly on her lap'. As Nel commented in retrospect, 'We of his personal staff were called upon to put forth the maximum effort of which our frames, nerves and minds were capable. I do not think this was only because it was wartime; I believe he has always been a fairly exacting employer.'[29]

Staff had to adapt quickly, not just to the punishing hours and workload but to the idiosyncrasies of their employers. One of Georgina's distant relatives, a child at the time, recalled visiting her at Downing Street during the war (Winston was away), and being allowed to go round drawing the blackout blinds with a maid while her mother and Georgina shared a cup of tea in the servants' quarters. She remarked of Georgie that 'she thought the world of Mr Churchill, although she often told him off when he absent-mindedly wandered around stark naked. He would always apologise to her profusely.'[30] She was not the only member of the household to grow used to seeing Winston's decidedly generous frame streaking from bathroom to bedroom, sometimes followed by an exasperated Sawyers, armed with a towel.

The extent to which the Churchills' diet was affected by rationing is debatable: an anecdote that has long done the rounds has Winston in bed (from where he did much of his work) and asking what exactly the ration looked like. Up it came, on a tray, to which his response is that it 'isn't too bad for a day'. The reply, of course, is that 'this, sir, is for a week'. The person missing from the usual telling is Georgina, who was in charge of the rations, the kitchen and the scales to weigh out the correct amounts. It was Georgina who brought him the tray for she always brought him his breakfast, and the anecdote is hers. (She used to tell it after a few sherries, one of the few stories she would let out.) He was, she reported, astonished.[31]

Winston was certainly involved in ministerial discussions over rationing, possibly more than Lord Woolton, the Minister of Food, appreciated. Woolton was the promotor of the vile 'Woolton Pie', a typically joyless wartime concoction of root vegetables topped with oats, whose edibility depends entirely on the level of Marmite in the gravy, but he was also a very able minister.

Winston became particularly exercised by the topic of rationing in May–July 1940, writing letters on food choices: 'the way not to get fish eaten is to put it into competition with game or meat'; surpluses; and his own, brutally honest, if not entirely scientifically supported, view of what should be prioritised – 'almost all the food faddists I have ever known, nut-eaters and the like have died young after a long period of senile decay. The British soldier is far more likely to be right than the scientists. All he cares about is beef.' He went on, with feeling: 'The way to lose the war is to try and force the

British public into a diet of milk, oatmeal, potatoes, etc, washed down on gala occasions with a little limejuice.'[32]

It's fair to say that while the British public didn't quite subsist on only that, the food situation of most of the population from 1940 until 1954 was one of severe shortages, especially of fresh fruit, eggs and high-grade meat. Churchill described himself quite happily as a beef eater ('I expect my wife to provide me with butcher's meat once a day when I am at home'), and his wine bill was not a small contribution to his near-permanent semi-bankruptcy: he was not someone who would easily have coped with only what was available on the ration.[33]

However, even the poor supplemented their allowances: the ration simply guaranteed fair distribution of certain key food at controlled prices, and all over the country people supplemented it by keeping rabbits, growing fresh produce and buying items, such as offal, that were unrationed. Mary, exiled to Beccles in Suffolk for most of 1940, recorded helping 'to pick & salt down 12 lbs butter beans. Then went to Walton market in search of rabbit to add to already quite large wartime stock – found rabbit, which was transported home carefully wrapped in sacking!'[34]

The rich inevitably ate better than the working or middle classes, for they were able to draw on their estates and farms as well as their friends abroad, in addition to going out to restaurants, which were less restricted, and managed to serve fabulous food – at a price. After 1942, restaurants were restricted to charging no more than five shillings for three-course meals, and far more people took advantage of an enjoyable way to inject some life into their diet.

The Communal Feeding Centres that were set up specifically to provide varied meals for low prices were renamed 'British Restaurants', after Churchill declared that 'everybody associates the word "restaurant" with a good meal, and they may as well have the name if they cannot get anything else'.[35] He tended to favour the Savoy and Claridge's, but in this, and in the general way in which he ate during the war, he was only reflecting his class and social position, together with a firm belief, shared by his staff, and indeed most of the population, that he wasn't quite like other people: all that blood, toil, tears and sweat had to be fuelled by something.

As with every other household in Britain in 1940, ration books were issued, and in the following years many written discussions took place between Winston's secretaries and the Ministry of Food on diplomatic allowances and extras. In common with other households where cooks were kept, in June 1940, the ration books of all the permanent residents and staff were handed to Georgina, so that she could pool allowances and plan ahead.

Along with Winston, Clementine and Mary, Nellie Goble, Frank Sawyers and Georgina were listed as having handed their ration books over, plus Frances Burrows, Lucy Bell and Marjorie Usher – forming, presumably, the rest of the domestic staff. In addition to this, after a plaintive request to the Ministry of Food ('both at Chequers and at No.10 the rationing makes it very difficult to entertain officially to the extent which

Mr Churchill finds necessary'), diplomatic ration coupons were issued on a regular basis, to cover the needs of guests – and the Churchills dined so rarely alone that Clementine marked the occasions out in her engagement diary.

By 1943, Georgina was using an average of 'about 24 coupons a month for each of the main commodities (meat, sugar, butter etc), or less than 6 a week of each commodity which, I think you will agree, is not unreasonable for the Prime Minister's guests at No.10'.[36] Eggs were not included until 1941, and then an extra dozen a week were supplied, on strict instructions that they were for entertaining.[37] Either this rule was bent a tad, or the supplies coming in from the farms at Chartwell and Chequers were remarkably reliable, for Mary's diaries suggest that fresh eggs were not lacking, especially at breakfast. On 21 July 1942, on one of her periodic overnighters at the Annexe (she was stationed with her ATS troop in Hyde Park, and had regular trips home), she woke to 'delicious breakfast in mummie's bed – fried bacon & eggs – brown bread & butter – white currant jelly – coffee – peach!' On another occasion she 'ate fried egg, bacon & honey for breakfast'. That this was not the norm away from Downing Street was made clear by her joyful underlinings.

A few miles away, Vere Hodgson wrote morosely that 'my one egg during a fortnight was bad – and they refused to give me another!'[38] On at least one occasion, a class of primary school children sent fresh eggs to Downing Street from their school hens, each with a child's name on it, and each child received a personal letter in return.[39] Points coupons were also part of the system, with each individual having a set number of points to put against produce as they chose. It meant that foods that were in erratic supply could still be controlled, and gave shoppers the illusion of choice: vital, it was deemed, for morale.

For ministerial purposes, again, there were diplomatic points coupons on offer, though they were not immediately used. Kathleen Hill noted in 1943 that 'up to the present, I have not given Mrs Landemare any Diplomatic Points Coupons. For one thing, she does not know of their existence, and she has not complained to me of a shortage of tinned foods, and further I know she did lay in a stock some time ago which was slightly replenished by gifts from America.'[40]

Georgina was very conscious that things had to be done properly: rationing worked because it was seen to be fair, with the same allowance for all.

> See, we had our rations and they had their rations but if there was anybody special coming there was diplomatic coupons. But I had to be careful because I never knew when I was going to be called up. Like she, Lady Churchill could have said to me 'Well you know, how much butter are you using?' things like that but she didn't. I was very careful.[41]

It was a careful balancing act between need, want and public image. There were various times, especially when the war wasn't going well, when Churchill's personal popularity was key to his political survival, and it would have been suicidal to have been seen publicly flouting restrictions. As Georgina added, 'we had to be very particular you know, you see, because, I mean, he could have been in trouble and I could have been in trouble couldn't I?'

Things never went as far as they did at Buckingham Palace, where the royal family practised a very conspicuous austerity – probably one reason why George VI was so keen to dine with Winston on a regular basis. When it came to wine, careful negotiations with the Government Hospitality Fund resulted in extra supplies being stored in the Chequers cellars for use strictly when overseas visitors were present.[42] They almost invariably were.

In addition to fruit and vegetables from the farms at Chartwell and Chequers, extra eggs, honey from the Chartwell bees and discretionary diplomatic coupons for the constant flow of guests, there were other ways to supplement the official ration. Parcels of food from abroad flowed to Britain during 1940, sent by relatives and friends in unrationed countries, such as America and South Africa. The Ministry of Food stepped in, both because the parcels were taking up valuable shipping space on ships from America – at a time when, despite the convoy system, shipping losses were still very high – and because 'it is not desirable for individual members of the public to be allowed to have large quantities of rationed goods over and above the amount available for other citizens'.[43]

Gifts were henceforth limited to those that could come via parcel post, although there were other routes:

in May 1942 Winston wrote to Lieutenant-General Henry Arnold, saying 'General Chaney has been good enough to pass on to me the case of oranges. Oranges are all too rare at present and it was most kind of you to think of sending them to me. Thank you so much.'[44] Gifts came from within Britain too, some from relatives, such as the Duke of Marlborough ('Thank you, dear Bert, for the plovers' eggs'), some from well-wishers among the public, and some from the king, who sent regular gifts of game from Balmoral ('The Prime Minister has received some venison from the King, for which Mr Churchill is very grateful indeed. Perhaps you would tell His Majesty what pleasure and gratification it has given Mr Churchill to receive all these delicious and most welcome presents from Balmoral'). Grouse and other game came down by train, carefully labelled with the date of shooting.[45]

Food wasn't the only thing sent to Downing Street, and in addition to various official gifts, such as a Maori Staff of Defiance, people sent clothing for him, and an apparently endless stream of cigars. His security staff became worried about the cigars, fearing that they could be poisoned (for he tended to chew them rather than just smoke them), and various expedients were tried, to see if tampering could be detected – they were X-rayed and chemically tested – but to no avail. They advised he donate them all to the Red Cross, but after he pointed out that wasn't exactly fair to the potentially poisoned injured soldiers either, the decision was taken to (mainly) send them all back (exceptions were made if they had been sent from a consulate).

Eventually, the policy was extended to all unsolicited gifts, although in reality many were sent on to suitable charities, and letters of thanks and explanation dispatched. This was largely precipitated by one particular wheel of Stilton, sent to the Churchills by a Mr Gouldburn, of Gouldburn's Ltd, Food Purveyors, in Manchester. Gouldburn sent the offending Stilton to Winston as a Christmas gift in December 1940, and, as was the habit at that point, he was thanked and sent a book (one of Winston's, obviously) in return.

Not long afterwards, a letter from a Mr Heywood, an irate local, winged its way south: Gouldburn's Ltd was displaying a very prominent sign claiming that they had executed a cheese order for Mr Churchill, gratefully received (unsubtle subtext: get your Stiltons here, etc.). If this were true, said Mr Heywood (rightly), it was an outrage! Lord Woolton had just declared that cheese should be left for manual workers, who needed the calories – and despite Churchill's much-publicised bricklaying efforts, he was hardly on the same level as the miners.

It was exactly the kind of incident Churchill's team dreaded, and someone was dispatched immediately to Manchester to deal with the issue (it was never resolved, for the offending window was obliterated in a bombing raid). Meanwhile, no more unsolicited Stiltons. The Churchills were in agreement:

> The Prime Minister thinks it would be most ungracious to refuse all gifts which are sent to him, and each must be considered on its merits. It is clear,

however, that great care must be taken to see that
no goods which are rationed are accepted, and that
gifts are not accepted which are sent to him for
advertisement purposes, the acceptance of which
might be used for such purpose.

That little bit of wiggle room would come in useful,
however. Winston habitually finished his meals with
blue cheese (plus the predictably Edwardian ice cream
– when available – and fresh fruit), and, despite the 1940
incident, there were other Stiltons. Elizabeth Nel recalls
spending one Friday in May 1945 – 'the silliest I've ever
known' doing very little other than

> disposing of portions of a monstrous cheese which
> had been sent to him as a gift. It really was a
> whopper, and about 15 chunks had to be dispersed
> or delivered, lists of names submitted, changes
> made, rechanges, etc, telephone calls, trips between
> no.10 and the Annexe (I think I went five times the
> double journey), until I could have chucked the
> whole blinking cheese into the river.[46]

Cheese, then, was clearly part of the average dinner.
Unfortunately, no record survives of the daily menus,
but it's possible to get an idea of what Georgina was
cooking from the reports of the Churchills' guests, as
well as from Mary's diaries and letters. Mary and Clementine's relationship was, as was so often the case in
upper-class families, distant throughout much of her
childhood, but they started to form a stronger

connection from the late 1930s, when Clementine made a point of taking Mary on short holidays, including teaching her to ski.

Mary was as interested in food as her mother was, and throughout the war, while Mary was stationed away from home, they kept up a steady correspondence, a not insignificant amount of which centres on food. Of course, food was a preoccupation for the whole country, bereft of fruit and butter and flavour as the rationed diet was, and wartime letters and diaries are all full of rumours of oranges, and fleeting moments of happiness around a fresh onion.

Mary and her mother bonded through food, though, summed up by Mary at the end of the war, when she wrote to her ex-nanny, now close family friend (and Clementine's cousin), Maryott Whyte, 'How I long to be a ex-servicewoman & retire to Chartwell. Will you teach me how to cook? Mummie's letters often have long, delicious descriptions of the seductive food with which you tempt her.'[47]

Mary's diaries are a joy to read, her life rammed with partying and romance, as well as hard work in uniform, and all of the angst of a sensitive teenager struggling with unexpected periods and the unwanted glare of publicity due to being the prime minister's daughter. They are also a good reminder of the way in which the large events of the war had less impact on most people than the small minutiae of everyday life: 'May 30th 1940, The evacuation of Dunkirk. Dinner with Shirley.'[48] She rarely lists entire menus, but there are a few, such as this one, from 1942, eaten alone as her parents had gone to

Chequers: 'Ate comforting supper – onion soup – omelette (!) chips – carrots – stewed peaches & cafe au lait.' Georgina would have been at Chequers, having prepared most of this earlier, to be reheated.

Two days later, this time with her parents back, she noted a 'scrumptious supper (chops – chips – sweet pancakes & coffee) & now BED'.[49] Suppers were informal meals: had this been a meal with guests, she would have called it a dinner. It wasn't uncommon for Georgina to cater for split evening meals, with Clementine eating alone or with Mary, when she was home, and Winston dining with guests. There was a routine, of sorts, but it was frequently disrupted.

In theory, breakfast was at 8 a.m., with both Clementine and Winston eating separately, in bed, with their food on trays. Orange juice was often served, sometimes fresh, more often from concentrate. In February 1945, John Bell & Croyden of Wigmore Street sent some specially prepared orange juice concentrate, waiving any payment. Eggs, as detailed above, were always present, whether boiled, poached or fried, along with Chartwell honey, toast, butter and preserves. Other options were available, and Clemmie wrote to Mary in 1941 'it is now 8.15 and I picture you ... devouring a large (& I hope succulent) breakfast of porridge & perhaps kippers or sausages'. This was Downing Street breakfast fodder, though: Mary in her camp was eating 'bacon & potatoes, jam & bread & butter'.[50]

Winston invariably also had a peach, as Mary, on leave in 1944, comments: 'Papa sitting up in bed in his beautiful and brilliant bed-jacket. He gave me a peach off his breakfast tray – O WOW.'[51] Breakfasts could be more substantial, and Winston declared to his nurse in 1942 that 'he hates "pap" – can't stand milk or porridge, kind of "steak and beer" for breakfast type'.[52]

When he was recuperating from illness in Tunis in 1943, he carefully set aside an 'exquisite filet of cold underdone beef', for his breakfast the next day. It disappeared overnight, whether due to cats or light-fingered local chefs it was never discovered.[53] Setting aside part of the previous night's meal for breakfast the next day was a habit, and Georgina recalled 'if he had a cutlet at night, he wouldn't always eat the whole thing coz on one or two occasions he sent me back with a little bit and said "Tell Mrs Landemare to keep that for my breakfast" … on his plate, which I used to'.[54]

The breakfasts that Georgina provided during the war were varied, but they were not huge in terms of quantity. As so often with Winston, however, there were conflicting views: at the White House in 1941, with unrestricted food available, and with a firm eye on his reputation as a solid eater, he ordered his temporary valet to provide 'something hot, something cold, two kinds of fresh fruit, a tumbler of orange juice and a pot of frightfully weak tea. For "something hot" he had eggs, bacon, or ham. For "something cold" he had two kinds of cold meats with English mustard and two kinds of fruit plus a tumbler of sherry. This was breakfast.'[55] It was also playing to the crowd, for he knew reports would slip out, and it's not recorded how much of what was provided he actually ate. He habitually had sherry or, more often, one of his trademark extremely weak whisky and sodas – described as 'mouthwash' – with his breakfast, moving onto champagne or white wine with lunch.

Lunches, held nominally at 1.15, slipping to 2 p.m. at Chequers, were more substantial, and also more important. There were private lunches – Mary and her mother ate salmon fish cakes, new potatoes with butter, and poires condés (pears stewed in red wine with a border of rice and filled with cream) in June 1942, but most of the lunches Georgina catered were for guests.[56] Both Clementine and Winston hosted lunches independently, as well as together, and regarded them as important political tools, both for advisory discussions and simply to keep people on their side.

Clemmie held 'hen luncheons' for women only, and on other occasions deliberately invited people 'whom I thought needed petting'.[57] The food was obviously crucial, needing to strike the right balance between excellent and restrained, and playing an important role in how each event went: 'I have just had what I feared might be a rather stiff luncheon … but it was a wild success. Everybody said it was lovely & Mrs Landemare (back from a week's holiday) surpassed herself.'[58] Some of the most important occasions were those at which Winston hosted George VI, which became regular Tuesday events, only very occasionally interrupted by having to withdraw to the shelter.

On 6 March 1941, they ate 'fish patty, tournedos with mushrooms on top and braised celery and chipped potatoes, peaches and cheese to follow'. Drinks were sherry, white wine, port and brandy, plus coffee.[59] Georgina was not immune to the weight of expectation, and after another of the lunches, Clementine wrote:

> I forgot to tell you that the King & Queen lunched alone with papa & me last Tuesday. Mrs Landemare was in a flutter & produced a really delicious luncheon & it was really all most enjoyable ... The Queen is so gay & witty & very very pretty close up ... papa tried to interfere with the menu but I was firm & had it my own way, & luckily it was good ... The King did not say much. He looked thin & rather tired.[60]

As a wartime repast, this seems pretty lavish, and it was, by the standard of the general population, but it is worth bearing in mind Georgina's pre-war luncheon menus for the Churchills: in May 1937 one of her lunch menus had featured risotto with tongue, chicken in white wine with vegetables, and a soufflé Florentine. Another had eggs in aspic, breaded veal escalopes with sauce maréchal (a typically complex preparation usually finished with diced mushrooms), liver and bacon and a peach savarin with velouté sauce.

The 1940s dishes were both simpler to cook and used fewer ingredients. The vegetables were also more seasonal and less esoteric, although there were a few throwbacks, such as sea kale, an Edwardian favourite. Although easy to grow, it requires the prompt application of a forcing pot to correctly blanch the stems (it is not dissimilar to early forced rhubarb as a technique), but even with reduced staff, it wasn't difficult to find someone to pop a cover over some shoots, making it an easy way to add a bit of nostalgic glamour to the table. Many of the meat dishes relied on game, a mainstay of the upper-class table before the war, and doubly important now, for it was freely available on their landed estates, and unrestricted apart from the seasonal game laws.

Jugged hare was eaten even among the populace at large, along with pigeon and more seasonal game. Winston was not a huge fan of fish, other than as a starter, preferring beef, which he liked rare – quite difficult to achieve given his habitual lateness. Georgina had her methods though:

> It always had to be underdone, see, and I never had to overcook things and in the war when things was getting very bad I used to have to watch, I used to watch if I, say, I'd got a small piece of beef, only a small piece, or say a birds, if it was plovers, or whatever it was, watch till I knew he was in then he'd have to have his bath, and then I knew exactly to put the meat in the, I used to keep the ovens going, you see, the meat in the oven because everything had to be to the point and not above the point.[61]

Georgina's name and her reputation spread well beyond Downing Street. When in Tunis in 1943, Clementine reported to Mary that 'the food, however, is "vurry" American. Last night we had a partridge for dinner which Sawyers informed us was cooked for an hour and a half! The result was concrete! Sawyers rather rashly informed the American cook that Mrs Landemare cooks partridges for only fifteen minutes. Your poor father literally cannot eat the food.'[62]

There were dinners, too, at Downing Street and Chequers, some of which again involved visiting dignitaries, and were important diplomatic tools. They worked – William Lyon Mackenzie King, the Canadian prime minister, was invited to dine in 1941, writing to Winston and Clementine afterwards that the privilege of his being welcomed into their family life left him awed, and that 'I hope that you will both feel that, though separated by the waters of the Atlantic in these perilous times, I am constantly by your side just as all Canada has been and will continue to the end, to be at the side of Britain'.

Much has been made of Britain being alone prior to the entry of America into the war, but this neglects the very real, and at times devastating, involvement of the Empire and the Dominions. Later, in 1944, the results of another visit saw Mackenzie King write to Clementine that 'the weekend at Chequers, the reception, the Prime Minister's dinner and the luncheon at Downing Street, have all left memories which will be deeply cherished. My associations with Winston and yourself have been so full of meaning and so precious that you have both become, if I may say so, almost a part of my life.'[63]

Dinner was usually around 8.30 p.m., although when Clementine was away they slipped by an hour. When no dignitaries were being entertained, the couple was still surrounded by advisors and ministers, and it was rare for Clementine to write, as she did in March 1941, 'alone with W and plovers' eggs' (unrationed, unsurprisingly, as rare, expensive and not exactly easy to guarantee a supply).[64]

There were private dinners in Winston's rooms at the Annexe; Anthony Eden supped on champagne and oysters, and Field Marshal Alanbrooke ate yet more plovers' eggs, chicken broth, chicken pie and chocolate soufflé – plus champagne, port and brandy.[65] This wasn't exactly diplomatic entertaining, of the sort that all those extra coupons were intended for, but fell into a grey area, where money, influence, careful management of diplomatic allowances and a very skilled cook made a lot of difference.

For Winston's birthdays, the gift rules seem to have been relaxed. For his 68th birthday, Mary recorded that 'despite rationing and austerity, people sent him delicacies of every kind – not only rare and sophisticated presents of oysters or rare vintages, but more homely and just as much appreciated gifts of butter, cream and eggs. Mrs Landemare had a field day, and we all had a scrumptious dinner.'[66] The birthday dinner two years later featured oysters, goose and one of his favourites, caviar (a liking he shared with Adolf Hitler, although when Hitler found out its price, he banned it, on the grounds that it was at odds with his aesthetic reputation – and vegetarianism).[67] There was also an 'ICED cake – wow', something virtually unknown at a time when even wedding cakes tended to be covered with a cardboard cover piped with plaster of Paris to resemble icing.[68]

Many everyday Downing Street dinners were with

tried and tested companions, and acted as a means of relaxing and resetting after a day of work: on one occasion in 1940, 'dinner began very lugubriously, W eating fast and greedily, his face almost in his plate, and every now and then firing some technical question at Lindemann, who was quietly consuming his vegetarian diet … however, champagne and brandy and cigars did their work and we soon became talkative, even garrulous'. It wasn't the first time Winston started foully and ended in a better mood: dining in the Downing Street garden in 1942, 'Papa and Mummie were in terrific form … one or two enjoyable flare ups – during one of which Mummie said: "oh you old son-of-a-bitch". Dinner ended in mellow and happy silence.' [69] It was necessary, for after dinner, Winston would return to his rooms and work until 2 or 3 a.m., striding about with a drink on hand, dictating to the duty secretary, before finally going to bed.

Churchill's late hours, afternoon naps and apparent obliviousness to the routines of others is well known. He struggled – somewhat unsurprisingly given his rich diet and levels of stress – with indigestion and unexplained stomach troubles for much of his life. As a result, on his various travels during the war, he took to ignoring time zones, except where they were imposed by dint of formal meals, instead referring to 'tummy-time'. Snacks between meals had already been proposed by his doctors in the 1930s, as a way of alleviating some of his stomach issues, and he never had a problem eating just one more meal. While rarely a glutton, he was used to good food, and plenty of it, and at times he would quite happily eat

– quite literally – for England when the occasion demanded it.

Inevitably, he was not the only leader at the time to use the dinner table as a political weapon, and at the various conferences or political visits in Quebec, Washington, Yalta, Potsdam and many others, his performance at dinner was part of an elaborate set of negotiations, wherein informal occasions were just as important as the formal dialogues that were the ostensible purpose for the meetings. Some of the countries had more food available than others, and in America the British party revelled in the unrationed provisions on offer.

The notoriously dreadful White House cook, Mrs Nesbitt, employed by Eleanor Roosevelt, at least partly as a means of revenging herself upon her unfaithful husband, recorded in 1941 that 'every time the Churchill group came, it seemed we couldn't fill them up for days. Once we cooked for guests who didn't come, and offered it to some of the Englishmen who had just risen from the table, and they sat right down and ate the whole meal through, straight over again.' Given the standard of her food, which even Mary called 'really nasty', this was quite a feat.

After Winston suffered from what was probably his first heart attack, at Christmas 1941, he went from Washington to Florida to recuperate, where, having done his public duty over the composite salads of the White House, he firmly rejected the dizzying heights of clam chowder, and requested Bovril instead (marketed then as effectively beef tea, a recognised invalid food).[70] Through this, and other incidents, he gained a reputation as a liker of plain food, someone who embraced the idealised British notion of a beef-eating stalwart, with no truck with fancy French sauces. He worked hard to encourage this image, which, like his carefully stage-managed brick-laying photo opportunities, helped to cement the idea that he was not just another aristocratic offshoot, cut off from the common man, but someone whose aspirations and enjoyment were firmly rooted in good, solid manual labour, beef and liberty.

He did genuinely prefer a plainer version of cookery than what was consumed by many of his peers, with a marked love of beef, and shared with Clemmie her belief that 'vegetables were not meant to build up the soul, but to nourish the body in war-time', and he successfully made the relatively plebeian Irish stew, one of the dishes with which he is most often associated, despite it not appearing much on his 1930s menus. In the 1940s, though, he served it when he hosted guests, including General Eisenhower, who he knew would report on his habits. Georgina's must have been particularly excellent, for she recalled 'of course he did like Irish stew when he had his guests there and he always used to say "Tell the butler to keep me some for the next day" but I never did coz you couldn't heat it up, you see, he always said that, he loved Irish stew, see'.[71]

He also carefully managed his drinking reputation, enjoying his apparent standing as a hard drinker. There's no doubt that he consumed a large amount of alcohol, with Doris Miles, his nurse at Chequers in 1943 listing his 'fluid intake chart, it goes something like this: champagne oz 10; brandy oz 2; orange juice oz 8; whisky and soda oz 8; etc. Doesn't that make your tongue hang out?'[72] However, while he drank a great deal, certainly enough to awe onlookers on occasion, he was very rarely drunk. Mackenzie Scott's comment sums up the general view: 'He took a great deal of wine to drink at dinner. It did not seem to affect him beyond quickening his intellect and intensifying his facility of expression. It really is such a delight to hear him converse.'[73] Roosevelt's views ran along similar lines. He may well have been reliant on alcohol, but so were most of his class. However, unlike many of them he could take it, and never became – as had his father, and as would his son – an unreliable alcoholic.

As the Churchills' in-house cook, Georgina also catered for the immediate household. She provided breakfasts for the other staff members, as well as the duty secretaries when they arrived very early, or if they'd stayed over at Downing Street after a very late night, and she also fed the nurses who attended him in 1943. The breakfasts were no less sumptuous for them, with Doris Miles rhapsodising 'my breakfast has just arrived – to make your mouth water I'll tell you what it is – grape-fruit (<u>real</u> one), boiled egg, toast, butter, marmalade – I'm afraid when I get back ... I'll turn my nose up at the food.'

The other meals were equally removed from the food she was used to although, as was to be expected, there were different meals provided for staff and the family. Distracted from writing by 'a succulent odour of roasting chickens', Doris reported later that,

I was right about the chicken, but we had wild duck
in aspic, which was equally tasty! The food seems to
get better and better, and I'm becoming the most
disgusting glutton. I'm just pushing back hot coffee
and biscuits, while waiting for the Patient to finish
his whisky and come and do his exercises before
bed.[74]

There were 'scrumptious pâté sandwiches consumed
with many cups of tea', and 'delicious chicken sandwiches', something Georgina must have spent a fair
amount of time making: Churchill took picnics with
him when travelling, including cold beef sandwiches en
route to Cairo in 1942, when he commented that 'the
bread must very be wafer-thin: it is nothing more than a
vehicle to convey the filling to the stomach'.[75] At other
times, the catering was done by the crew on board the
various trains and ships on which he travelled, or by staff
provided by whomever he was meeting.

Mary, too, benefitted from Georgina's skills, despite
not living at home. A constant procession of cakes, biscuits and jam wove its way to wherever she was stationed,
and when Clementine visited her, picnics of grouse and
potted shrimp, crackers and cream cheese came too.
Naturally, there were also boxes of fruit, and Mary
thanked her mother in characteristic fashion in September 1941: 'Thank you ... for the scrumptious peaches.
Judy & I behaved like pigs – as soon as we'd finished our
tea we vamoosed for ½ hr into the woods, and gobbled
them all up at once! Actually fresh fruit is one of the
things I rather miss – so the peaches were very welcome.'[76]

The high standard of food, produced under difficult conditions, was something everyone who ate regularly at Downing Street remarked upon. Those who spent time with Georgie, who by 1945 was fast becoming an institution, found her delightful as well as talented, and it's no wonder that by the end of the war she was named properly in the Churchills' letters and diaries, no longer just dismissed, as her predecessors had been, as simply 'the cook'. Even the cat that she had adopted, a grey Persian called Smoky, became part of the family – somewhat inevitably, given Winston's attachment to animals. Smoky was something of a menace, badly behaved and given to drawing blood as he clawed through precious secretarial stockings, and he slept on Clementine's bed when Winston was away, biting her toes through the brocade covers.[77]

By no means everyone who served Churchill during the war years could stand the pace, and even Georgina admitted that 'some were hectic days, being up at early hours and going to bed past midnight'. She called it her 'war work'. She had to be up hours before the family, preparing breakfast, and didn't go to bed until after his last whisky. Luckily, she could survive on very little sleep – unlike Winston, she didn't get to nip off for a post-prandial nap most afternoons.[78]

By the beginning of 1945, however, the strain was showing for everyone. Churchill, whose doctors had kept from him, with the connivance of his family, his worsening heart condition from 1943, was behaving ever more erratically, and there are suggestions that he was suffering, if not from dementia, at least from partial mental breakdown. When Roosevelt suddenly died, in April 1945, he collapsed. His attitude to work became even worse, and as the war drew to a close, those around him found him increasingly impossible to deal with.[79]

It's hard to convey the sheer sense of utter physical and mental exhaustion that gripped the British population in the last few months of the war: as the blackout was gradually lifted, and foods not seen by most people for years – ice cream and oranges among them – made occasional appearances on the streets, people spoke of longing for peace, and not necessarily victory.[80]

On 8 May 1945, they got it. On VE Day in London, 20,000 people gathered to watch Winston Churchill's speech, given from the Ministry of Health balcony. His secretaries, staff and ministers pressed around him, worn out, jubilant, relieved and above all caught up in the moment. Georgina, characteristically, hadn't made it, but fought her way up from the kitchens to catch the closing sentences. Elizabeth Nel witnessed the point where he broke away from his coterie, came over to Georgina, and shook her hand. He insisted she come out onto the balcony, saying he simply couldn't have achieved victory without her efforts over all the years. Almost in tears, she turned to Elizabeth and said that those words meant more to her than seeing the crowds. It was his hour, and whatever came next, it would be one of his finest.

What came next was, in many ways, not a surprise. The worn-out staff were given holiday – Georgina took two weeks from 9 July. Meanwhile, a general election was held in July 1945, with the Labour Party promising to do a comprehensive job of delivering the recommendations of the Beveridge Report, effectively creating the modern welfare state. As grateful as the nation might have been to Churchill on a personal level, politically they wanted change. Labour swept into power on a landslide, and 26 July, results day, was a very gloomy one in the Churchill household.

Georgina, like the rest of the family, was convinced the Tories would be returned. In 1973, when she was interviewed by Joan Bakewell for the BBC, her distress was evident:

> It wasn't leaving Downing Street, but I, the way that he was treated, after what he'd done, I felt it because, but I was so convinced that we would go back. I was so convinced we'd, you see, and it was such a shock to me. Terrible, it was a terrible shock and I sat up till midnight and when I heard the first Labour gains … nobody knows how I felt. And I had people for lunch. I never did know how I did that lunch.

Lunch was, according to Mary, 'choked', and the day was sunk into 'Stygian gloom'. Clementine tried to raise the general spirits, saying it might be a blessing in disguise. Winston replied simply that 'at the moment it's certainly very well disguised'.[81] Mary, who also was present, wrote in her diary that 'Papa spent the afternoon watching the results – M [mummie] went to rest. I wandered from sitting room to the Private Office – from the kitchen (where Mrs Landemare moved unhappily among her saucepans) to the Map Room and then back again.'

Later the same afternoon, Georgina made honey sandwiches and declared, 'I don't know what the world's coming to, but I thought I might make some tea'.[82] After a shattered final weekend spent at Chequers, they moved out, initially to Claridge's and then to Sarah Churchill's flat. Winston spent time at Chartwell, where the furniture was still swathed in druggets. Clementine grimly packed boxes and discussed where they would live next. On 3 August, the balance of the diplomatic coupons and points was handed over for the new prime minister's use.[83] On 17 August, Jock Colville, now a member of the new administration, visited Churchill's successor, Clement Attlee, at Chequers. He found his 'lack of ostentation or ambition' attractive, thought Violet Attlee distinguished-looking, but lacking Clementine's 'unflagging perfectionism', and above all, lamented that 'Mrs Churchill's superb cook had vanished and the ATS replacement, though she did her best, was not in the same class'.[84]

7

Peace at Last

'Mousse de Maple', from Georgina Landemare's 1930s handwritten recipe book. A chilled mousse flavoured with maple syrup.

> *4 eggs, 1 pint of cream, gelatine, 1 cupful of hot maple syrup, the hot syrup poured on the yolks. The cream, gelatine and whipped whites last 4 hours freezing.*[1]

The immediate aftermath of the election defeat was hard work – 15 August 1945 was VJ Day, when Japan surrendered after the devastation of two nuclear bombs. Churchill, still an MP as well as Leader of the Opposition, attended Parliament and carried on working, but he was fractious and angry, and turned on his family. Years earlier, he'd declared that 'it is well to remember that the stomach governs the world', and now, shorn of diplomatic coupons for meat and fat, eggs and petrol, his own stomach was not happy.[2]

In August, Clementine wrote to Mary from Chartwell:

> I cannot explain how it is but in our misery we seem,

instead of clinging to each other to be always having scenes. I'm sure it's all my fault, but I'm finding life more than I can bear. He is so unhappy & that makes him very difficult. He hates his food, (hardly any meat) has taken it into his head that Nana tries to thwart him at every turn. He wants to have land girls & chickens & cows here & she thinks it won't work & of course she is gruff & bearish.[3]

'Nana' referred to Maryott Whyte, who, in keeping with Mary's end-of-war wish, was teaching her to cook, as well as cooking for the family at Chartwell while Georgina remained in London. She was a capable caterer, but clearly not up to Georgina's standards. As a family member and long-standing friend, she was more accessible for Winston to rage at than Georgina, though – Nana wouldn't leave if he insulted her.

In September, not without relief on both sides, Winston left Clementine to continue with the business of moving house in London and unpacking in Kent, and went off to Italy to paint and try to come to terms with life outside No.10. During the trip, he gave up his habit of afternoon napping, never to start again, and gradually managed to accept his new position.[4]

Meanwhile, the household domestic staff, equally as shocked by the events of the past few months, also had to decide what their futures held. Very few staff had hitherto lasted more than a few years with the Churchill household. Apart from Georgina, the most notable exception was Grace Hamblin, taken on as a temporary part-time secretary when she was 24, in 1932, the year before Georgina first worked for the family, and quickly made permanent and full-time. By 1945, she'd switched to working as Clementine's private secretary, and remained with her now in the post-war era. The children knew her as Hambone.[5] She and Georgina got on very well.

Another apparent stalwart, Frank Sawyers, the butler-valet, had joined the household in 1940 and was seen as Winston's shadow, but despite loyal wartime service, decided to leave. He was 43 in 1945, and went on to have a career that took in Rhodesia and America, so he may well have had itchy feet, after accompanying Winston across the world in the name of diplomacy (which always required a well-pressed shirt). He'd gained a reputation as an excellent Winston-manager, and was known to many of Winston's colleagues by name, but there are hints that Clementine, at least, wanted something different. When one of the Chartwell cottages was being renovated, she suggested that 'when we part with Sawyers I think we should get a much better type of servant if we got a married butler and could offer this cottage to his wife'.[6] There were rumours of misconduct, including low-level theft, but he was much liked, and was the godfather to one of Georgie's grandchildren.[7] Two valets further on, Norman McGowan's wife was, indeed, put up on the estate, although whether he counted as a better type of servant remains moot. Sawyers' 1946 reference, written by Winston, simply stated that 'He has a good memory and always knows where everything is. He is leaving me of his own accord and I am sorry to lose him.'[8]

Georgina was twenty years his senior – seven years younger than Churchill himself. Rationing was still in place, and showed no sign of being lifted while British troops were still abroad, especially since part of their remit was to feed starving people in Germany and France, where Paris had once more developed a market for cat meat.[9] There were limited prospects for an ageing jobbing cook, whose significant pre-war reputation was of little use in a shattered post-war country, and she got on well with, and admired, her employers, who both appreciated and liked her in return. Unsurprisingly, she decided to stay with the family, cooking mainly in London, where the bulk of the entertaining would henceforth be done.

By October, things were settling down. There were still domestic shocks, such as the level of moth damage in the carefully packed Chartwell boxes, and the censorious nature of public opinion when a journalist gained access to the new London home at 28, Hyde Park Gate and slammed the couple for spending so much updating it when 'lesser folk' could hardly find housing at all.[10]

Winston remained grumpy, although there was little difference between his post-war dinner performances and that of many of his wartime meals: 'tonight we dined with Winston at Chartwell ... dinner began badly, with reading of the newspapers and monosyllabic answers; but when the champagne had done its work, Mr C brightened up and became his brilliant, gay and epigrammatic best'.[11] Rationing did not extend to alcohol, and during two months of 1949 his alcohol bill included 454 bottles of champagne, 311 bottles of wine,

58 of brandy, 56 of whisky, 58 of sherry and 69 of port. (A lot was for entertaining.)

Colville, still a regular visitor, remarked that 'although he [Winston] was never inebriated (or, indeed, drank between meals anything but soda-water faintly flavoured with whisky), he would still consume, without the smallest ill-effect, enough champagne and brandy at luncheon or dinner to incapacitate any lesser man'.[12] Winston was still habitually late for meals, despite the best efforts of his valets – when Frank Sawyers left William Greenshields took over, followed by Fred Raven, then Norman McGowan, whose memoirs of his 'beloved guv'nor' cover his time with Winston from 1949 to 1952.[13] Clementine colluded with them in a series of measures, which ranged from setting the clocks fast (he simply looked at his watch instead) to lying about when meals would be served. It became something of a game. Georgina seems rarely to have been fazed, and McGowan commented that 'in his home while I was there the cook was Mrs Landemare, a woman who excelled at her craft. She knew my Guv'nor's tastes to a nicety and perfectly cooked meals arrived with machine-like precision no matter how varied the times they were required.'[14]

He was not the most attentive party leader, spending weeks at a time on holiday painting, and he was also busy writing up his history of the Second World War and negotiating ways through his still tricky finances. Although his writing brought in significant sums of money, the family still lived beyond their means, with Clemmie remarking that 'it is silly to have two homes just now ... because of the rations which all get eaten up in one place & becos' of the servants'.[15] It didn't stop them, and in fact they expanded. Winston won his battle over land girls and fowl (Lord Beaverbrook sent him over a few chickens to get started) and started buying up neighbouring farms.

When Mary married Christopher Soames in 1947, the couple moved to Chartwell Farm, at the bottom of the garden, where their enthusiastic love-making could sometimes be heard up at the house, to Clementine's amusement and Winston's exasperation.[16] They had five children, and Christopher became embedded in the family, first as farm manager, and later entering Parliament and becoming a significant political figure. In the late 1940s, however, much of his time was spent trying to make the Churchill farming empire profitable (it never really was).

One great help was that in 1946–7 Chartwell was purchased for the nation, to be given to the National Trust when the Churchills vacated it. They were able to live there for a low rent until the end of their lives, and now, with the property secure, they set about making it more suitable for post-war reduced-cost living. Bedrooms were moved, a home cinema installed for the regular film showings to which family, professional and domestic staff were all invited and, in a slightly drastic, but practical move, the kitchen, scullery and pantries on the lower ground floor were abandoned in favour of more modern provision elsewhere.

The floor was not completely vacated – cold stores and the butler's pantry and the servants' hall stayed in use, but the old kitchen, with its coal-fired range and easy access to the kitchen courtyard for deliveries, was shut up and used as a store.[17] In 1946, the hatch between the scullery and kitchen was blocked up, and the scullery became a police room for Winston's permanent bodyguard. The cellars remained vital, for storing all of that alcohol, and, in a nifty bit of make do and mend, the dugout in the garden was converted into an additional wine cellar.[18] There were at least two electric fridges somewhere in the kitchen complex: one on hire-purchase from the Sevenoaks Electricity Company, which had been paid off in 1942, and a 'frigidaire de luxe' from Keating & Miskin in Blackheath, who had sent a service engineer out to demonstrate how to use it to the cook in 1938. One of them was primarily used as a wine fridge for Moselle and Winston's beloved Pol Roger champagne.[19]

Siting the new kitchen was a cause of a lot of discussion between Clementine and the builders working on the refurbishment. It was at one stage proposed, at least, for the second (top) floor, but doesn't seem ever to have actually been sited there. Instead, a self-contained caretaker's flat was installed on the top floor, along with bedrooms for servants and guests, and the Churchills' main kitchen was rather bizarrely squeezed into a small landing halfway up the back stairs. It wasn't brilliantly ventilated, and it was very small – the newly situated pantry on the first floor was bigger (but had very little natural light). It had a dumb waiter, enabling dishes to reach an alcove in the corridor by the dining room without the need for parlourmaids to negotiate the tight stairs or get in the way of anyone cooking in the restricted space, but it must still have been an irritation to cart produce up the stairs from the kitchen courtyard, and it may be that the former larder by the old kitchen remained in use as a prep area and occasional scullery.

Winston adored Chartwell, although Clementine was never quite as keen, and the couple spent a great deal of time there. However, it was not their primary home, nor was it their main entertaining space: that was Hyde Park Gate. The residences were staffed separately, with between three and seven permanent members of staff in London (they still struggled to retain maids), and eight to ten at Chartwell (which included the gardens team). There were land girls and German POWs working on the estate at Chartwell, and the bulk of the indoor domestic servants were Swiss, so it was a multi-lingual team.

The Swiss girls, part of a large influx of au pairs in the 1950s, were brought over for a year each, and then departed due to work permit restrictions. The model was very popular at the time, as the numbers of British women entering domestic service declined, and those who wished – and could afford – to keep servants found they were increasingly in a sellers' market.[20] They had the advantage of being cheap – averaging around £2 a week – but Clementine found herself once more managing servants who needed training if they were to meet her exacting standards.

Georgina, based up in London, rarely came down to Chartwell during the 1940s and 1950s, but she did play a role in teaching the maids, and stayed in long-term contact with some of them. They blurred into an endless procession for family and more permanent staff alike, though McGowan records a Martia, a Doria ('an attractive blonde') and a Martha, who unfortunately let Winston's adored poodle Rufus off the lead one day, whereupon he leapt happily over the road to greet a fellow servant and was promptly killed by a passing car.

Georgina taught them the best way to make macaroni cheese and Irish stew, and several of her recipes – including koulebiaka (salmon with rice in pastry), borscht, sole florentine, guard's pudding and soupe bonne femme – appeared in the menu books kept by the Chartwell staff. Evocatively, if confusingly, they are written in mildly garbled Denglisch, with headings such as 'orangenkompott & biscuits', 'fishsalat' and 'apfeltarte'.[21] There were clearly phases with the various cooks: that of December 1949 was a pastry aficionado, and served up cheestart, oniontart, spinachtart and appletart to the servants one lunchtime. Happily, the leftovers were spread out over a few days.

Chartwell was very much a family home, and, while food was provided for the live-in domestic staff, it was a bit more rackety for professional service staff such as the secretaries. With the exception of Grace Hamblin, whose parents lived in Westerham (as did she from the 1950s), they were based in London, and came down to Kent on a rota system. They struggled with food provision, and wrote to Clementine in 1946, saying that, although they were provided with enough bread, potatoes, milk and seasonal green vegetables, they found that the need to bring their own rations, as well as to find time to buy unrationed produce, was too much. The letter went on, listing the foods they habitually needed to buy as 'e.g. tinned soups, fish, offal and unrationed protein food, suet, fruit, cake, sauces, salad cream, condiments, vegetables (except cabbage or cauliflower or such like), lemonade or orangeade, cocoa, semolina and similar cereals, flour and all the other things which go to make up a store cupboard'. The accompanying list of their purchases bears witness to their differing tastes, including half a pound of coffee as well as a jar of Nescafé and a tin of cocoa, a tin of custard powder, hip syrup, Marmite, two dried haddocks and a 'bottle of hors d'oeuvres'.[22] They decamped to the pub in Westerham for most of their meals, but it was not ideal.

Back up in London, with Georgina in charge, things ran more smoothly. The secretaries were still left to fend for themselves, but now had a choice of all the restaurants in Kensington (or of bringing meals from home). For those who lived at Hyde Park Gate, both servants and the family, meals were cooked by Georgina: 'every morning Lady C would have a long meeting with Mrs Landemare, the cook, who had been with the family for many years and was affectionately known as Mrs "Mar". Food was extremely important to the Churchills and it was always extremely good'.[23]

Mary Soames, who gave Georgie an engagement calendar for Christmas in 1945, complained that she was putting on weight (Clemmie had already gone on a diet, having gained a stone over the course of the war – she blamed it on too much work, not enough exercise and far too much entertaining). Mary was still with the ATS at the beginning of 1946, but recorded a day off at Hyde

Park Gate: 'dear Mrs Landemare sent up kippers and coffee – also honey & butter & toast – which I resisted. I have attacked my figure with vigour and considerable success during the last month – to my great joy.' Lunch was 'eggs & fish & peaches before a fire in the library'.[24]

Winston, Clementine, Mary and their immediate band drew closer together in the aftermath of the war, in what Clemmie called a 'rough and stony' world.[25] Georgina, unlike the Chartwell cooks, was part of the coterie, and, while the division between servant and served was always clearly demarcated, her name now appeared much more frequently in family letters and diaries. Other domestic servants, more temporary and fleeting, remained invisible. Georgie herself recognised the shift, recalling of Clementine that 'I can never forget taking her the menu book in the morning and she would correct little mistakes in such a kind way, one couldn't help feel the friendship, she knew so much about food & all that means so much to a cook.'[26] Georgina became known, now, as the Churchills' cook, and something of a quiet celebrity in her own right. She was a stalwart, a 'lynch-pin', and those who joined the staff during her time there struggled to visualise what it would be like without her.[27]

She welcomed all the various maids who passed through the household – she usually had two kitchen maids assisting her, but, as ever in the Churchill household, their stays were fleeting and names largely unrecorded. There was a daily char or housekeeper, Mary Dorgan, who lived in Belgrave Road. She'd worked for the Churchills since 1940, retiring in 1948 through ill-health. She and Georgie had become close friends.[28] All those who knew Georgina recalled her genuine interest in others, her friendliness and that she was 'open and generous-spirited', always interested in what else was going on around her, while sharing with the rest of the longer-serving members of staff a deep-seated loyalty and utter refusal to gossip or give away titbits of information to anyone outside the clan.[29]

She commanded the kitchen, and was now confident, informed – and angry – enough to write to *The Times*: 'Sir, would not the meat situation be somewhat eased if hotels and restaurants were allowed to serve only fish luncheons and dinners except, of course, for permanent residents in hotels? It seems to me that working men and women are really not having enough to eat. Yours Truly, G. E. Landemare. 28 Hyde Park Gate, SW7.'[30]

The various grandchildren were taught always to go to the kitchen and thank her for her sterling work, and guests, including Field Marshal Montgomery and Charlie Chaplin, were asked if they would like to meet her.[31] On some occasions, people she'd cooked for in her pre-war life came to dine, and to their delight would be invited down to the kitchen to renew her acquaintance.[32] She was one of very few domestic staff who Winston knew by name, and took the time to converse with on the rare occasions that their paths crossed. He liked her, which was novel, for mainly he simply ignored his staff, and liking or disliking was irrelevant as long as they did their jobs. Meanwhile the relationship with Clementine went even deeper, and the two were entirely at ease with each other, albeit still within the boundaries set by their class and employment relationship.

Georgina's food was exquisite, and her calm legendary. Heather Wood used to go and watch her preparing apples 'with such precision and expertise – like everything else she did', describing her as 'round and cheerful and very calm indeed, whenever there was a mini-crisis'. Temporary cooks who filled in for her when she was away went to pieces and threw tantrums when guests were announced at late notice. Georgina did not: 'Mrs Landemare was very calm and organised. If I went into the kitchen half an hour or so before a big dinner, I would quite often find her sitting, with everything under control, reading the *Sporting Life*.'[33]

Her interest in horseracing was one that Winston now shared, having been introduced to the joys of the turf by Christopher Soames. Characteristically, once interested, he threw himself into it, buying a stud and several horses, and reviving his father's racing colours of brown and pink. His most successful horse was called Colonist II – Georgina sent a telegram ('hearty congratulations') on behalf of herself and the valet Walter Meyer (and Florence – presumably a maid) to congratulate him on its success in 1951.[34]

She effortlessly took on the mantle of staff spokesperson, writing to thank him for the 'lovely party you so kindly gave' after Christmas 1948 (this was a yearly event). She also gave Mary cooking lessons, which Mary thoroughly enjoyed, and they, too, became close. In May 1946, Mary wrote that 'dear Mrs Landemare has given me a wonderful, battered book "Mémorial de la

Pâtisserie", which used to belong to her husband'.[35] It contained 3,000 recipes, and was an iconic French culinary manual. Meanwhile, Clementine wrote down Georgina's birthday (9 April) in her yearly engagement diary.

No.28 Hyde Park Gate was shortly expanded into 27 Hyde Park Gate, fortuitously put on the market in 1946, as the need for more office space became apparent. The street was a short cul-de-sac opposite the south side of Kensington Gardens. The Albert Memorial, where Georgina had played with Algy as a child, was a five-minute walk away, and Ashburn Mews, where the family had then lived, was a gentle fifteen-minute stroll. The house had been built in the 1830s, and inevitably had a basement kitchen, although it had a window overlooking the garden, which Clemmie had landscaped and filled with roses around a stone terrace. The basement also contained a scullery, slate-shelved larder, pantry, servery and china store, and the wine cellar, as well as the butler's pantry, strong room, staff sitting room and WC. Bedrooms for live-in staff were on this floor as well as in the attics, and there was a separate entrance for provisions (and servants).

Georgina's kitchen fittings were entirely modern: no more coal-fired ranges to manage. There were gas and electric water heaters and electric radiators.[36] Clementine even acquired a pressure cooker and an electric toaster, sent to her by Frank Clarke, who hosted her and Winston in Quebec in 1946.[37] The food situation, however, was worse than it had been during the war. It was worse for everyone, not just the Churchills: bread and potatoes, both unrationed during the war itself, went on the ration in 1946 and 1947, and all of the allowances were repeatedly cut.

One London woman wrote that 'our rations are now 1 oz bacon per week – 3 lbs potatoes – 2 oz butter – 3 oz marge – 1 oz cooking fat – 2 oz cheese & 1/- meat – 1 lb jam or marmalade per month – ½ lb bread per day. We could be worse – but we should be a lot better considering we won the war.' Dinner for her that day was two sausages, 'which tasted like wet bread with sage added', mashed potato, half a tomato, a cube of cheese and a slice of bread and butter.[38]

Even the restaurants struggled – although not all of them. While Georgina was on holiday, Mary put on a party at The Berkeley in early 1946, which she enjoyed greatly; later in the month, now with Georgina back, she hosted a dinner for Prince Charles of Belgium. Georgina prepared oysters, turtle soup (which would have been tinned), sole bonne femme, roast duck and one of her signature recipes, maple mousse. Midnight refreshments, bought in from Fortnum's, included the evocatively named 'savoury frivolities', sandwiches, fruit cake, chocolate cake, ice cream, champagne and coffee. Mary declared her nervousness to her mother, for 'I did so want to do you and papa and Mrs Landemare credit'.[39]

Fresh produce was not an issue for Georgina at Hyde Park Gate. With the expansion of Chartwell came a shift toward commercial gardening, a not uncommon fate more generally for the kitchen gardens and greenhouses of many country houses at the time. The wartime emphasis on agricultural productivity, including, on an individual level, the infamous 'dig for victory' campaign, was if anything increased after the war (to 'dig for victory' were added the words 'over want').[40]

Small amounts of now old-fashioned vegetables, such as sea kale, were produced for family consumption, but most of the produce was more mainstream. Winston reported in 1947 that he'd sold a crop of lettuces for £200, and that 'the hot houses are dripping with long cucumbers. The grapes are turning black and a continuous stream of peaches and nectarines go to London.'[41] Grace Hamblin was co-opted into driving baskets of fruit and vegetables up to London on her journeys between Chartwell and Hyde Park Gate, along with milk and cream from the Jersey cows (Maybelle, the first, was a present from the Royal Jersey Agricultural and Horticultural Society in 1946, and was followed by others).[42] Eggs, poultry, ducks and game – especially rabbits, which were caught in their hundreds per month – also came from the estate, although Winston was always worried in case he was eating an animal he knew.[43]

There was a great deal of entertaining: one of the bodyguards, Edmund Murray, remembered that there was 'a galaxy of famous people attracted to the Churchill residence', with stars including multiple royals, both British and foreign, actors such as Laurence Olivier and his then wife Vivien Leigh, statesmen and their wives, military commanders and authors. In addition to this (none of them brought their own rations), the live-in domestic staff needed feeding. As in the war, rations were pooled, though it was at Georgina's discretion as to how exactly the results were apportioned, meaning that 'often, indeed, we individually had less than our ration, and I should stress that everybody in the household from the most junior kitchen maid to my Guv'nor and his wife, shared and shared alike, so that the cook had to exert miracles to stretch the food out for the numerous guests which they entertained'.[44] Miracles were duly performed: 'every meal was planned to perfection and every time I ate with them, I came away feeling I would love to eat the whole thing all over again'.[45]

One crucial way in which Georgina was able to supply such memorable meals was through the continuing stream of edible gifts. In the 1940s and 1950s, Winston Churchill became, to some extent, and mainly to those who did not know him personally, a living legend. As Britain plunged further into austerity in 1946–7, those who fervently believed that he was the saviour of Western civilisation said so, with material proof. Typical was a letter from the chairman of the Permutit company, who supplied a water softener to the Churchills at Chartwell, offering it for free 'as a token of the high esteem in which they are held', because they have 'on so many occasions sacrificed their personal comfort in their devotion to the Cause of Freedom, and realising also that we in common with every citizen of this country owe them a debt that can never adequately be repaid'.[46]

They were asked to lend their names to a whole host of clubs and societies, and to patronise charities across the globe. Such duties risked being onerous, as well as cheapening what was a very carefully curated public image, and were mainly turned down, though there were exceptions. In 1955, Winston enthusiastically accepted the invitation to join the Hastings Winkle Club, a charitable organisation that already counted certain of Churchill's circle – Field Marshal Montgomery and the Duke of Windsor – among its numbers. Members received a winkle shell, which they had to produce if challenged to 'winkle up'. Failure to do so resulted in a fine, which went to charity. (Members also signed off their letters to each other with the term 'winkle up'.) Winston, being a particularly high-profile member, was not given a mere shell: he was the proud recipient of a golden winkle, which can still be seen at Chartwell today.[47]

Material gifts, however, were a different matter. Although Clementine had some scruples about exactly who gifts were from, Winston rarely cared, and, now that official policy on accepting presents no longer applied, he pretty much took everything that was offered. Through the post came endless cigars, a veritable library full of books, some of which he pounced on (he loved Hornblower, and invited C. S. Forrester to dine), and others of which simply joined his extensive collection. There were also trinkets and objets d'art, some from official quarters – Commonwealth organisations in particular – others from more general well-wishers as well as relatives and friends. Dorothy Allhusen (author of *Scents and Dishes*) sent a paperweight that had belonged to Disraeli. Again, some items came out for display, while others remained in packing crates at Chartwell. Still others were passed on, and he gave

Georgina an ornate wooden tray. More significantly, food gifts poured in.

Wealthy friends and allies, especially with connections abroad or significant shooting estates, formed a reliable backbone for edible gifts. Amy Guest, widow of Frederick Guest, one of Winston's political colleagues, was now living in America, and regularly sent hams, rice and sugar; media baron Lord Beaverbrook arranged for game, whisky and champagne from various producers, to be sent directly to the Churchills; American statesman Bernard Baruch set up an agreement with Bloomingdale's to send items such as hams, tongues, honey and olive oil; US naval commander Admiral Stark sent sugar, tinned butter, bacon, tea and biscuits; and Averell Harriman, who had been a US special envoy during the war (and the Churchills' son Randolph's estranged wife Pamela's lover – they went on to marry in 1971) contributed many welcome sides of bacon, sugar, tinned meats, fat and other produce, which he sent with the US Air Force flying into Britain. The Chinese ambassador managed regular deliveries of preserved ginger, and Field Marshal Smuts, the South African prime minister, made sure that dried fruit was not in short supply. Winston replied, 'your parcels of good things continue to cheer us'.[48]

Meanwhile, Sir Bernard Freyberg, Governor-General of New Zealand, arranged for his parcels to go via New Zealand House, and was a stalwart. He sent tongues and hams, chocolates and sweets, and a 10½lb loaf cheese, into which he recommended pouring a little port. They were all duly passed to Georgina, with the report coming back to Winston that 'Sir Bernard particularly asks you to let him know if the ham and tongues arrive in good condition. Mrs Landemare says they are.'[49] Landed aristocrats with estates in Scotland packaged up venison and grouse (a favourite Churchillian breakfast delicacy, which he shared with the cat), and the Christmas turkey was invariably provided by connections in the States. In 1947, it came via Edward Stettinius, ex-America Executive Secretary to the UN, who also sent them (frozen) to Lord Halifax and Anthony Eden, among others. This was political networking in all its glory.[50]

Not everyone who helped swell the tables at Hyde Park Gate was known personally to the family. Gifts also came from producers, including apples from Kirkham and Co., fruit brokers; a chocolate bulldog from Bunny's of Brighton, and fish from W. H. Cartmell in Fleetwood ('thank you for allowing me this privilege, God Bless You').[51] Even Mr Gouldburn (of the unsolicited Stilton) tried his luck again, although exactly what he sent – and was duly thanked for – is not recorded.[52] Churchill's cigar suppliers sent food too: Mr Kaplan from New York sent a bottle of kirsch, fourteen pounds of bacon and ten pounds of rice, 'which has been unobtainable in this country for about two years', while Antonio Giraudier, his Cuban middleman, entered into lengthy correspondence about exactly how much Winston liked brandy (a lot, after luncheon and dinner, came the response), before sending him two dozen bottles of the best he could get, as well as a huge ham. He also sent parcels for the staff.[53]

It wasn't always obvious where things had come

from: in 1947 half a smoked salmon turned up with a
note saying it was from 'The Colony Restaurant' in New
York. The secretaries worked overtime deciphering
handwriting and, in this case, sleuthing for clues. It was
eventually attributed thanks to an article in the *Evening
Standard*, in which a Mr Cavallero of 'a New York restaurant' declared his intention of sending a salmon to Mr
Churchill (the article pondered how he'd get round the
weight restriction – evidently the answer was just to
send half).[54]

The Churchills weren't alone in receiving food from
abroad: with the restrictions on weight and shipping
gradually lifting in the 1940s, now that space was no
longer required for guns, and convoys no longer under
threat from U-boats, countries including America,
Canada and Australia set up schemes whereby food
relief could be easily sent to the UK. Some parcels were
sent from friends and relatives; others went under the
banner of schemes such as CARE (Co-operative for
American Remittances to Europe), which saw individual
Americans pay for food aid to be sent to Europe (and not
just the UK – Germany benefitted, as did France and
other occupied nations). Recipients of the resulting
boxes were encouraged to write back personally, forging
many a pen-pal friendship en route. For some, especially
those born just before or during the war, this was their
first taste of tinned peaches and other goods still
regarded as luxuries.[55]

Some people went further. Another source of food
gifts to the Churchills were members of the general
public, usually in Australia or Canada, who decided that

Winston – and sometimes Clementine – deserved a food parcel too. The range of contributors in the last six months of 1947 alone was significant: there was a Mrs Foster from Queensland who said, 'you may wonder who and what I am – so I will just introduce myself as a stenographer and private secretary who has been working for about 390 years and who hopes to keep going for quite a while yet', and declared she'd been sending food parcels to relatives for a while, but only just plucked up the courage to send one each to the Churchills; and Lady Lyle, also in Australia, who sent a weighty parcel of four pounds of apricot jam, a one-pound tin of honey, a one-pound tin of cheese, a one-pound tin of beef loaf, a one-pound tin of dried milk, a one-pound tin of grease and four ounces each of currants and sultanas.

Miss Viola Moses, a New Zealander, was typical: 'being a grateful admirer of your wonderful war work and knowing of your trying times since, I feel I would like to send you a Christmas food parcel', as were the Clays, 'an Australian family which greatly respects and admires you, & who firmly believe this chaotic condition would not have happened had Britain been guided by yourself'.[56] They included in their parcel a Camp Pie, a tinned Australian speciality not dissimilar to Spam. Realistically, and taking into account fluctuations in the supply of food parcels, the main thing Georgina lacked was fresh red meat, which could be problematic, bearing in mind Winston's love of beef. One butcher did try to supply extra, but whether through a sense of fair play or the demands of public image, he was turned down.[57]

Part of Georgina's daily routine was to keep detailed records of what was eaten. Family and staff menus were written into separate hardbound books, to be signed off in red pencil by Clemmie. None of the family menu books from Georgina at Hyde Park Gate survive, although there are a couple from Chartwell, where the food was slightly more basic. However, one of her staff menu books does still exist, painting an evocative picture of life below stairs for the domestic staff who ate her food.[58]

Breakfasts were substantial, in keeping with what was expected at breakfast in 1946: despite the war, and despite the publicity given to breakfast cereals, with their faint hint of American glamour, the average British adult expected (or at least wanted) a cooked breakfast. They were monotonous, but not nearly as monotonous as the pre-war British norm, which centred on bacon and eggs to the exclusion of all else. Georgina varied it, not least due to the lack of bacon: on any given day she cooked one dish from a selection of dried haddock, toast with marmalade, bacon and fried bread, porridge, sausages, kippers, herring, bacon and fried potatoes and fresh eggs. She also served up dried eggs, for most people a rationing staple, generally buttered (essentially scrambled), and recycled any leftover fish into fish cakes, bulked out with potato.

Family breakfasts were all of this and more, with not just one but a selection of dishes, always served with toast, butter and the inevitable honey. Not only was honey included in many of the food parcels, but the Chartwell hives were rejuvenated and restocked, with help from the local beekeeping association.[59] Freshly ground coffee was a given for family breakfasts, and grapefruit made a spate of appearances, tied to deliveries of fresh citrus from well-wishers in countries with ready supplies.

The midday meal was called 'luncheon' both upstairs and down. The family would have been well used to this, but for the working-class household servants, midday still meant dinner, always the main meal of the day. In many families, men still habitually returned home for their midday dinner, prepared by their wives (who still combined work with household duties in a lot of cases, though the aspiration remained to stop work and only keep house). For the Churchill below-stairs staff, although the midday meal was given the more socially elevated title of 'luncheon', in recognition of their lower status it remained the most substantial meal of the day, and was always served hot. It invariably consisted of two courses, always with either meat or fish, followed by a simple sweet.

On Sundays, Georgina provided a roast, usually a shoulder of mutton but occasionally lamb, or even more occasionally beef. She served it with mint sauce; potatoes either baked or roast, or new when they came through; vegetables – usually of a decidedly brassica persuasion; and sometimes a Yorkshire pudding. The traditional – and much lampooned – pattern of servant or upper-working-class cookery was then to eke out the remains of the Sunday joint until everyone was heartily sick of the sight of it. Georgina, unsurprisingly, was rather more inventive. Certainly, anything remaining of the joint was integrated into meals later on in the week – leftovers were regarded simply in the light of conveniently pre-cooked ingredients, and not regrettable bits to use up – and the usual, time-honoured dishes of toad-in-the-hole (which could use any meat available, not just sausages), hashes, cold meat (with hot sides) and hot pots appeared at other meals. But the Sunday joint would not have been that big, and wise cooks such as Georgina didn't seek to serve more than would be eaten.

Her other staff luncheon dishes were very varied, although always plain and often long-cook, to make the most of cuts such as brisket and neck, or old, tough rabbits. She served things such as stewed rabbit and boiled sausages, pork pie and Danish pork, roast venison (and cold venison a few days later), liver and bacon, sausage and onions, and corn beef hash. Fried fish, sometimes battered, was also very frequent. All of these were served with vegetables and often potatoes. The sweets were variations on a theme: lots of stewed fruit with custard (including apples, pears, damsons, rhubarb, cherries and blackberries). Much of this must have been bottled when in season, for there was no seasonal pattern to the appearance of the various fruits in the staff menu book. There were fruit tarts, too, served with ideal milk (condensed milk). Starchy and milky puddings were popular too – blancmange, rice pudding, canary pudding (Mary learned to make one in 1946), sago pudding, spaghetti pudding and couscous pudding – Winston was given some to take home and try when he was in France in 1948.[60]

In the winter months, she cooked mince pies and Christmas pudding. She also made use of branded mixtures, including Creamola, who made both a just-add-milk instant rice pudding and a caramel-flavoured instant dessert that was marketed during rationing on the grounds that it was cheap and required no eggs.

The final staff meal was high tea, which was smaller and more inclined to be cold or make use of remains of other meals. Frequently, Georgina noted simply 'remains of family luncheon', though sometimes she gave the actual dish – Irish stew, curry, fish, risotto, two pieces of chicken, two pieces of hare. The upstairs roasts were minced and served downstairs, accompanied by spaghetti, potatoes or other vegetables. Tinned meat, including Spam (and presumably that Australian Camp Pie) and tinned sardines, were also high tea staples, and the sweets were drawn from the same repertoire as those served at lunch.

The pattern of meals was not that different to that which Georgina would have experienced when she was a kitchen maid herself, although the unlimited supplies of bread and cheese upon which Edwardian servants subsisted outside formal meals was definitely absent. It took very able management to produce three meals a day for staff and three meals for the family (plus cake and biscuits in case of need), as well as handling both expected and unexpected guests.

There were also celebratory events. Birthdays meant cake – for example, for Clementine's birthday in 1946, Georgina made a cake in London and was then driven down to Chartwell complete with cake, Mary and Sarah.

Christmases, too, needed catering, and as well as dealing with gifts of frozen Virginian turkeys and huge hams sent from abroad, there was also the family dinner on the 25th, and a lavish servants' party before or after Christmas itself. In 1950, it was held on 8 January, and Georgina provided 'roast turkey, sprouts, peas, roast potatoes, bread sauces, Christmas pudding and mince pies; followed by a high tea of 'malt bread and butter, scones and butter, 2 Christmas cakes, 2 gateau d'amandes, boudoir bis[cuits] & cheese bis[cuits]' and finally a cele-bratory supper: 'turkey sandwiches, jellies, fruit salad, chocolate creams, triffles [sic], stewed cherries & rasp-berries, mock cream, all sorts of fruits & nuts'.[61]

The Churchill staff ate very well, but it was a reflec-tion of the status of the household, both financially and in terms of widespread connections. They did not flout rationing, nor did they bend its rules, but they did eat better food, and more of it, than the vast majority of the population. Winston's food was reputed to be plain and simple, which fitted his public image, but the concept was open to interpretation, and his was not quite the plain and simple of his staff, or indeed, most of the country.

Winston remained a committed diner, and showed little sign of losing his appetite for entertaining as he celebrated his 75th birthday, despite at least one small stroke and his ongoing heart issues. Georgina, adhering to the public line when she was interviewed in 1973, said that, 'I don't think he was a big eater, see, he wasn't a big eater like some men', and, measured by the standards of his class and era, he wasn't. Jane Portal, one of his secre-taries at the time, reported that he wasn't interested in fine dining, and his motivation at dinner parties was more about the company, the atmosphere and the opportunities offered to network and socialise.

That said, he was discerning, knowledgeable and knew what he liked to eat. He would not have relished being labelled abstemious either: 'as everyone knows Sir Winston Churchill is blessed with an excellent digestion and has a lively regard for the pleasures and benefits of good food and good wine. Not for him is the ascetic regime of so many famous men of advancing years. He unaffectedly enjoys his meals – and the conversation over brandy and a cigar which can follow.'[62]

Having a hearty, meaty appetite was the very definition of British aspiration (Hitler's vegetarian diet was held up as a sharp contrast), and there never seems to have been any criticism of the fact that he, and others of his class, were able to eat the meals others only dreamed of. Breakfasts continued to be varied, if not huge, with the 'something hot and something cold' of the war years still in evidence, along with orange juice and fruit. Luncheons were smaller than dinners, the reverse of the below-stairs pattern, but could also be rather elaborate, if guests were invited. Typical dishes were roast chicken or beef, cutlets, smoked salmon with eggs, fried fish, roast game and vegetables including gratins. The risottos and spaghetti dishes that reappeared on the servants' tea table were often luncheon dishes. Sweets were savarins (a variant on a rum baba) or meringues, fruit fools and ice creams – elevated versions of what the staff were eating, with more textural contrasts, fresh ingredients and a lot less starch.

There were many foreign influences, not just at Chartwell from the Swiss maids, but also at Hyde Park Gate, where Georgina deftly worked in recipes to use ingredients such as maple syrup, which repeatedly occurs in the gift lists. She made maple ice cream, as well as mousse de maple (maple mousse), the recipe for which she wrote into her manuscript cookery book: it's a beautifully light concoction that relies on maple syrup for its flavour, rather than merely using it instead of honey or sugar.

In contrast to all of this, one 1951 book, *100 Meat-Saving Recipes*, simply said that 'most housekeepers today lead lives of quiet desperation'.[63] A Gallup poll a few years earlier on people's fantasy meal had revealed a quiet longing for pre-war middle-class comfort: 'sherry; tomato soup; sole; roast chicken with roast potatoes; peas and sprouts; trifle and cream; cheese and biscuits; coffee'.[64] Many of these dishes were regularly served at family meals at Chartwell and Hyde Park Gate, both for luncheons and dinners, the menus for which follow the pre-war pattern of soup, fish, meat, vegetables and sweet (plus cheese and fruit, left unsaid). On one day at Chartwell in 1951 they ate vegetable bouillon; fried fish with tartare sauce; roast partridge with bread sauce; rösti; and vanilla ice cream, and on another it was turtle soup; turbot with hollandaise; beef escalopes with potatoes and salad; and fruit salad with cream. Winston 'had a passion for cream. In fact, on occasions he was almost rude about it. He would always almost empty the jug himself and look round the table. "Does anyone want cream?" he would ask, rather pugnaciously', and it was often served at his meals.[65]

In October 1951, the Labour Party, having scraped a victory in the February elections, called another snap election and were voted out by a working class electorate who were desperate for new housing, and a middle class unconvinced of the benefits of free healthcare and a well-educated working class. All were angry with continuing food shortages and eager to see the end of rationing.[66] Few of Churchill's immediate family or close advisors were convinced he should return to No.10, but he let them assume he would shortly hand over to Anthony Eden.

Touting an agenda of 'houses and meat and not being scuppered',[67] he swept back to Downing Street, family and staff, including Georgina, in tow. She'd been happy at Hyde Park Gate – 'it was more like a home, you know, very happy', but she was very pleased to go back, and 'they welcomed me at Number 10 and I, I can't remember the gentleman that was in charge of Number 10, he was Sir Somebody, but he said "Welcome back Mrs Landemare" and I was so pleased, you know'.[68]

She was, however, slowing down, and under the new regime she no longer cooked at Chequers – it was all arranged in-house. Nor did she cook for state banquets or large-scale diplomatic entertaining, for the Government Hospitality Fund organised caterers. At Downing Street, the old kitchen had been abandoned, shortly to be converted into offices, and Clement and Violet Attlee had moved into a self-contained flat, with its own, very modern, kitchen, which was much easier to manage and heat.

Typically, Winston wasn't satisfied, writing 'look at all the distinguished people I have had to entertain in our poor little attic. I am sure they are surprised at the difference between the accommodation and the menu.'[69] The state rooms were partially reopened, and a kitchen inserted on the ground floor to service them.[70] They took on more staff, but relied on outside caterers for large events – Winston's birthday party food in November 1951 was provided by the Government Hospitality Fund, and included turtle soup, fried fillet of sole with anchovy cream sauce, cold roast partridge and 'baked-in-jacket-potatoes', celery and beetroot salad, watercress salad, plum pudding with brandy butter and small iced cakes. Compared to Georgina's menus, it was hardly inspiring: one reason perhaps, why she was paid a £5 bonus the next year for 'Mr C's birthday dinner'.[71]

Georgina was 70 in 1952, and had been seeing a specialist in Harley Street for heart problems, paid for by the Churchills. She was still close to her siblings, all of whom had survived the war unscathed. Algy was in Wandsworth, with his wife Rosina; Maud and Thomas Moss were in Northampton; Archie and Agnes were in Putney; and Eve and Richard Mott were still in Chiswick. Meanwhile, she'd become a grandmother, for Yvonne and Ted now had two daughters, Edwina, born in 1943 (Georgina telegraphed 'so happy god bless you and Edwina – mother', and Clementine sent a jacket 'I'm afraid it's much too big for her; but it will come in useful for the autumn'), and Elisabeth, born in 1948.[72] They lived in Bristol, and Georgina would travel down to see them, settling into a grandmotherly role much more easily than she had a motherly one, a trait she shared with Clementine Churchill, who spent much more time with her grandchildren than she had with her own offspring.

Edwina recalled that 'my father and I would go together down to Temple Meads to meet her off the London train – a warm, plump, cuddly figure, delighted and excited to come down to stay with us', and that despite rationing she always carried 'interesting parcels ... butter, treacle, Italian amaretti biscuits, fresh produce that had come up from the Chartwell farm or unusual presents like the delightful money box the carpenter at No.10 had made for me from one of Churchill's cigar boxes'. The edible gifts that poured into the Churchills' larders were very welcome when gifted elsewhere. Clementine sent personalised Christmas presents as well: 'I remember taking *Black Beauty*, signed "to Edwina from Clementine Churchill" into school as a 10 year old, and being stunned by the admiring response of the staff – up until that time "the Churchills" were just nan's employers.'[73]

Georgie went on holiday with her family in the summer, when she had two weeks off, and, after the move back to Downing Street, when the Churchills started spending Christmas at Chequers, she also had time off over the festive season. Yvonne and Ted were solidly left-wing, though, and, despite her illustrious employer, and high-flying career, 'there was no celebration of everybody that she clearly was cooking for ... none at all'.[74] Georgina's life in London was never discussed, and, looking back, Edwina suggested that it wasn't clear how welcome Georgie really was in Bristol.

She rarely cooked for her family, although she did provide a series of suet puddings for her grandchildren after school, and occasionally sprang other dishes on them as well. There was a memorable 'family horror', 'a fantastic orange pudding that we were all loving until she told us the main ingredient was potato and we all stopped eating'. Were the family guinea pigs for a new recipe? It's possible, though it was clearly successful in her view, for Georgina wrote two versions of a sweet potato pudding into her manuscript book, noting that they could be served as a sweet or savoury course. Perhaps she just thought she'd surprise them – sweet potatoes were not exactly common in 1950s Britain.

Yvonne and her family also visited Georgina in London, and Mary reported that 'Mrs Landemare has had her daughter Yvonne and an adorable grand-daughter to stay'.[75] Edwina remembers sitting in Winston's chair after his return to Downing Street, and that her grandmother basked in the warmth of the police and staff when she came back, but also that 'she was more familiar with Edwina Sandys [Diana's daughter] than with her granddaughter, Edwina Higgins'.[76]

On 7 January 1953, Clementine's engagement diary and the wage books both recorded a simple statement: 'Mrs Landemare leaves.' Georgina, like Winston, had returned to Downing Street in a blaze of glory, and now, thirteen years after she started with the Churchills, she decided to retire. It didn't entirely take. On 18 March, Clemmie recorded '11.30, Mrs Landemare', and then on the 24th, '3.30, interview cook'. There was a new kitchen maid on 20 April and then another entry for 'Mrs Landemare' on the 29th. These could be seen as innocuous meetings between two old friends, interspersed with finding new permanent staff (inevitably, they'd fallen back on temps in the meantime), except that on 9 May Georgie reappeared in the wage books, now on £5 a week instead of her previous £3, and took up her role once more. The Churchills had managed four months without her, and now enticed her back on a significantly increased salary. In the meantime, Archie Young had died, aged only 63: perhaps Georgina was determined to make the most of life, and that meant working in a job she loved.

The next few months would prove fraught in the Churchill household, however. Winston, who was by now rather deaf, had suffered mild aphasia (language impairment, generally caused by a stroke) the year before, leading to unresolved discussions about his future in office. On 23 June, following a successful dinner with the Italian prime minister at No.10, he suffered his most significant stroke yet, and, although he presided over a Cabinet meeting the next day at which no one noticed he was ill, he was struggling to walk, and was clearly unable to function properly.

The family decamped to Chartwell amid a total press blackout, enabled only by the fact that he was so close to the Fleet Street press barons. Slowly he struggled back to health, but for several months was technically not making the decisions put out in his name. He and Clemmie, who was suffering from painful neuritis (inflammation of the nerves, in this case in her shoulders and neck – she had to wear a brace, which she hated), had fierce rows, underpinned by his refusal to simply retire from office. After one meal, he remarked to her 'you will not be angry with me, dear, but you

ought not to say "very delicious". "Delicious" alone
expresses everything you wish to say.' She (understandably) let rip on the subject of manners, 'eyes blazing',
and, for once, he did not interrupt.[77]

Tensions were not helped by the breakdown of both
Diana's and Sarah's marriages (Diana had married
Duncan Sandys in 1935, and Sarah had married Anthony
Beauchamp in 1949). Diana had a nervous breakdown,
threatening to attack her mother with a knife, while
Sarah turned to alcohol and would spend time in prison
as it eventually took its toll.[78] They moved to Chequers
in August, with Clemmie insisting that they give the
domestic staff a break before they walked out, and by
October they were back in Downing Street.[79]

As the year closed, and 1954 started, things seemed to
be getting back to normal. Winston revelled in Georgina's skills, writing happily to Clemmie in May that 'we
had a jolly weekend. Mrs Landemare distinguished
herself as usual.'[80] His weight was an issue: Clementine
put him on a diet, with an emphasis on fruit and vegetables. His response was to go round every pair of scales
in both houses, looking for the one that gave the most
optimistic reading, before buying a new set, which took
a full stone off his weight in comparison to the worst of
the others. He decided that her set was broken, sent
them to be checked and declared that if he was right she
would need to review her conclusions and abandon her
regime. According to his new scales, he was 14¼ stone
(92 kg: he was about 1m 72, and according to modern
medical advice this is classed as obese). He wrote mutin-
ously that 'I have no grievance against a tomato, but I

think one should eat other things as well'.[81] Georgina, too, was suffering. She'd been back just over a year, but was now struggling. In a postscript to his scales rant, Winston wrote that it had been arranged 'that the Chequers cook and kitchen maid shd come down here to Chartwell and cook all week for us, so that I was able to give Mrs Landemare 9 days complete holiday. She was not vy well, and was delighted.'[82] It wasn't enough: this was in early June, exact date of the days off unknown. On 26 June 1954, the wages book recorded 'retired'.[83] She'd started working for the Churchills a month after rationing started: she finished a mere eight days before it finally ended.

8

Retirement

'Chocolat cake good', from Georgina Landemare's 1930s hand-written recipe book. Intensely chocolately cake, not included in the 1958 book, but based on that given by Clemmie's mother Blanche to Dorothy Allhusen for her book in the 1920s.

> *½ lb of butter [beaten] to a cream. 7 eggs yolks & whites and beaten separately, ½ lb of best chocolat grated and heated then beaten up with the butter, with 8oz of sugar, and 8 oz of dried flour, 4 oz of ground almonds, 1 teaspoon of sal volatile, bake in a slack oven.*[1]

Having lived in-house with the Churchills for fourteen years, Georgina was now homeless. She was their longest-serving domestic servant, and their lives had been intertwined for over two decades, but she was now simply too ill to continue. In keeping with the traditions of the working class of her generation, she turned to her family for support, staying with both Eve and Algy in the first year of her retirement.[2] She struggled to adjust and, a month after leaving, wrote wistfully to Mary with congratulations on the birth of her daughter

Charlotte: 'I am pleased to say I am feeling better and I am going down to Yvonne's for 8 weeks & then back here for the winter. I so often think of you all.'[3] She continued to visit and, despite the employment of a permanent replacement, a Mrs Troger, in London, and then Katharine Anderson from September 1954, she was enticed back on a number of occasions to cook for particularly distinguished guests during the autumn of 1954.

Katharine Anderson later wrote down some of her memories of that time. The Churchills had a terrible reputation as employers, and had reached the stage where the various agencies they were reliant upon had essentially blacklisted them. Anderson was recruited directly through the Cordon Bleu cookery school, where she had had a year of basic training. Having been rejected for two jobs already, she was as keen for employment as the Churchills were to find a replacement cook. She was taken on to cook at Downing Street, working mainly in the small, first floor kitchen which served the private apartments, as well as to cater at Chartwell, for two weekends a month. Like Georgina, she had the services of one kitchenmaid, but unlike Georgina, she struggled. She admitted freely that she was 'young and inexperienced', and that she 'wanted to die' when the meat in the Chartwell cold larder went maggoty, henceforth relying on the fridge and ordering smaller quantities instead. Although there was now an electric oven at Chartwell, fridge space was lacking, and she found the rather ramshackle mixture of 1920s and 1950s technology hard to manage. Mealtimes were erratic and Winston and Clementine Churchill demanding. Their ingrained habit of planning meals and menus on a daily basis, rather than well in advance, was not something Katharine had been taught.

She did her best, serving menus comprised of French dishes – canapés epicuriennes, poulet sauté aux champignons et riz (chicken with mushrooms and rice), plus fried potatoes, green beans, a chocolate bavarois and cheese and coffee for her first small-scale dinner party. But she pepped up her consommés with Bovril, a bad habit instantly spotted by Clementine. Clemmie brought in Robin Adair, the long-term partner and professional collaborator of Marcel Boulestin, who had trained so many of Clemmie's cooks as well as Clemmie herself in the 1920s. Adair had been interned during the war, and never fully recovered, and shocked Katharine with his apparent alcoholism as well as his air of what she termed 'sophistication'. It was not surprising, therefore, that Clementine turned back to Georgina. Her initial reason was that it was Winston's eightieth birthday and, as Katharine put it, 'the amount of cooking required for a big reception was beyond my experience and capabilities'. In came Georgie, described by Katharine as 'a round little woman who could have rather a rough manner and tongue, but she and I never had a cross word and she was most generous in her help to me'. Together they catered the family lunch – fried sole, cold baron of beef (most of a cow, usually weighing in around 300 lb or 550 kg), chicory salad, soufflé potatoes followed by a grape and peach compote and a sweet – plus the inevitable round of Stilton cheese.[4]

A pattern was now set for the next six months,

whereby Katharine would do the bulk of the family cooking, and Georgina anything requiring a bit extra (larger functions were usually still catered by the Government Hospitality Fund, despite their shortcomings). Georgina couldn't stay away from a household in which she felt wanted and valued, and it was quite clear to everyone that the Churchills really did need her skills.

Clementine admitted freely that 'she is an inspired cook. When she retired in 1954, I was completely at a loss.'[5] After much prevaricating, Winston finally stood down as prime minister in April 1955, much to the relief of his family and colleagues. The night before the announcement, on 4 April, a quiet dinner for the Queen and Prince Philip had been planned, but was boosted into a much larger party, part-celebration, part-commiseration, with around fifty guests drawn from political, military and personal spheres. It was unthinkable that anyone other than Georgina should cater it, and it was her farewell to Downing Street as much as his.

On the 6th, there was a tea party for all of the support staff, from telephonists to drivers, so that the Churchills could thank them before leaving.[6] Then Winston left for Chartwell, while Clemmie stayed in London ready to reclaim Hyde Park Gate. Georgie went back to Algy (and his bright-green pet parrot). She still wasn't emotionally quite ready to leave though, despite being physically too ill to continue. In July the following year, she wrote to Winston, who had sent her one of his books: 'I shall so enjoy reading it, as I have already done your war books, and it gives me such pleasure in the many hours of leisure I have, since I gave up my life's ambition'.[7] He also sent her a silver V sign, which joined her signed, dedicated photographs of the couple, given to her during the war.

By November that year, as unable to keep away as they were to cope without her, Georgina was – temporarily – back on the payroll, and didn't fully leave their service until 17 December, when she was 73.[8] By this time Katharine Anderson, who despite needing help from Georgina was remembered as a 'very good' cook, had left, replaced initially by a German au pair at Chartwell, and more fully by Josephine Schwartz in December. As had been the case before the war, few cooks lasted long: constant moving about, meals at short notice, entertaining under pressure and the tension between Winston's desire for specific dishes cooked in specific ways versus turning out fashionable foods for the discerning 1950s and 1960s guests took their toll.

After December 1955, Georgie never formally cooked for the Churchills again. Following the death of Algy's wife in 1956, Georgina moved in permanently to Algy's house in Montserrat Road in Putney, where she cooked basic meals for them both, in between visits to Bristol to see Yvonne and her family. All four surviving Young siblings were now on their own, Maud's husband having died in 1944, and Eve's in 1955. Maud remained in Northampton, although with extended stays with Eve, who was still in Chiswick, living with her unmarried daughter, Marjorie.[9] Unlike her sisters, Georgie had never given up work in favour of unpaid domestic duties, and she remained attached to her working life, in the shape of the family for whom she'd worked for so long, regularly exchanging letters and visiting Hyde Park Gate.

Winston, while still sporadically active in Parliament, spent much of his time holidaying in the Riviera and painting. He was a real celebrity, still feted and with no shortage of eager dinner guests, and with constant press interest in his life – and food. As ever, Clementine helped to promote his public image, channelling press interest into controllable paths. She ensured that his birthday cakes, ordered since the early 1950s from Maria Floris, a Hungarian-born pastry chef with a well-known shop in Soho, became something of a publicity phenomenon, each one more fantastic than the last. There was a chocolate-iced bowler hat topped with sugar flowers bearing honours and the names of people close to him for his 77th; a drum with the spines of his published books around it (and a model of Rufus the poodle (mark II), trying to reach one of the cakes on top) for his 79th; and then others, including a spiral with thirty-two models of his most famous hats; and another with a bunch of roses and a banner proclaiming his promotion of 'the cause of United Europe'; and yet another a 3D map with a bridge between America and Britain and sugar replicas of his honorary citizen document (he was made an honorary citizen of America in 1963).

For his 80th, there were two cakes, both ringed with candles and sugarwork crests and emblems reflecting his life. One was for the family; the other, intended for the 150 guests at his party that year, weighed over 50 kg and had to be carefully proportioned to fit through the doors at Downing Street. His 90th was positively muted in comparison: merely a beautifully moulded sugar oak leaf and acorn wreath or two, a rose on top and the number '90' above a scroll reading 'in war: resolution; in defeat: defiance; in victory: magnanimity; in peace: goodwill'. It was two feet in diameter and eight inches deep. Naturally, all of them were rich fruit cake. Press releases went out ahead of time, with photographs after the event, for each cake was kept a closely guarded secret until the big reveal.[10]

Press fever over cake helped to stave off prying journalists looking too closely into Winston's health, which was declining. From 1958, a permanent nurse was added to the staff, and he suffered another stroke in 1959. Clementine, too, was suffering, both from the neuritis she'd had for a few years and from sheer exhaustion. While Winston enjoyed the sunshine of the Côte d'Azur, she stayed in England, disliking the brashness of Nice. She frequently took holidays of her own, or stayed with Mary and her family, but she was lonely and sometimes depressed, and her secretaries often found themselves in the role of surrogate children.[11]

She stayed in close contact with Georgina too, and in 1955 suggested that she write up some of her recipes into a cookery book. As Mrs Landemare, Georgina had appeared briefly in the second volume of Winston's war memoirs, *Their Finest Hour* (1949), when he recounted his version of the Downing Street bomb story: she had a clear and unique selling point, and a guaranteed market, given the continued interest in Winston Churchill. It would also supplement her income: she had the basic state pension, which in 1958 was £2.50 per week, along with £2 per week from the Churchills.[12] Clementine also sent her £5 for Christmas every year, although the Churchills' generosity longer-term took no heed of inflation – the state pension had risen to £4 in 1965 and was £17.50 by the time Clementine died in 1977, still paying £2 a week to her ex-cook. Georgina also had some savings, having had few living costs for the term of her employment with the Churchills.

They decided to call the proposed book 'Recipes Rich and Rare', and Clementine sent it, when it was roughly ready, in 1957, to Collins, which at the time was run by Mark Bonham Carter, Violet's son, and rather a fan of Georgina's cooking, which he'd experienced as a child. No one was going to refuse Clementine, especially with such a solid proposition (with the added benefit that she wrote the Foreword), and Collins rapidly agreed to publish the book, with an amended title to reflect Georgina's association with Downing Street. The eventual title, therefore, was *Recipes from No.10: Some Practical Recipes for Discerning Cooks*, and there would be a number of changes required before it was published.

Compiling the book to the point that it was ready to send to Collins, and then making their amends, took three years, with Georgina, Yvonne and Clementine all involved. There were piles of newspaper clippings and handwritten recipes collected from friends and colleagues to sort through, including 'Mrs Beeton's Dressed Crab', copied out by Mary Soames, and pre-war articles on the return to favour of the iced bun.

Georgina's manuscript book formed the basis for just

under a third of the recipes, mainly those in the cakes, puddings and fish sections, but she changed many of these, especially the fish, quite substantially from her 1936 versions. It was hard work to create a cookery book for a general readership from her personal notes, especially since Georgina rarely used a scale and measured things by the handful. Like Clemmie's former cookery teacher, Marcel Boulestin, she was of the opinion that 'the dangerous person in the kitchen is the one who goes rigidly by weights, measurements, thermometers and scales'.[13] Down in Bristol, Yvonne had to persuade her mother to measure her ingredients, taking notes as she cooked so that the recipes could be replicated by her readers. She made her weigh her handfuls, for Georgina 'wouldn't have had a clue'. Georgina also tweaked the names (the saddest loss was 'fluffy eggs', which became the less descriptive and less frivolous 'cream eggs'). Her 'Eperlans sur Hâtelets à la Météor', for example (see top of chapter 2), when given measurements and grammar, became the more replicable:

EPERLANS À LA MÉTÉOR

For six people. 6 large smelts. ½ lb mushrooms. 2 ozs breadcrumbs. 2 shallots. 6 anchovy fillets. Chopped parsley. Lemon juice. Egg yolk. Anchovy sauce. Seasoning.

Clean some smelts, remove the bone. Mix together chopped cooked mushrooms, lemon juice, parsley, breadcrumbs, chopped shallot, oil and seasoning. Place a little of this farce on each smelt, cover with an anchovy fillet and roll them up, fastening with a skewer. Flour, egg and breadcrumb and fry in deep fat. When cooked, remove skewer and serve with fried parsley and anchovy sauce.

The 1936 version, itself essentially Edwardian, had been fussier: after being rolled and skewered, the smelts were deep fried as in the published recipe, but the skewers were then removed and replaced with silver hâtelet skewers, intended for display, and instead of a bought (or made) anchovy sauce, a much richer velouté was used. Paring down the recipes from their previous incarnations was vital in this post-war age. Hâtelet skewers were virtually unknown at this point, a relic of the nineteenth century and a marker of a long-gone style of upper-class serving. There is a misplaced accent on 'farce' in this recipe, a very rare mistake in the French.

Georgina's idiosyncratic spellings had been corrected by Clementine, who had also gone right through the final typescript and added in all the accents in black pen. Although the names were mainly in French, as they had been in her original manuscript, and indeed on her pre-war menus, in other ways the recipes chimed with the times: margarine instead of butter in the 'Eggless Chocolate Cake', assumed ease with the use of garlic, and the inclusion of lots of vegetables and salads were all features of the post-war cutting-edge culinary landscape. But they were also (apart from the margarine) features of high-end 1930s food, and in many ways the book looked backward as much as forward.

It wasn't unwise to do so: while branded products

and shiny kitchen gadgets were coming into the market, the vast majority of people still lived much as they had before the war. Georgina claimed to one journalist that she disapproved of 'fridges, and canned food', and made ice cream in an old-fashioned ice bucket 'because it keeps the flavour so much better', and never used a mechanical whisk. This would have appealed to those who hankered after the fine life before the war, and wanted a book by a bona fide old-fashioned cook – 'a gallant lady of that old-fashioned breed that would not give in', and who 'spared no effort in producing what she knew he liked', as she was once described, but it also reassured those whose kitchens were still essentially those of the 1930s (or before). Unlike the Churchills, only 5.3 per cent of British homes had fridges in 1953, rising only slightly to 17 per cent in 1960.[14] This was, therefore, a canny nod to several potential audiences.

Apart from Clementine's Foreword, there was little in the book to hint at Georgina's personality. This was a common trait among the Churchills' more trusted servants, who rarely published memoirs or spoke openly to outsiders about their time with the family, and reflected her own, largely invisible presence as below-stairs staff. It was at odds, though, with many of the books that were flooding onto the market, now that rationing was over and British women were realising how much time they'd lost to saving every last scraping of bacon fat and pepping up breadcrumbs with marmite.

Even before rationing had fully ended, books such as *Quick Dinners for Beginners* (1950) had whispered revolt against the dried egg, and pre-war household names such as Ambrose Heath and Philip Harben had swept back into the market with recipes for egg-rich soufflés and the alarming-sounding 'beef with bananas'. Heath also published recipes for hamburgers and 'American Hash', a reflection of the ongoing obsession with American glamour.[15] Post-war writers poured personality into their books, with heartfelt introductions explicitly aiming at 'those who are starting out to cook for the first time, brides or bachelors, to those who have lost a servant or a mother, or who, having cut the cord of family life, are henceforward to keep and nourish themselves'.[16]

Servant-keeping was now a rarity, but there was also a sense, at least in the immediate post-rationing era, of novelty in being able to proudly keep house in a new era of plenty, and women's magazines extolled the virtues of wifely goodness. *Woman's Own* happily declared about the kitchen, 'a woman's place? Yes it is!', fit now for happy wives, who didn't need a servant because they now could aspire to Formica and fitted units instead.[17]

Harben hedged his bets with his *Entertaining at Home* (1951), which was for 'the host and hostess who do their own cooking, for themselves and for their guests, employing no professional cook either because they cannot afford one, or because they cannot get one, or – the best reason of all – because they enjoy doing the work themselves'.[18] Even Constance Spry and Rosemary Hume's encyclopaedic *Constance Spry Cookery Book* (1956) contained numerous asides and personal commentary, looking back to Spry's Edwardian upbringing, and contrasting it with the joy of now:

> Remembering as I do the days of immensely long, boring, wasteful dinners, remembering too the starvation which was all too often at our very doors, I cannot forbear to remind you how much respect ought to be paid to food, how carefully it should be treated, how shameful waste is. Forgive me for this, but you see it is fortunately unlikely that your hearts will be wrung or your consciences nudged by the sight of starving people.[19]

It was the era of Patience Gray, Elizabeth David and Alice Toklas, all writing lyrically about the food of France and (in the case of David) the Mediterranean more widely, and read as much for a sense of ill-defined authenticity as for the recipes – David later admitted that she was essentially writing fantasy food in the early 1950s. The 1955 paperback edition of her *Mediterranean Food* was a bestseller among the urban middle classes, who could obtain her specialist ingredients quite easily in Italian and other shops in London and other big cities.

Far more popular though, and also personality-driven, were the books – and, from 1955, TV shows – of Fanny Cradock, a veritable culinary phenomenon in the late 1950s and 1960s. In 1956 she held a televised cook-off against Raymond Oliver, a French chef who claimed women could not cook as well as men. He wore chef's whites, she wore a pink satin ball gown (wipe-clean). She lost, but the publicity was fantastic, and she came to define another of the various strands of cookery at the time: a heightened reality, fantastical style, as far removed from the drab war years as possible.[20] Housewives loved her. For all those who sought exotic peasant food, written in beautiful, well-researched prose, there were more who fell for Fanny and her desire to 'bring a little colour and excitement into cooking without the expenditure of excessive time, labour or your hard-earned money'.[21]

Georgina's book carried neither the whiff of sun-kissed lavender fields nor the promise of winning at competitive entertaining (although she did include a flambé, the ultimate party dish in the 1960s). Hers was not at all personal, simply solid. Clementine's original Foreword to *Recipes from No.10* included the words 'I hope housewives will find it of value, but I expect they will have to try and try again before they get the magic touch'.[22] For the published version, she changed 'housewives' to 'readers'. Georgina's recipes could be cooked by anyone – but it certainly helped if they knew their way around a kitchen, and it would easily have fitted into a professional cook's library. It was part of another strand of recipe writing in the late 1950s, one into which her matter-of-fact prose and solidly excellent recipes fitted well, and which looked back to the pre-war upper- and upper-middle-class love of decent, well-presented and excellently cooked Anglo-French food – exactly what the Churchills and their circle consumed in home and at restaurants.

While those without servants experimented with piped green mayonnaise and thought they were the first to cook bouillabaisse outside the south of France, those who had grown up with money, servants and a restaurant habit happily re-embraced the food of the 1930s. Many, like the Churchills and their children, still had servants, often trained before the war, and who shared Georgina's belief that 'the best of food was carefully prepared and simply and beautifully cooked', and that the secret lay in good preparation. She did admit, though, that intuition played a huge role, along with 'the ability to adjust with discretion the ingredients to hand and so achieve perfection' – hard work for the novice bachelorette in a bedsit.[23]

It's hard to avoid the suspicion that her book was of most use to very experienced housewives and professional cooks. When *Woman's Journal* published an article on the book, they requested three recipes not found within its pages: 'Chateaubriand with Shallot Butter' (served for Clemmie's 70th birthday, and a particular favourite of Christopher Soames, who had asked Georgina for the recipe), 'Whitebait of Sole' (made for the christening of Randolph and Pamela's son Winston) and 'Beef Steak and Kidney Pudding' (served by request to General Eisenhower, cooked according to Winston's desire for a meat filling that was cooked for so long that it fell apart – it was also one of Clementine's favourites). The article included a rare nod to the uninitiated: 'Mrs Landemare always uses a pepper mill; and for beginners suggests that the sauce [Hollandaise] should be made in a double saucepan.'[24] The book itself offers no hint of the advice she would habitually give when talking about food – her granddaughter still remembers the vehemence with which she was told never to put lettuce in a salade niçoise.

The *Woman's Journal* article added detail to the recipes, labelling koulebiaka (a superlative salmon and rice pastry roll) as 'Lady Churchill's Favourite', and discussing Winston's preference for raspberry jam in the *gâteau hollandaise* (a layered fatless sponge), instead of the more usual marmalade. (It was then served with hot raspberry sauce and whipped cream.) The *oeufs bénédictine* recipe carried the caption 'muffins seem to have gone out of favour! Mrs Landemare suggests small baps, cut in half, as an alternative', while apparently *côtelettes de boeuf à la Russe* (beef patties with a cream and beetroot sauce garnished with onion rings) 'were frequently served at No.10'.

These were not comments Georgie put into her book. *Recipes from No.10* did, to a large extent, reflect the food at Downing Street, though. She included rum baba, *boeuf bourguignon* and a selection of chocolate cakes: all dishes Clementine enjoyed, while Boodle's orange fool was loved by both Winston and Clemmie. There were two recipes for consommé, to be served hot or cold (although only the beef version would jellify properly to give the true Churchill jellied soup effect). The twenty-eight egg dishes, including *oeufs sur le plat Jockey Club* (fried bread spread with chicken liver pâté, topped with a fried egg, a slice of sautéed veal kidney and cooked mushrooms), certainly mirrored the abundance of eggs served during and after the war, and, in a nod to Winston's days in the army, there were a number of Indian-ish dishes involving curry paste – 'Cervelles à la Connaught' (brains, as per chapter 3) among them.

None of the thirty-nine vegetable recipes were taken from the manuscript book, but the overwhelming presence of brassicas and potatoes certainly fits with the diet at Hyde Park Gate and Chartwell in the 1950s. Sea kale (rather directly translated as 'Choux de Mer', rather than the more usual 'Chou Marin') was in there, along with salsify – both increasingly rare in 1958 but classics of the Edwardian upper-class table. She did include some basics – thirty-seven French-style sauces taken indirectly from her copies of Saulnier and Escoffier, as well as how to make almond, choux, nouille, puff and shortcrust pastes (nouille was another Edwardian classic, used for lining tartlet tins as well as making noodles; it was, like modern pasta dough, made simply of egg and flour). There was a section on salads, thankfully geared toward the 1950s and not the 1930s (no pineapple in sight), and a lengthy list of sweets, which erred toward fruit and cream.

There were also notable omissions: no mention of the recipes for *oeufs Ottawa* or Canadian cakes, both in the manuscript, and surely influenced by Winston's trips to Quebec for wartime conferences; and few nods to American dishes such as hamburgers, which were gaining favour in the 1950s. Clemmie had reported fulsomely on Eleanor Roosevelt's 'stove on wheels' in 1944, 'for grilling hot dogs, trout or indeed anything. It is like a tall, gigantic wheelbarrow with a big metal tray with holes. This is filled with charcoal, and then there is a giant griller on the top, on which you can ~~cook~~ broil 20 or 30 hot dogs at a time.'[25]

But American barbecues were not exactly a good fit with Georgina's pared-back, elegant dinner party style, and this was a book designed to reflect dining at Downing Street at its best and most aspirational, rather than covering the full range of Churchillan experiences abroad. It was also selective in terms of regular dishes served: no plovers' eggs, little caviar, not that much game (all rather at odds with Churchill's carefully maintained reputation for plain food). There were no instructions on roasting, despite Winston's love of roast beef done exactly how he liked it (as 'pink perfection') – to the extent that Georgina would cook it in London, and it would be driven down to Chartwell to be eaten cold. Clemmie liked grouse, and roast game was regularly eaten – but this was an aristocratic hangover from before the war, when it would have been present at every dinner, and, like the plovers' eggs and caviar, didn't really have a place on the majority of middle-class tables, the ostensible audience for the book.

She didn't include the mousseline pudding she'd been cooking when the bomb fell in October 1940, something even she admitted needed to be served immediately, air raids notwithstanding, and presumably considered as rather too fiddly (or traumatising). Also missing, though, more curiously, were the more plebeian dishes, including the Irish stew that Winston had grown to like so much during the war. It was another of Eisenhower's favourites, cooked laden with onions, and with more added just before serving 'to float on top and make their presence known'.[26]

There were few servants' dishes: none of the meat puddings or pies, or the starch-based sweets with sago and tapioca. No cold meat or leftover dishes either – no toad-in-the-hole, no hashes, and certainly no kippers or kedgeree. She was actively contributing to the myth of

Churchill, erasing the servants from No.10, and with them something of her own experience.

Collins launched the book in autumn 1958, priced at 18 shillings. As usual with such arrangements, Georgie's royalties were staggered: 10 per cent for the first 3,000 copies sold, 12.5 per cent to 7,000, and 15 per cent thereafter. By the end of the year, she'd sold 2,585 copies on the domestic market, and 440 on export, justifying a second print run in 1959.[27] Further profits came from the interview with *Woman's Journal* (a whopping £250), and with *Housewife* (20 guineas).

The book was illustrated by Selma Nankivell, a tutor at Brighton College of Art, whose whimsical, rustic drawings captured the spirit of the time. Each section had a picture: a woman in a 'new look' style full-skirted dress with token apron watering the greenhouse for 'salads'; two smiling male chefs putting a decorated cake on a stand for 'cakes'; a woman in a square-necked frilly dress arranging fruit for 'puddings'; a behatted woman with a basket shopping for 'vegetables' (with a very un-Georgina set of scales at her side); a jolly butcher surrounded by carcasses for 'meat' and others on the same theme. 'Savouries' and 'pastes' were almost certainly based on Georgina herself: in the former, a cook in a high-necked dress and practical apron, recipe book to the side, transfers canapés from a rack to a plate, while in the latter she rolls out pastry on a board. Stout, smiling and practical, she is exactly as described by all those who knew her when she worked for the Churchills.

However, although the reviews were generally excellent, with Ambrose Heath saying, 'I praise and recommend it very highly', nearly all the reviewers agreed that this was not a book for the inexperienced. The *Birmingham Daily Post* called it a 'mouth-watering collection of 360 recipes – "creations" is perhaps the word', but also suggested that 'Mrs Landemare makes no concession to the beginner and no doubt scorns those who set the oven by a number and not their own skill; at least she gives no oven temperatures. But it is a book to give you ideas.' *Tatler's* reviewer called it 'a cook's manuscript, set out in print form in a book – and I like it'.[28] Sales dwindled rapidly though, and in the first half of 1960 only 107 home and 22 export copies were sold.

By the mid-1960s it had largely been forgotten, except by people who had known her and experienced her cooking. Even fifty years later, Heather Wood wrote that she cherished her copy, and still used it, especially for the iced cream of cucumber soup (*crème de concombres glacée*). Nicholas Soames, Mary's son, added, 'I am still a great fan, and I have her cookbook. It is a work of art, full of delicious, old-fashioned recipes and with a splendid section on savouries, which you simply don't get in any ghastly modern cookbook.'[29]

Another book, in a similar vein, was published in autumn 1958, and reviewed in many of the same publications. This was Lily MacLeod's *A Cook's Notebook*, summed up by the *Birmingham Daily Post* as 'a most workmanlike and also imaginative compilation of recipes and advice'. Unlike *Recipes from No.10*, MacLeod managed 'a nice blend of haute cuisine and good plain fare, starting with caviar, but devoting three pages to the

cheap and uninteresting cod – in her hands it is trans-
formed'. The reviewer still grumbled that she only gave
oven temperatures for electricity, and not gas, though: a
truer reflection of 1950s technology would have been to
include guidelines for solid fuel as well, which was still
commonplace in many homes.

Born in 1907, like Georgina, MacLeod had worked in
the 1920s and 1930s as a jobbing cook, in her case mainly
in country houses, and started her book with her own
Introduction: 'the happiest time of my working life was
spent cooking in the stately homes of England and how
pleased I am that I knew a way of life that has since virtually disappeared'. She was a Scot, born in the Hebrides
and trained in Cookery and Dietetics at Glasgow and
West of Scotland College of Domestic Science. Her
husband, George, was a valet when she met him, doubtless in service. He was also diabetic, and she followed up
A Cook's Notebook with *Cooking for the Wayward Diabetic*
in 1960.

In 1958, her book was a direct competitor with Georgina's, in the market for what reviewers called 'high end'
and 'books written by professional cooks'. In 1964,
however, as Mrs Douglas, her married name, she became
the latest in the line of London cooks for the Churchills:
she inherited Georgina's mantle, and cooked Georgina's
recipes, directly from her book, as well as bringing her
own excellent skills, honed in such a similar context, to
Hyde Park Gate. She continued to cook for Clementine
after Winston's death, and remained with her until 1976,
when Lily died from cancer, second only to Georgina for
the longevity of her service.

Britain was changing, and with it its food and kitchens. Although many people still lived in what were effectively Edwardian conditions, especially among the poor – 22 per cent of homes still had no running water as late as 1961 – in general, living conditions were improving.[30] By 1965, 56 per cent of the population had a fridge, and the number of married women in paid employment just kept on growing. Modern kitchens had serving hatches and easy-to-clean surfaces, and those who could afford it were encouraged to buy more and more gadgets to make cooking easier. Georgina's recipes seemed old-fashioned and overly time-consuming, and the world that she had known, of country house parties and endless entertaining, was becoming a thing of the past. The last debutantes were presented at court in 1958, and, while professional cooks and servants continued to be employed, there were far fewer of them – only 100,000 in the 1961 census.

Chartwell was not the only country house to be reborn as a site of leisure for the masses under the management of the National Trust. However, it was rare for the Trust to open up the servants' quarters of their stately homes, dominated as they were in the 1960s by an ethos that revered the aristocratic way of life, and viewed country houses as valuable for their artistic treasures, static monuments to beauty and not as places through which to explore complex, people-focused social history.[31]

The 1960s and 1970s narrative of life in service emphasised exploitation and lack of choice, with memoirs full of poverty, abuse and resentment being written by former servants. The idea of individual agency, or the huge differences in experience, even the mere fact that the majority of employers only had one or two servants on their staff, were glossed over in favour of the very real misery and lack of opportunity that many had faced. Those who, like Yvonne, had parents who had worked as servants sought to distance themselves from the perceived humiliation of their parents' occupation.

Ted Higgins was by no means alone in regarding the pre-war era of masters and servants very much in the light of the 'bad old days'. However, Georgina was also not alone in feeling bitter that her version was being ignored.[32] Lily MacLeod summed up her feelings, so similar to those of Georgina:

> this is all ended. Beautiful houses that once teemed with life and gracious living are left to the chance of an auctioneer's hammer. In the quiet of the night I fancy that the ghosts who walk in them now are not ladies in green or headless cavaliers but dignified butlers, bossy cooks, haughty lady's maids and austere housekeepers sighing for a life that has gone.[33]

Georgie sought solace in her friends and ex-colleagues from Downing Street and beyond, including Mary Soames, to whom she wrote in 1959,

> last Wednesday Her Ladyship invited me to tea, you can imagine how pleased I was to go and what was so nice I saw Sir Winston. I thought Her Ladyship looked wonderfully well and so full of life, it so

cheers me up to see them. I often read of Captain Soames when he speaks in the House and I think of bygone days.[34]

In 1958, Yvonne and Ted moved to London, to Stanmore, where Georgina's savings eventually went into building an extension above the garage, with a self-contained granny flat, complete with tiny kitchen in anticipation of her moving in with them. However, for the next decade she remained very independent, with a wide range of friends to both visit and correspond with – including ex-colleagues from the past, some of the Swiss au pairs from Chartwell, as well as Paul's family in America. She was still living partly with Algy in Putney, but took a great deal of pleasure in teaching Edwina to cook before she went off to university. These weren't the dishes of the recipe book, but the fruits of a long life cooking for very different groups of people, and she taught her 'main courses on a budget, starters that can be prepared hours or even days in advance, the multiple uses of choux paste (cheap and versatile), the benefits of concentrating on more labour intensive, but memorable puddings which work out so much cheaper'.[35]

She now lost much of the weight that had troubled her, having visited a new doctor who took her off all the medication prescribed by the Harley Street heart specialist, dismissed her assumption that her figure was entirely due to tasting all those creamy dishes, and put her on a high-fibre diet, with a new diagnosis of diverticulitis (pockets in the lining of the large intestine: it causes stomach pain, bloating and both diarrhoea and constipation).

Relations with Yvonne and Ted continued to be strained at times, coming to a potentially embarrassing head in 1961. The TV series *The Valiant Years*, based on Winston's war books, was airing on ITV, and Richard Burton, who narrated it, gave Clementine a colour TV on which to watch it. She already had two, so she offered to drive it over and give it to Georgina, who accepted enthusiastically. But the local elections were on, and the Stanmore house was covered in red, for it was Labour HQ. Lady Churchill had to be put off until polling day was over.

In 1965, Winston Churchill, who had been declining for some time, had another stroke and died. It was not unexpected, but it left Clementine reeling, for Diana had committed suicide two years before, and Clemmie had – finally – been formally diagnosed with depression in 1961. Georgina received an official invitation to the state funeral, having attended his lying in state with Edmund Murray (his ex-bodyguard), Joe Bullock (his driver) and their wives. She wore black, with a tiny veil, and commented sadly that, 'I was with Sir Winston when he moved from the Admiralty to No.10. Those were the good times. Now I don't do much cooking – only for myself and my brother.'[36]

Later, Edwina took her to the churchyard at Bladon, the parish church associated with Blenheim, to visit his grave. In the wake of his death, his doctor, Lord Moran, published a book of memoirs, which, although factually problematic in places, revealed for the first time the extent of Winston's health issues, including the way in which his 1953 stroke had been kept from the public. Georgina, as with most of the Churchill family, was furious – she must have known what was happening at the time, but to her, loyalty was paramount to the very end – regardless of her retirement, or the fact that Winston was dead.

Algy died in 1969, though by then Georgina had been living with Yvonne and Ted in Stanmore for two years. She also paid regular visits to Edwina (Eddie), to whom she was very close. Edwina had married in 1964, and her first child, Stephen, was born in 1967. Gary and Kate would follow in 1968 and 1972. As the family moved around, Georgina would go up to Nottinghamshire, Hertfordshire and Northamptonshire for the weekend, cooking for them, and settled happily into her role as a devoted great-grandmother. After a few drinks she'd regale any guests with carefully selected tales of her time at Downing Street. Edwina's sister Elisabeth also married in 1970, and moved to Hertfordshire.

However, Georgie was still the Churchills' beloved ex-family cook too. Clemmie and her secretary, Nonie Chapman, were regular visitors to her bedsit: she'd cook them chocolate cake because she knew it was something Clemmie loved. Otherwise, her skills were seldom used, and she normally ate with Yvonne and Ted. For her 90th birthday, in 1972, Edwina did most of the cooking, to a menu very carefully – and enthusiastically – planned. Georgina drew pictures of how 'Poulet Stanley' (with onions, rice, mushrooms, truffles and a velouté sauce) should be laid out and garnished, on an oval plate, and went through all 135 ways of cooking a potato, as detailed in *Larousse Gastronomique*, her copy of which she now gave to Edwina.

By the early 1970s, attitudes toward domestic service were shifting slightly. While the overall emphasis remained firmly on the bad, there was, at least, the start of a desire to show servants in popular culture, rather than simply try to forget they had existed, and to try to humanise the way in which they were shown. The 1971–5 series *Upstairs Downstairs* was conceived explicitly to 'see servants as people', and, although it still contained rather tired tropes, including sexual shenanigans and ill-educated but cunning maids and footmen, it was phenomenally popular, and did mark a move toward re-examining and revaluing lives below stairs.

For some, though, it was nostalgic, albeit falsely, and for those who still hankered after servants – but could no longer afford them – it reinforced the idea that there had been a halcyon era when everything was jolly, and servants well-treated, and everyone knew their place – a narrative that would vie with the equally black-and-white idea of universal oppression in the late 1970s and 1980s.[37] There were rumours that Mrs Bridges, the *Upstairs Downstairs* cook, was loosely based on Georgina, although the writers, Jean Marsh and Eileen Atkins, had had relatives in service themselves, and would have known many elderly ex-servants with similar training and views.

In 1973, with interest in historic domestic service rising, Georgina was interviewed by Joan Bakewell for a 'Below Stairs' episode of the BBC TV show *Times Remembered*, a documentary series that featured various people, usually in their 70s or older, discussing their lives. It was her 91st birthday, and she was surrounded by cards. Clementine, as organised as ever, had sent a tele-gram. Over the course of ten minutes, she talked about working for the Churchills, her memories of the family, the bomb incident and how upset she had been at the election result in 1945 (she blamed it on the soldiers). She was steely-eyed throughout, every inch the dedicated family retainer, except when she recalled leaving Downing Street. The *Evening Telegraph* adored the slot, wished that it could have been longer, and called it 'a superb little cameo'.[38]

In 1977, Georgina was 95. She still corresponded with a large number of people from throughout her life, spread across the world, and she was still in contact with a now deaf and almost blind Clementine, as well as the other long-standing servants from the 1940s: Grace Hamblin, Victor Vincent (the Chartwell head gardener) and Joe Bullock. Grace and Victor had stayed at Chart-well under the National Trust, and they, as well as many other ex-Churchill staff, were on Georgina's Christmas card list every year. That list, however, grew ever shorter.

Maud had died in 1975, leaving only Eve and Georgina, the youngest and oldest of the five Young siblings. When she sat down to write a memoir of her life, urged on by Kathleen Hill, one of Winston's wartime secretaries, it was partly to record for posterity the people she'd known, now long dead, not just in the era that had made her such an interesting TV contributor, but before that, from when she was born, and grew up, nearly a century before. She also wrote explicitly to combat the view that life in service had been exploitative or denigrating, angrily adding asides directly addressed to Ted and his views on life in the past: 'we have gained a lot but perhaps not', and:

> my brother and I would go up to a dell where we
> used to pick lovely violets that smelt and also prim-
> roses but cars have spoilt all that – progress as they
> call it. I'll leave you to decide as I am close to passing
> on, when the good God calls me. How I could relate
> all the small things that mattered in life that today
> mean nothing. Driving in a car you see only clouds
> of dust and dry road, no beauty. Their only concern
> is petrol and if their car is as good as their
> neighbour's.

But the memoir isn't rose-tinted, and Georgina's prose, while lacking commas, and at times very difficult to read, flows freely when she's drawing on her memories of childhood, and she's matter-of-fact about the every-day life of her family, and relationship with the upper classes. Even twenty years after retiring from service, she consistently capitalised her Ladies and Gentlemen, marking them out from the women and men of her own social milieu.

She had a confident, straightforward written voice, not oozing nostalgia, and the places and people she remembered, as well as the chronology, were all per-fectly placed: her memory was startlingly good. It's a testament to how invested in her career she remained, as well as how mentally acute she was, that while her friends' letters were full of illness and laments about the price of cake, she sat down and started to write a substantial manuscript because 'I have been asked many times to write about my life'. She may also have been using it as a displacement activity: Yvonne had been diagnosed with breast cancer, and it was not a happy time. After Georgina had written the record of her life, Yvonne then told her no one would be interested, and so Georgina tore the whole thing up and pushed it down the plughole of her sink, stopping with only a handful of pages left to go after Edwina's last-minute intervention.

By autumn 1977, Yvonne was seriously ill with a sec-ondary chest infection, which meant that she could no longer cope with having Georgina at home. Hastily installed in hospital, Georgie held court on the geriatric ward, the only lucid person there, gleefully recounting stories about her life to the cleaners and nurses, doctors and catering staff, including – with discretion – a few titbits from her time with Churchill. Some of her audi-ence would barely have remembered the man himself, for they would have been children when he died. When it became obvious that she could not go back to the house in Stanmore, she was moved to Anmer Lodge, a nearby residential home.

On 12 December 1977, Clementine Churchill suffered a sudden and major heart attack while lunching at home. She died the same day. A few days later, Georgie received Clemmie's last Christmas card, which must have been sent just before her death. Unlike in previous years, this one wasn't a specially commissioned reproduction of one of Winston's paintings, but a generic holly wreath with a robin in the middle. The writing was frail, and it lacked the usual personal dedication. Edwina was with her as she opened the card and silently cried.

Mary Soames sent Georgie a glass rose in a globe and an angora cape from among Clementine's personal possessions – keepsakes to remember her by, and letters came to Anmer Lodge commiserating on Georgina's huge loss. She wrote back, saying she was lonely.[39] She couldn't go to Clementine's funeral, though she received a descriptive letter from Penelope Barwick, one of Clemmie's ex-secretaries, saying that it was very sad, and that 'inevitably there were not many of Lady Churchill's contemporaries as she had outlived them all'.[40]

On 24 January 1978, there was a memorial service for Clementine's life, and on the 25th Georgina's daughter Yvonne died. Grace Hamblin wrote to Georgina in sympathy, saying that this winter had been so full of traumatic events that she was calling it a 'black winter'. She also said that she'd tried to get *Recipes from No.10* reprinted for sale at Chartwell, but to no avail.[41]

Georgina changed her will, written after Edwina's birth in 1943, to reflect the death of her daughter, but she was by now physically ageing, and her sight was almost gone: while she managed to sign it, she had to have the codicil read out loud to her rather than reading it herself.[42] Ted was named as executor but would never fulfil his duties, for he, too, died that year, at home, of coronary disease in July.

Before then, on 20 April, Georgina herself died, peacefully, of heart failure while she slept. Grace Hamblin summed up her feelings when she wrote, 'Mrs Landemare was one of the very few links left with that remarkable life we were given thro' our connection with the Churchills, and it is very sad to know that she is no more.'[43]

Epilogue

After Clementine's death in 1977, Mary Soames wrote to Georgina, giving her details of Clemmie's peaceful death, and declaring 'Dear Mrs Landemare – my mother was devoted to you and admired you so much – was so grateful for all you did for her and Sir Winston all those years you were with us.' For Georgina, cooking at the very hub of power, influencing the interactions of the people leading the country at a time of turmoil and crisis was the achievement of her lifetime. It was something she put above family or money or recognition. She was, in her turn, valued and respected by the family for whom she cooked for over two decades.

Seven years after her death, in 1985, the Cabinet War Rooms, newly renamed the Churchill War Rooms, opened to the public, and when they later reinstalled the kitchen, Georgina's granddaughter Edwina gave them the items she had at home to add to their display. Back went Winston's bedside candlestick holder, and back, too, went some of the cooking equipment that Georgina had acquired throughout her long life in kitchens. There were copper pans, including one with 'Système Café Voisin' engraved upon it, possibly a token from

Paul's training a century before, and pastry jiggers, knives, a waffle iron and the wooden tray, battered and worn, which Frank Sawyers had given her during the war. All were now polished and accessioned and put on show in a kitchen Georgina would have known – but very rarely have used.

The kitchen at No.10 was long gone, the Annexe had returned to offices, and at Chartwell the kitchen was that of the 1930s. Hyde Park Gate was in private hands, and Chequers remains the official country residence of the sitting prime minister, kitchen firmly out of bounds to the interested public. The kitchen in the bunker was – and is – the closest it's possible to get to Georgina's wartime service with the Churchills.

In the last ten years there has been yet another reassessment of the way we regard domestic service. Finally, the nuances are being shown, amid an understanding that the sheer scale of the subject means generalisations are dangerous. Unfortunately, popular presentations, from heritage sites to TV shows, still tend to be simplistic, and err on the side of entertainment. Servants are still stock figures, bobbing and curtseying, and the complexities of the employer–employee relationship are rarely well explored.

There is also still a lack of period specificity – servants are generically Victorian or vaguely twentieth century – and with it a misunderstanding of the ways in which servant life changed from the Victorian period to the 1950s. However, interest continues to grow, both popularly and academically, and it's now (hopefully) unthinkable that anyone of Georgina's longevity and experience could believe that their life story was not valuable.

We cannot read Georgina's shredded memoir, and it's impossible to entirely fill in all of the gaps in her well-lived life. We can see her talking in that 1973 interview, and we can try to put ourselves in her place among her scuffed pans in the War Rooms kitchen (I've hefted them, and felt their weight).

As a woman, especially a working-class one, in the early twentieth century, she remains frustratingly out of reach at times, but she's not alone. Even a life as well-documented and examined as that of Winston Churchill has gaps, not so much in terms of what he was doing, but certainly as to his domestic life, and his food. There are the (few) menus, and apparently authoritative lists of his likes and dislikes – but they are often contradictory, and so much politics underlies them that solid conclusions are hard to draw. There's also little recognition of the fact that, like his politics, his feelings about food would have changed throughout his life: what was true in 1955 wasn't necessarily true twenty years earlier. That does not mean that such things are not recoverable though, and it's certainly worth trying. Studying Churchill through his food brings a new way of looking at him, and Georgina's story enriches his, just as cooking for him and Clementine deeply enriched hers.

Georgina was precluded by her gender for much of her life from cooking at the very top of the culinary hierarchy: she never became head chef at the Ritz, or led a ducal kitchen. Even in the 1950s the profession remained dominated by men at its highest – and best-paid – levels.

She only published one book, and never made a TV show: hers was never a household name. Yet she was able to proudly state that she'd cooked for sixteen monarchs, men (and a few women) at the absolute peak of society. She never listed them but, in the 1940s, with monarchs toppling like crazy, and exiled leaders holed up in hotels in London, it's not hard to draw up a list, and there were royal visitors after the war too.[1] The power and influence of hereditary monarchies had been waning for a while, and, while the prestige of cooking for them was still enormous, it was men such as Winston Churchill who were the real leaders now. In 1895, Georgina had set out to work in significant households; she ended up in the most significant in the country.

Cooking was more than a job for Georgina: it was a vocation. When she looked back at her time with the Churchills, it was as a calling, and a culmination of her training and personal experience to date. Like all of the long-standing staff, she looked back at Chartwell, No.10 and Hyde Park Gate with joy, despite the long hours and exhaustion. Like Winston, she was utterly focused on the job at hand and, like him, was left empty and frustrated when through ill-health she was forced away from it.

She'd cooked her way through Edwardian splendour, two world wars, a depression and the age of jazz. She'd seen country houses built and demolished, and been part of the voting public as the Labour Party grew and the Liberals declined. She'd left school before she was 14, but her granddaughter would be awarded a PhD. She herself embraced the extra value given to her life by the fact that it was her fools and stews, and puddings and blanquettes and soups and boiled eggs that sustained Winston Churchill during the war.

Even as the war ended, he'd become a living legend, the man and the idea overlapping, but not quite the same, in people's minds. Still today there's a fever about him, although it's now acknowledged that his personal support network – Clemmie, his daughters, his secretaries – were crucial. We should add to these his cook: invisible, unassuming but a vital part of the team.

However, as much as Georgina's life was, by her as much as by others, defined by her time as the Churchills' most beloved family cook, it's also worth celebrating it in its own right. She devoted her life to food, and to others, finding joy in her skills and her relationships with those around her – employers, fellow servants and friends. As a servant she was discreet, loyal and quietly brilliant. As a colleague she was interested, warm and welcoming. She's remembered with joy by those who knew her. Here's to a life well-lived, for it was one that, looking back, she was able to describe as valuable and enjoyable – and one with absolutely no regrets.

Notes

Introduction

1. Inevitably, not everyone agrees that this is a good idea – or that it's even happening. See, for example, Graham Smith (2016), 'Beyond Us and Them: Public History and the Battle for the Past on Twitter', https://historiansforhistory.wordpress.com/2016/09/06/beyond-us-and-them-public-history-and-the-battle-for-the-past-on-twitter-by-graham-smith/; or Tristram Hunt's 2010 article 'History used to be the study of great men. Now it's of everyman', https://www.theguardian.com/commentisfree/2010/nov/21/tristram-hunt-praises-serious-biographies

2. The costumed cooking teams at Historic Royal Palaces and Audley End House (English Heritage) are the only professional teams, but the National Trust has a few volunteer teams doing sterling work at sites such as Ickworth and Attingham Park, as well as Quebec House (other NT sites are of patchier quality). English Heritage are also responsible for the wildly popular 'Victorian Way' videos on YouTube, which centre on the 1880 cook, Avis Crocombe, and try to give a nuanced view of her life through both first-person performance and third-person discussion. For excellent books on servants' lives, see (for example) Delap, Lucy. 2011. *Knowing Their Place: Domestic*

Service in Twentieth Century Britain. Oxford: OUP;
Steedman, Carolyn. 2009. *Labours Lost: Domestic Service
and the Making of Modern England*. Cambridge: Cambridge
University Press; Light, Alison. 2007. *Mrs Woolf and the
Servants*. London; New York: Penguin/Fig Tree.

3. Summers, Anne. 1998. 'Public Functions, Private
Premises: Female Professional Identity and the Domestic
Service Paradigm in Britain, *c*.1850–1930.' In *Borderlines:
Genders and Identities in War and Peace, 1870–1930*, edited by
Billie Melman, 353–376. New York & London: Routledge;
Benson, John. 1989. *The Working Class in Britain, 1850–1939*,
Themes in British Social History. London; New York:
Longman, 23.

4. Delap, Lucy. 2011. *Knowing Their Place: Domestic Service in
Twentieth Century Britain*. Oxford: OUP, 211; Lethbridge,
Lucy. 2013. *Servants: A Downstairs View of Twentieth
Century Britain*. London: Bloomsbury, 116; and see, for
example, Jackman, Nancy, and Tom Quinn. 2012. *The
Cook's Tale*. London: Coronet.

5. Soames, Mary. 2002. *Clementine Churchill*. Rev. and
updated ed. London: Doubleday, 33.

1: Beginnings

This chapter draws predominantly on Georgina's handwritten memoir, in the possession of her granddaughter, Edwina Brocklesby. All quotes not otherwise footnoted are from the memoir. For a overview of the period, G. R. Searle, *A New England: Peace and War 1886–1918* is useful, and for a general perspective of growing up and living in London in the 1870s–1890s, Molly Hughes's (1978) *A Victorian Family* is excellent. Molly was thoroughly middle class, but her experiences nevertheless mirror those of Georgina – pastries, open-top buses and the sheer excitement of a big city. For Aldbury and Tring, Jean Davis's books are useful guides, and Chris Reynolds's Hertfordshire Genealogy website has enough links and extracts that it's easy to become lost for several eye-opening hours (http://www.hertfordshire-genealogy.co.uk). The genealogical data has been drawn from the various censuses of the time, now available online in a number of places.

1. From Georgina's 1936 unpublished manuscript. The version in her 1958 published books reads: '12 oz butter, 4 eggs and 4 yolks of eggs, 3 oz caster sugar, 1 lb flour, 1 oz yeast, ½ oz grated lemon rind, ½ oz cinnamon, pinch of salt, 6 almonds shelled and splintered, a little cream. Make ready the yeast by dissolving in the cream which should be warmed slightly and a pinch of salt added. Place the butter in a basin with the cinnamon and lemon rind and beat for 10 minutes. Add the sugar and a quarter of the flour and 2 of the eggs. Beat all well together. Work in gradually the remainder of the flour, eggs and the extra 4 yolks. When all has been mixed, continue to beat for a further 10 minutes. It will be found easier to work with the hands than with a spoon. Smooth out the mixture in the basin making a slight well in the centre, place in the dissolved yeast and again work all this well together. Butter a large timbale mould [straight sided, deep and round: a high-sided cake tin will work for modern purposes] and sprinkle with the splintered almonds. Place in the mixture but only to halfway up the mould. Leave in a warm place until the mixture rises to the top of the mould. Bake in a moderate [180°C] oven for about ¾ hour.'

2. Cited in *Kelly's Directory*, 1890, online at http://www.hertfordshire-genealogy.co.uk/data/places/places-t/tring/tring-directory-1890.htm.

3. A silk mill and three windmills. One mill (now Heygates) still survives, though it is now thoroughly mechanised. http://www.british-history.ac.uk/vch/herts/vo12/pp281–294.

4. Ward, Humphry Mrs. 1895. *The Story of Bessie Costrell*. London, 1.

5. Statistics from the 1881 census as given in the introduction of the census, online at http://www.visionofbritain.org.uk/census/EW1881PRE/3. As a comparison, in 2014, the rural population stood at 9.3 million out of a population of 54.3 million (https://www.gov.uk/government/publications/rural-population-and-migration/rural-population-201415).

6. Now known as Gamekeeper's Lodge.

7. Davis, Jean. 1988. *Aldbury People 1885–1945*. Aldbury: J. Davis.

8. Earnings varied considerably, but a good guide (with further references) can be found here: https://countryhousereader.wordpress.com/2013/12/19/the-servant-hierarchy/

9. Battersea, Constance. 1923. *Reminiscences*. London: Macmillan, 126; Jenkins, Roy. 2002. *Churchill*. London: Pan Macmillan, 15.

10. Davis, Jean. 1988. *Aldbury People 1885–1945*. Aldbury: J. Davis, 60.

11. Rothschild, Miriam. 2008. *Walter Rothschild: The Man, the Museum and the Menagerie*. London: Natural History Museum.

12. Mellish, Katharine. 1901. *Cookery and Domestic Management*. London: E. & F. N. Spon, 972–973.

13. Roscoe, Thomas, and Peter Lecount. 1839. *The London and Birmingham Railway*. London: Charles Tilt, 67–68. For a full account of the coming of the railway to Tring, see also Ian Petticrew and Wendy Austin. 2013. *The Railway Comes to Tring*, online at http://gerald-massey.org.uk/railway_local/

14. David, Elizabeth. 1978. *English Bread and Yeast Cookery*. London: Book Club Associates/Penguin.

15. Cookery, Buckmaster's. *c.*1875. *Being an Abridgement of Some of the Lectures Delivered in the Cookery School at the International Exhibition for 1873 and 1874*. London: Routledge, 105.

16. Francatelli, Charles Elmé. 1861. *A Plain Cookery Book for the Working Classes*. London: Bosworth and Harrison, 42.

17. Actually Andrew John, listed in the 1891 census as a garden labourer, aged 25.

18. Sweet, M. 2001. *Inventing the Victorians*. London: Faber & Faber.

19. 'The Potteries and the Bramley Road Area and the Rise of the Housing Problem in North Kensington', in *Survey of London: Volume 37, Northern Kensington*, ed. F. H. W. Sheppard. 1973, 340–355. Available at *British History Online* http://www.british-history.ac.uk/survey-london/vol37/pp340–355, accessed February 2018; White, Jerry. 2016. Life in 19th century slums. History Extra, available at http://www.historyextra.com/period/victorian/life-in-19th-century-slums-victorian-londons-homes-from-hell/, accessed February 2018. Although changes were made, and successive schemes adopted to alleviate poverty, it remained poor. Housing clearances didn't help, including the building of a block that would later gain notoriety for similar reasons, of institutional neglect, governmental failures and unnecessary loss of life. It was called Grenfell Tower, and the fire there in June 2017 killed seventy-one people.

20. Dated 1891. Quoted at http://www.british-history.ac.uk/survey-london/vol42/pp168–183#h3–0015

21. Booth's Poverty Maps, 1886–1903, consulted online at https://booth.lse.ac.uk/map/13/-0.0569/51.5015/100/0, accessed February 2018

22. She was at a typical Victorian red-brick school, several storeys high, on Clareville Grove.

23. Hughes, Molly. 1979. *A London Family in the 1890s*. Oxford: OUP (First published 1946), 147.

2: The Kitchen Hierarchy

Georgina's memoir covers part of the period discussed here, and the quotes from her are all taken from this. See Nicola Humble for an overview of books and cooking throughout the Edwardian era and beyond, and for servants anything by Pamela Sambrook and Pamela Horn is both readable and reliable. Lucy Delap's *Knowing Their Place* puts Edwardian service into a longer context. There are lots of servants' memoirs, generally for a slightly later era, and of varying quality, but among the best are Mollie Moran's *Silver Spoons and Aprons* and Rosina Harrison's look at life with Lady Astor.

1. For the 1958 published version, see chapter 8.
2. Delap, Lucy. 2011. *Knowing Their Place: Domestic Service in Twentieth Century Britain*. Oxford: OUP, 56–57.
3. Rennie, Jean. 1977. *Every Other Sunday*. London: Coronet, 29.
4. King, Carla (2010) 'Stephen Gwynn', in the *Oxford Dictionary of National Biography*. Consulted online February 2018; UK census for 1901 and 1891.
5. Horn, Pamela. 2012. *Life Below Stairs: The Real Lives of Servants, the Edwardian Era to 1939*. Stroud: Amberley, 14.
6. Anon. 1884. 'The Nurse-Maid's Place', *Bow-Bells*, Vol. 40 (1029), 17 April 1884, 403.
7. Heren, Louise. 2016. 'My Ancestor Was a … Nanny', *Who Do You Think You Are Magazine*, 20 December 2016, accessed online via https://www.pressreader.com/uk/who-do-you-think-you-are-magazine/20161220/281539405591857, February 2018; Anon. c.1881. *The Management of Servants*, London, Warne & Co., 23.

8. Herbert Walter Dumergue, born in Fareham, educated at Oxford and by the 1890s a doctor in Kensington. His father was born in Middlesex.

9. Brocklesby, Edwina. 2018. *Irongran: How Triathlon Taught Me That Growing Older Needn't Mean Slowing Down.* London: Sphere.

10. Jenkins, Roy. 2002. *Churchill.* London: Pan Macmillan, 37.

11. Lough, David. 2015. *No More Champagne: Churchill and His Money.* New York; London: Picador / Head of Zeus; Lethbridge, Lucy. 2013. *Servants: A Downstairs View of Twentieth Century Britain.* London: Bloomsbury, 16; Mrs Earle. 1901. 'Family Budgets IV: Eighteen Hundred a Year', *Cornhill Magazine* 11 (61), 48–61.

12. Harrison, Rosina. 2011. *The Lady's Maid: My Life in Service.* London: Ebury. (First published 1975.)

13. This is based on ideal budgets, so isn't a hard and fast guide to household income.

14. Lethbridge, Lucy. 2013. *Servants: A Downstairs View of Twentieth Century Britain.* London: Bloomsbury, 17; Jenkins, Roy. 2002. *Churchill.* London: Pan Macmillan, 9.

15. MCHL 5/7/27, GL to MS, 7 June 1968.

16. Wadlow, Flo, and Alan Childs. 2007. *Over a Hot Stove: A Kitchen Maid's Story.* Norwich: Mousehold Press, 8.

17. Sambrook, Pamela. 2005. *Keeping Their Place: Domestic Service in the Country House.* Stroud: Sutton, 73.

18. Rennie, Jean. 1977. *Every Other Sunday.* London: Coronet, 91.

19. Jackman, Nancy, and Tom Quinn. 2012. *The Cook's Tale.* London: Coronet, 84.

20. Powell, Margaret. 2011. *Below Stairs*: Pan, 65.

21. Gray, Annie. 2017. *The Greedy Queen: Eating with Victoria.* London: Profile.

22. Jones, Stephanie. 1992. *Merchants of the Raj: British Managing Agency Houses in Calcutta Yesterday and Today.* Basingstoke: Macmillan, 29–30.

23. Muthesius, Stefan. 1982. *The English Terraced House*. New Haven; London: Yale University Press, 44.

24. Delap, Lucy. 2011. *Knowing Their Place: Domestic Service in Twentieth Century Britain*. Oxford: OUP.

25. Lubbock, S. 1939. *The Child in the Crystal*. London: Jonathan Cape, 148.

26. Lethbridge, Lucy. 2013. *Servants: A Downstairs View of Twentieth Century Britain*. London: Bloomsbury, 35.

27. Senn, Charles Herman. 1904. *The Century Cookbook: Practical Gastronomy and Recherché Cookery*. London: Ward, Lock & Co.

28. Marshall, A. *c.*1888. *Mrs A. B. Marshall's Cookery Book*. London: Marshall's Cookery School. The recipe is 'Little tongues à la Financière'.

29. Ibid.

30. de Salis, H. 1902. *À La Mode Cookery*. London: Longmans, Green & Co., 160.

31. Laudan, Rachel. 2016. *Servants in the Kitchen: Professed Cooks and Plain Cooks*, available at http://www.rachellaudan.com/2016/05/servants-in-the-kitchen-professed-cooks-and-plain-cooks.html accessed February 2018.

32. Hamilton 20/1/1–8 diaries of Lady Hamilton, 3 December 1903. The Hamilton archive can be found at the Liddell Hart Centre for Military Archives at King's College London.

33. Ibid. 1 January 1904.

34. Stelzer, Cita. 2011. *Dinner with Churchill: Policy-Making at the Dinner Table*. London: Short, 31.

35. Hamilton 20/1/1–8, 3 October 1905.

36. CHAR 28/11/42–43 Lord Randolph Churchill to Jennie Churchill, 7 November 1891.

37. In 1911, Robert and Bronia give their nationality as Italian, but according to the 1891 census he was born in Salonica, and she was from Krakow. They probably both held dual

nationality through their parents or grandparents, and were part of a European-wide family of merchants, similar to the Rothschilds and the Rallis.

38. Gerard, Jessica. 1994. *Country House Life: Family and Servants, 1815–1914*. Oxford: Blackwell, 172.

39. In the 1901 census, the family were in Shanklin with their governess and nanny.

40. The photograph was taken by Schuth's Photographic Galleries, which were active in London from 1892 to 1908. For help in dating I am indebted to Ian Chipperfield.

3: Paul

For the food scene in Paris in the late nineteenth century, the website www.victorianparis.wordpress.com is useful, containing lots of primary material across a variety of topics. Luke Barr on *Ritz and Escoffier* is a good introduction to London and the new wave of restaurants there, and Amy Trubek also gives a great deal of background information on restaurants. Much of this chapter has involved drawing out tiny details from census and military record data, and a huge hoorah to both findmypast and ancestry.co.uk, as well as the detailed digital archive of the Archives de Paris.

1. This is the manuscript version. It was published as 'Cervelles Connaught: for four people: 2 sets of brains, butter, 1 oz flour, 1 tsp curry powder, a little chopped mango chutney, 3 tbsp cream. Wash and cleanse the brains. Melt a little butter in a saucepan, put in the brains, salt and pepper and cook very slowly for about ½ hour. Put aside to cool. Make a sauce with a little butter, one tablespoon flour and curry powder mixed. Add a little chopped mango chutney and juice of the brains. Cook for 15 minutes, pass through a strainer and then add 3 tablespoons cream. Cut the brains into slices, reheat in a

covered dish in the oven. Place on serving dish and coat with boiling sauce.'

2. Robb, Graham. 2010. *Parisians: An Adventure History of Paris*. London: Picador, 144.

3. Marcus, Sharon. 1999. *Apartment Stories: City and Home in Nineteenth-Century Paris and London*. Berkeley; London: University of California Press, 135–142.

4. Thank you to Daniel Nomdedeu at Entraide Généalogique for helping elucidate Paul's siblings.

5. On Paul's marriage certificate, Mathurin is listed as living on his own means in Tournan, in Seine-et-Marne, about thirty miles southeast of Paris (and fifteen miles south of what is now Disneyland).

6. Jarrin, Guglielmo A. 1861. *[the Italian Confectioner ... New Edition, Revised and Enlarged.]*. New edition, revised and enlarged. ed. London: Routledge, Warne and Routledge; Gouffé, Jules. 1873. *Le Livre De Pâtisserie*. Paris: Hachette.

7. *Annuaire-Almanach du Commerce Didot-Bottin*, 1864, 1227–1228. Consulted at http://gallica.bnf.fr/ark:/12148/bpt6k6333170p/f1237.item, May 2018

8. Walton, William. 1899. *Paris from the Earliest Period to the Present Day*, cited at https://victorianparis.wordpress.com/2014/09/04/paris-police-order-in-the-street/

9. Jackson Jarves, James (1852) *Parisian Sights and French Principles*.

10. Faure, Alain. 2006. 'Local Life in Working Class Paris at the end of the Nineteenth Century'. *Journal of Urban History* 32 (5), 761–772; Ferguson, Eliza. 2011. 'The cosmos of the Paris apartment: working class family life in the nineteenth century'. *Journal of Urban History* 37 (1), 59–67.

11. Escoffier, Auguste. 2011. *Souvenirs Culinaires*. Paris: Mercure de France. (First published 1985), 29.

12. Pépin, Jacques. 2003. *The Apprentice*. New York: Houghton Mifflin, 59.

13. Labouchère, Henri. 1871. *Diary of the Besieged Resident in Paris*. London: Bradbury, Evans and Co., 13 October 1870. Available at http://www.gutenberg.org/files/19263/19263-h/19263-h.htm

14. Menu from 25 December 1870, *99me jour du siège*. Published by the Musée Escoffier de l'Art Culinaire.

15. Gluckstein, Donny. 2011. *The Paris Commune: A Revolution in Democracy*. Chicago, Ill.: Haymarket Books.

16. Ibid. 6 January 1871.

17. Ibid. 19 January 1870.

18. Cited in Polansky, Iva (2017) 'The Bloodbath of the Paris Commune', at https://victorianparis.wordpress.com/2017/03/18/the-bloodbath-of-the-paris-commune/. For the current thinking on the numbers killed, however, see Robert Tombs (2012) 'How Bloody Was la Semaine Sanglante of 1871: A Revision'. *The Historical Journal* 55(3) 679–704.

19. Spang, Rebecca L. 2000. *The Invention of the Restaurant: Paris and Modern Gastronomic Culture*. Cambridge, Mass.; London: Harvard University Press.

20. Trubek, Amy. 2000. *Haute Cuisine: How the French Invented the Culinary Profession*. Philadelphia: University of Pennsylvania Press, 42.

21. Charpentier, Henri, and Boyden Sparkes. 2001. *Life À La Henri: Being the Memories of Henri Charpentier*: Modern Library. (First published 1934), 58.

22. Paul doesn't appear in any of the surviving archives from the Savoy hotel, which Escoffier headed from 1890, and his name does not crop up in the Escoffier Foundation's material. From 1901 the census suggests he was working in private houses, and no longer in the restaurant trade.

23. Rue Neuve-St-Mérri is now called just Rue St Mérri, and the northern part, where Paul lived, was demolished in 1934. Many thanks to Gerard Walraevens for help in identifying this. The Les Halles market was demolished

in 1971, and is now a mixture of scrubby park and the maze-like shopping centre Forum les Halles. Most will know the area only from having been sucked into the multi-layer confusion that is the RER-métro station underneath, the horror that is Châtelet-Les Halles.

24. Then written as Lacondamine.

25. This section relies on Paul's military service record, for a copy of which I am indebted to the voluntary association Le Fil d'Ariane.

26. Burnett, John. 2004. *England Eats Out: A Social History of Eating Out in England from 1830 to the Present*. 1st ed. Harlow: Pearson/Longman, 110.

27. 'Dining Rooms and Restaurants', from Murray's *Handbook to London*, 1879, quoted at http://www.victorianlondon.org/food/dickens-restaurants.htm, see also http://uk-menu-archives.co.uk/product/williss-restaurant-ltd-diner-c1880s/

28. Ralph Blumenfeld, 3 October 1890, quoted at http://www.victorianlondon.org/food/dickens-restaurants.htm

29. Goiran, Joseph Henri. 1935. *Les Français À Londres: Etude Historique*. Paris; Trubek, Amy. 2000. *Haute Cuisine: How the French Invented the Culinary Profession*. Philadelphia: University of Pennsylvania Press.

30. Barr, Luke. 2018. *Ritz and Escoffier: The Hotelier, the Chef and the Rise of the Leisure Class*. New York: Clarkson Potter.

31. Trubek, Amy. 2000. *Haute Cuisine: How the French Invented the Culinary Profession*. Philadelphia: University of Pennsylvania Press, 64.

32. His name appeared occasionally in the culinary press, never with an attribution. He may have worked in the lower ranks of the staff at the Ritz or elsewhere, but certainly never as head chef.

33. Marshall, Agnes. 1891. *Larger Cookery Book of Extra Recipes*. London, 488; Senn, Charles Herman. 1904. *The Century*

Cookbook: Practical Gastronomy and Recherché Cookery.
London: Ward, Lock & Co., 823.

34. It was a birthday dinner for Edward VII (though he
wasn't actually present) known as the Gondola Party.
https://issuu.com/thesavoylondon/docs/savoy_stories_
ver.3_nov_2016_proof_ has a few more details.

35. *Victorian Party-Giving on Every Scale.* 2007. Stroud:
Nonsuch, 83–84. Originally published 1880.

36. Churchill, Randolph S. 1966. *Youth: Winston S. Churchill
1874–1900.* London: Minerva, 1991, 110.

37. *Food and Cookery,* July 1900, 196.

38. Harrison, Michael. 1977. *Rosa: Rosa Lewis of the Cavendish.*
London: Corgi, 74.

39. Fletcher, John. 2005. *Ornament of Sherwood Forest.*
Bakewell, Country Books, 88–89; Newcastle Collection
Ne3/A/101, 93 & Ne3/A/107, 97.

40. Baedeker, Karl. 1900. *London and Its Environs.*
(Republished 2002, Old House Books).

41. Suzanne, Alfred. 1904. *La Cuisine Et Pâtisserie Anglaise Et
Américaine.* Paris, 6.

42. *Food and Cookery,* January 1898.

43. *Food and Cookery,* 1897, vol. 2, 69.

44. Trubek, 124.

45. *Food and Cookery,* January 1901, 21.

4: Married Life

There is a wealth of literature on country houses and their
servants, of which Lucy Delap and Lucy Lethbridge's books
have been very useful. Adrian Tinniswood's *The Long Weekend*
is fascinating and brings to life the thriving social scene of the
era. This chapter also introduces the Churchills more, and for
them I have drawn most upon the books by their daughter,
Mary Soames, including her biography of Clementine, and her
edited collection of their letters, as well as more general biographies of Winston by Andrew Roberts, Richard Holmes and

Roy Jenkins (there are lots of others for anyone wanting more detail on his political life). David Lough's *No More Champagne* has also been very useful indeed.

1. From Georgina's MS book. The recipe did not make it into print, but is easy enough to replicate. It makes around fifty macaroons. Mix one small egg white with 8 oz almonds and 10 oz icing sugar in a saucepan, whisk two egg whites to stiff peak, and fold into the almond mixture. Heat the mixture up gently without letting it boil, until it thickens, and then fold in 3 oz of finely chopped angelica. Use a teaspoon to dollop the mix onto slightly greased baking paper or on rice paper (the latter is more authentic to the era): you should end up with about fifty roundish biscuits. Bake at 120–130°C for 30–35 minutes until just browning on top.

2. On her marriage certificate and emigration records, 'Angelique' becomes the more easily spelt 'Angelic'.

3. Secombe, Wally. 1990. 'Starting to Stop: Working Class Fertility Decline in Britain', *Past and Present* 126, 151–188.

4. Griffiths, Clare and Anita Brock (2003) 'Twentieth century mortality trends in England and Wales', *Health Statistics Quarterly* 18, 5–17. Available online at https://www.ons.gov.uk/ons/rel/hsq/health-statistics-quarterly/no--18--summer-2003/twentieth-century-mortality-trends-in-england-and-wales.pdf.

5. Purnell, Sonia. 2015. *First Lady: The Life and Wars of Clementine Churchill*. London: Aurum, 152; Soames, Mary. 2002. *Clementine Churchill*. Rev. and updated ed. London: Doubleday, 14.

6. Landemare, Georgina. 1958. *Recipes from No.10: Some Recipes for Discerning Cooks*. London: Collins, Foreword.

7. Lough, David. 2015. *No More Champagne: Churchill and His Money*. New York; London: Picador/Head of Zeus, 99.

8. The relevant bills are in CHAR 1/106 (see, for example, folio 73 for expenses incurred on board the *Enchantress*), and CHAR 1/110/118 is the bill from the House of Commons. The dissertation on dining chairs can be found in Churchill, Winston, Mary Soames, and Clementine Churchill Baroness Spencer-Churchill. 1998. *Speaking for Themselves: The Personal Letters of Winston and Clementine Churchill*. London: Doubleday, 259.

9. Ibid., 73.

10. Brackenbury, Alison. 2018. *Aunt Margaret's Pudding*. Fife: Happenstance Press, and pers.comm.

11. Parker, D. H. 1977 unpublished. *The Story of My Life in Gentlemen's Service*. Courtesy of Adrian Tinniswood.

12. Burnett, John. 1989. *Plenty and Want: A Social History of Food in England from 1815 to the Present Day*. London: Routledge, 244.

13. Beeton, Isabella. 1888. *Mrs Beeton's Book of Household Management*. London: Ward, Lock & Co., 1544.

14. Greaves, Simon. 2014. *The Country House at War: Fighting the Great War at Home and in the Trenches*. Swindon: National Trust Books, 12; Adam, Ruth. 2000. *A Woman's Place, 1910–1975*. London: Persephone Books, 46.

15. Lethbridge, Lucy. 2013. *Servants: A Downstairs View of Twentieth Century Britain*. London: Bloomsbury, 141.

16. Twilley, Nicola. 2013. 'The Lost Sausages of World War One', available at http://www.ediblegeography.com/the-lost-sausages-of-world-war-i/, accessed July 2018.

17. Burnett, John. 2004. *England Eats Out: A Social History of Eating out in England from 1830 to the Present*. 1st ed. Harlow: Pearson/Longman, 174.

18. Tschumi, Gabriel, and Joan Powe. 1954. *Royal Chef: Forty Years with Royal Households*. London: William Kimber, 135.

19. Churchill, Winston, Mary Soames, and Clementine Churchill Baroness Spencer-Churchill. 1998. *Speaking for*

Themselves: The Personal Letters of Winston and Clementine Churchill. London: Doubleday, 168.

20. Burnett, John. 1989. *Plenty and Want: A Social History of Food in England from 1815 to the Present Day.* London: Routledge.

, —. 2004. *England Eats Out: A Social History of Eating Out in England from 1830 to the Present.* 1st ed. Harlow: Pearson/Longman.

21. Lough, David. 2015. *No More Champagne: Churchill and His Money.* New York; London: Picador/Head of Zeus, 112.

22. WSC to CSC 23, November 1915, quoted in Churchill, Winston, Mary Soames, and Clementine Churchill Baroness Spencer-Churchill. 1998. *Speaking for Themselves: The Personal Letters of Winston and Clementine Churchill.* London: Doubleday, 164.

23. Ibid., 163.

24. Archie's records, accessed via ancestry.co.uk, January 2018. I couldn't find Algy.

25. Moran, Mollie. *Aprons and Silver Spoons: The Heartwarming Memoirs of a 1930s Kitchen Maid.* 2014. 17.

26. Greaves, Simon. London: Penguin. *The Country House at War: Fighting the Great War at Home and in the Trenches.* Swindon: National Trust Books, 194.

27. BBC Radio 4, *The Kitchen Cabinet* (17 June 2014) from Clitheroe. Available on podcast, for episode details see here: https://www.bbc.co.uk/programmes/b046j1k4.

28. Horn, Pamela. 2012. *Life Below Stairs: The Real Lives of Servants, the Edwardian Era to 1939.* Stroud: Amberley, 41.

29. Lethbridge, Lucy. 2013. *Servants: A Downstairs View of Twentieth Century Britain.* London: Bloomsbury, 157.

30. MCHL 5/7/27, Notes on staff, supplied by Mrs Clive Howes.

31. Undated, unreferenced newspaper clipping, (1958?) in family archives.

32. MCHL 5/7/27, GL to MS, 2 June 1968.

33. Tinniswood, Adrian. 2016. *The Long Weekend: Life in the English Country House, 1918–1939*. London: Jonathan Cape, 94.

34. Perkin, Harold James. 1989. *The Rise of Professional Society: England since 1880*. London: Routledge, 241–243.

35. Tinniswood, Adrian. 2016. *The Long Weekend: Life in the English Country House, 1918–1939*. London: Jonathan Cape, 27–8.

36. Rennie, Jean. 1977. *Every Other Sunday*. London: Coronet, 80.

37. Harrison, Rosina. 1976. *Gentlemen's Gentlemen: From Boot Boys to Butlers, True Stories of Life Below Stairs*. London: Ebury, 165.

38. https://winstonchurchill.org/publications/finest-hour/finest-hour-138/churchill-facts-residences-of-winston-and-clementine-churchill/; MCHL 5/7/27, details of servants from Gladys Blackwell.

39. Lethbridge, Lucy. 2013. *Servants: A Downstairs View of Twentieth Century Britain*. London: Bloomsbury, 197; and see the servant memoirs already cited in chapter 2.

40. Waterson, Merlin. 1985. *The Country House Remembered: Recollections of Life between the Wars*. London: Routledge & Kegan Paul, 58 (Lady Marjorie Stirling).

41. Buczacki, Stefan. 2007. *Churchill and Chartwell: The Untold Story of Churchill's Houses and Gardens*. London: Frances Lincoln, 28.

42. Lethbridge, Lucy. 2013. *Servants: A Downstairs View of Twentieth Century Britain*. London: Bloomsbury, 151; Delap, Lucy. 2011. *Knowing Their Place: Domestic Service in Twentieth Century Britain*. Oxford: OUP, 116.

43. Light, Alison. 2007. *Mrs Woolf and the Servants*. London; New York: Penguin/Fig Tree, 169.

44. See, for example, Lake, Nancy. 1930. *Menus Made Easy … Revised and Extended Edition, the Thirty-Fifth*. London; New York: Frederick Warne & Co.

45. de Salis, H. 1902. *À La Mode Cookery*. London: Longmans, Green & Co.

46. Sysonby, Ria, Oliver Messel, and Osbert Sitwell. 1935. *Lady Sysonby's Cook Book*. London: Putnam, 67, 154; and CSCT 9/3/1 menu book for 1936–7, 24 October 1936.

47. Boulestin, X. Marcel. 1931. *What Shall We Have Today?* London: William Heinemann Ltd, 9.

48. Rennie, Jean. 1977. *Every Other Sunday*. London: Coronet, 136.

49. Newspaper clipping in family archive, nd, 1956?

50. Moore, Lucy. 2009. *Anything Goes: A Biography of the Roaring Twenties*. London: Atlantic, 161; 173.

51. Ibid., 13–17.

52. CHAR 1/400A/46 note from Dr Otto Pickhardt, New York.

53. https://www.nationalarchives.gov.uk/currency-converter

5: Chef for Hire

As we sweep into Churchill-world, it's all of the books listed at the start of chapter 4, plus Sonia Purnell's biography of Clementine and Stefan Buczacki on the Churchills' houses. Nicola Humble is again helpful for the context of the recipe books. Mainly, however, this chapter uses the papers of Winston and Clementine Churchill, kept at the Churchill Archive at Churchill College in Cambridge, and the unpublished papers of Georgina Landemare, which are in the possession of her granddaughter, Edwina Brocklesby.

1. Published in *Recipes from No.10* as follows: 'For six people: 6 sponge cakes, 4 oranges, 2 lemons, ¾ pint cream, sugar to taste. Cut up sponge cakes lengthwise in slices and place in a glass dish. Put in a basin the grated rind of 1 lemon and 2 oranges and the juice of all the fruit. Mix with the cream and sugar to taste. Pour all over the

sponge cakes and allow to stand for 6 hours before serving (it is like trifle, but nice).'

2. MacLeod, Lily pseud. 1958. *A Cook's Notebook*. London: Faber, 9.

3. Anon. *c*.1958. 'Cook at No. 10', newspaper clipping in papers in the possession of Edwina Brocklesby.

4. Stelzer, Cita. 2011. *Dinner with Churchill: Policy-Making at the Dinner Table*. London: Short, 23; http://www. nationalarchives.gov.uk/currency-converter/.

5. Soames, Mary. 2012. *A Daughter's Tale: The Memoir of Winston and Clementine Churchill's Youngest Child*. London: Black Swan, 274.

6. Landemare, Georgina. 1958. *Recipes from No.10: Some Recipes for Discerning Cooks*. London: Collins.

7. The Hamilton papers are all in the Liddell Hart Centre for Military Archives at King's College, London, and the diaries are kept under Hamilton 20/1.

8. It's hard to show full workings in a narrative text, so here's the evidence: Mark Bonham Carter writes to GL during negotiations on publishing *Recipes from No.10* that he remembers her time as their cook (he was Violet's son); Lord and Lady Islington can be surmised from a recipe for 'Rushbrooke Gingerbread' in MS (unpub.) 1936; GL memoir refers to catering parties for the Rallis.

9. Horn, Pamela. 2012. *Life Below Stairs: The Real Lives of Servants, the Edwardian Era to 1939*. Stroud: Amberley, 75.

10. Royal Archive (henceforth RA) MRH/MRHF/MENUS/ MAIN/BP (Buckingham Palace menu book for the 1920s, 17 April 1927); RA QM/PRIV/QMD/1927 (Queen Mary's diary for 17 April 1927). Material used by permission of Her Majesty Queen Elizabeth II.

11. Tinniswood, Adrian. 2016. *The Long Weekend: Life in the English Country House, 1918–1939*. London: Jonathan Cape, 98–103.

12. Hamilton 20/1/6 Diary for 1935, 19 July.

13. Soames, Mary. 2012. *A Daughter's Tale: The Memoir of Winston and Clementine Churchill's Youngest Child*. London: Black Swan, 28.

14. Jenkins, Roy. 2002. *Churchill*. London: Pan Macmillan, 494.

15. Bonham Carter, Violet, and Mark Pottle. 1998. *Champion Redoubtable: The Diaries and Letters of Violet Bonham Carter, 1914–1944*. London: Weidenfeld & Nicolson.

16. I did make it with lard, to be fair. It almost induced a sugar coma. (The published version used margarine.)

17. Sir Alexander Spearman, Obituary. *The Times*, 6 April 1982; 'Two By-Elections: Early Writs for the Wrekin and Scarborough'. *The Times*, 9 September 1941.

18. Alexander Spearman to GL, 9 February 1978, in private family papers belonging to Edwina Brocklesby.

19. Unpublished memoir in private family papers belonging to Edwina Brocklesby.

20. '£1 in 1900 → 2017 | UK Inflation Calculator.' US Official Inflation Data, Alioth Finance, 7 August 2018, https://www.officialdata.org/1900-GBP-in-2017?amount=1.; *Food & Cookery* V (1901), 99.

21. Light, Alison. 2007. *Mrs Woolf and the Servants*. London; New York: Penguin/Fig Tree, 251.

22. Saulnier, L. 1914. *Le Répertoire De La Cuisine*. Paris, Introduction; Escoffier, Auguste. 1919. *L'Aide Mémoire Culinaire*. Paris.

23. Edwina Brocklesby, pers.comm; the Saulnier book is in the family papers.

24. (Or 'Playa Plate' – the 'Plate' is probably crossed out.)

25. Humble, N. 2005. *Culinary Pleasures: Cookbooks and the Transformation of British Food*. London: Faber & Faber.

26. Morphy, Countess. 1935. *Recipes of All Nations*. London: Published for Selfridge and Co. Ltd by H. Joseph, 8–9.

27. MCHL 5/7/27 GL to MS, 2 June 1968.

28. CHAR 1/182 and Sarah McKeon (house and engagement steward, Chartwell) pers.comm, August 2018.

29. Churchill, Winston, Mary Soames and Clementine Churchill Baroness Spencer-Churchill. 1998. *Speaking for Themselves: The Personal Letters of Winston and Clementine Churchill*. London: Doubleday, 281 (letter dated 17 April 1924).

30. Conversation with Lady Williams (née Jane Portal), November 2018.

31. CHAR 1/285; CHAR 1–351/50–52.

32. Lough, David. 2015. *No More Champagne: Churchill and His Money*. New York; London: Picador/Head of Zeus, 240.

33. CHAR 1/268/79–80; CSCT 9/3/1 menu book 1936–1937; RA MRH/MRHF/MENUS/MAIN/WC menus for Windsor Castle, 1920s.

34. Holmes, Richard. 2006. *In the Footsteps of Churchill*. London: BBC, 222.

35. Churchill, Winston, Mary Soames, and Clementine Churchill Baroness Spencer-Churchill. 1998. *Speaking for Themselves: The Personal Letters of Winston and Clementine Churchill*. London: Doubleday, 179.

36. Stelzer, Cita. 2011. *Dinner with Churchill: Policy-Making at the Dinner Table*. London: Short, 26.

37. Jenkins, Roy. 2002. *Churchill*. London: Pan Macmillan, 474.

38. Gilbert, Martin. 1976. *Winston S. Churchill: Vol. V. 1922–1939.* [S.l.]: Heinemann, 265.

39. There is some debate about the date. This seems to be fairly definitive: Stefan Buczacki (nd) Churchill Facts: Residences of Winston and Clementine Churchill, in Finest Hour 138, consulted at https://winstonchurchill.org/publications/finest-hour/finest-hour-138/churchill-facts-residences-of-winston-and-clementine-churchill/ June 2018.

40. CSCT 2/25 WSC to CSC 8 March 1935.

41. 1911 census. Doris, unusually, is also with Margaret (already widowed) in Belcher's household.

42. Burnett, John. 1989. *Plenty and Want: A Social History of Food in England from 1815 to the Present Day*. London: Routledge.

43. Lily is named in a letter of 1924, cited in *Speaking for Themselves*, 281; Jessie Cameron started 13 May 1935 CSCT 4/5 CSC engagement diary; M. Logan is hired through Massey's CHAR 1/314/140 and E. R. Phillip from Hunt's CHAR 1/337/24.

44. CSCT 1/26 CSC to WSC, 4 August 1942.

45. CSCT 1/5 CSC to WSC, 12 July 1911.

46. CSCT 1/6 CSC to WSC, 20 April 1912.

47. CSCT 1/7 CSC to WSC, 22 July 1913.

48. Holmes, Richard. 2006. *In the Footsteps of Churchill*. London: BBC, 28.

49. Jenkins, Roy. 2002. *Churchill*. London: Pan Macmillan, 396.

50. Penelope Barwick, née Hampden-Wall to GL, 29 December 1977.

51. Churchill, Winston, Mary Soames, and Clementine Churchill Baroness Spencer-Churchill. 1998. *Speaking for Themselves: The Personal Letters of Winston and Clementine Churchill*. London: Doubleday, 283–6.

52. CSCT 3/24 9.

53. The National Trust. 2014. *Chartwell* (official guidebook), 20.

54. MCHL 5/7/4 MW to CSC, 13 April 1935.

55. CHAR 1/337 and 338 – accounts paid.

56. CHAR 1/336/36.

57. Stelzer, Cita. 2011. *Dinner with Churchill: Policy-Making at the Dinner Table*. London: Short, 30.

58. Churchill, Winston, Mary Soames and Clementine Churchill Baroness Spencer-Churchill. 1998. *Speaking for Themselves: The Personal Letters of Winston and Clementine Churchill*. London: Doubleday, 330.

59. CSCT 3/2 notes by CSC on her early life.

60. CSCGT 4/4 engagement diary for 1933; Purnell, Sonia. *First Lady: The Life and Wars of Clementine Churchill*, 152.

61. MS Bonham Carter 63, 70 engagement diary 1932, 1939.

62. Boulestin, X. Marcel. 1936. *Myself, My Two Countries*. [S.l.]: [s.n.], 287.

63. Soames, Mary. 2012. *A Daughter's Tale: The Memoir of Winston and Clementine Churchill's Youngest Child*. London: Black Swan, 27.

64. Allhusen, Dorothy. 1927. *A Book of Scents and Dishes, Etc.* London: Williams & Norgate, 194; Georgina Landemare. 1936. Unpublished MS. Georgina's version of the recipe is given at the start of chapter 8.

65. Soames, Mary. 2012. *A Daughter's Tale: The Memoir of Winston and Clementine Churchill's Youngest Child*. London: Black Swan, 99.

66. All information on diners from WCHL 6/35 The Chartwell Visitors Book. 5 December also lists Christine Churchill and Christopher Hassall.

67. Gilbert, Martin. 1982. *Winston S. Churchill*. London: Heinemann, 295.

68. Holmes, Richard. 2006. *In the Footsteps of Churchill*. London: BBC, 227.

69. Landemare, Georgina. 1958. *Recipes from No.10: Some Recipes for Discerning Cooks*. London: Collins, Introduction.

70. *Irish Independent*, 24 September 1938, p.18; and 1 October 1938, p.17.

71. Soames, Mary. 2012. *A Daughter's Tale: The Memoir of Winston and Clementine Churchill's Youngest Child*. London: Black Swan, 152.

72. CHAR 1/337/228.

73. Jenkins, Roy. 2002. *Churchill*. London: Pan Macmillan, 546; Churchill, Winston, Mary Soames, and Clementine Churchill Baroness Spencer-Churchill. 1998. *Speaking for*

Themselves: The Personal Letters of Winston and Clementine Churchill. London: Doubleday, 172.

74. David Jenkins. 2011. William James Tatem, 1st Baron Glanely. Accessed at https://museum.wales/articles/2011–11–30/William-James-Tatem-1st-Baron-Glanely-1868–1942/, April 2018.

75. 1939 Register gives details of this, and Margaret and William's whereabouts.

76. 1939 Register.

6: The Wartime Cook

There are many books with memoirs and diaries from the war. Good examples can be found in Simon Garfield's edited volumes of the Mass Observation archive (*We are at War, Private Battles* and, for the post-war era, *Hidden Lives*). Virginia Nicholson's *Millions Like Us* uses primary accounts to focus on the war from the female perspective. For a general overview of food, both from a military and a domestic perspective, Lizzie Collingham's *The Taste of War* is useful. For the Churchills, the standard biographies give most of the details. However, I have drawn extensively on the papers of Mary Soames for details of their domestic life, often sidelined in the face of so much crucial politicking. For access to such a beautifully written and utterly charming set of diaries and letters, I am very grateful to Emma Soames. The interview with Joan Bakewell and Georgina Landemare was, at the time of writing, still online via the BBC iPlayer website.

1. From Georgina's MS cookery book. It was not published in 1958, but the recipe is fairly self-explanatory and extremely good. Fold in the whites very carefully, and grease the mould well. It will take quite a fancy mould, but the mixture should only come about 2/3 of the way up it (a pint or pint and a half is ideal). Cover with foil with a fold in to allow for expansion, and steam as per the

recipe. Turn out and serve immediately. Good with custard, wine sauce or a rich red fruit purée.

2. *Cambridge Daily News*, 28 September 1939; Nicholson, Virginia. *Millions Like Us: Women's Lives in the Second World War*. London: Penguin, 24.

3. Buczacki, Stefan. 2007. *Churchill and Chartwell: The Untold Story of Churchill's Houses and Gardens*. London: Frances Lincoln, 209.

4. CHAR 1/351/56.

5. MCHL 1/1/3 Diary for 1941 part 1: 11 July.

6. MCHL 5/7/6 Extract from the memoir of Charles Taylor, 1935.

7. Buczacki, Stefan. 2007. *Churchill and Chartwell: The Untold Story of Churchill's Houses and Gardens*. London: Frances Lincoln, 223.

8. Landemare, Georgina. 1958. *Recipes from No.10: Some Recipes for Discerning Cooks*. London: Collins, Introduction.

9. Soames, Mary. 2012. *A Daughter's Tale: The Memoir of Winston and Clementine Churchill's Youngest Child*. London: Black Swan, 185.

10. Holmes, Richard. 2009. *Churchill's Bunker: The Secret Headquarters at the Heart of Britain's Victory*. London: Profile; Pawle, Gerald. 1963. *The War and Colonel Warden: Based on the Recollections of Commander C. R. Thompson, Personal Assistant to the Prime Minister 1940*. London: Harrap, 166.

11. Nel, Elizabeth, and Winston Churchill. 1958. *Mr Churchill's Secretary*. London: Hodder & Stoughton, 43; Pawle, Gerald. 1963. *The War and Colonel Warden: Based on the Recollections of Commander C. R. Thompson, Personal Assistant to the Prime Minister 1940*. London: Harrap, 166.

12. Minney, R. J. 1963. *No.10 Downing Street. A House in History. [with Plates]*. London: Cassell, 400.

13. Anon. 1958. 'Recipes from No.10 Downing Street' (interview with Georgina Landemare). *Woman's Journal*, December 1958, 10–15.

·14. Interview with Georgina Landemare from *Times Remembered: Below Stairs: Georgina Landemare* (BBC TV 1973). Available to watch at https://www.bbc.co.uk/programmes/po3tpv61.

15. Soames, Mary. 2012. *A Daughter's Tale: The Memoir of Winston and Clementine Churchill's Youngest Child*. London: Black Swan, 240; Major, Norma, and Mark Fiennes. 2001. *Chequers: The Prime Minister's Country House and Its History*. New ed. Boston [Mass.]; London: Little, Brown.

16. Rose, Jill. 2018. *Nursing Churchill*. Stroud: Amberley, 183.

17. Soames, Mary. 2012. *A Daughter's Tale: The Memoir of Winston and Clementine Churchill's Youngest Child*. London: Black Swan, 241; Colville, John. 2005. *The Fringes of Power: Downing Street Diaries, 1939–1955*. London: Phoenix, 263.

18. McGowan, Norman. 1958. *My Years with Churchill*. [1st ed.]: London, Souvenir Press, 103.

19. Interview with Georgina Landemare from *Times Remembered: Below Stairs: Georgina Landemare* (BBC TV 1973). Available to watch at https://www.bbc.co.uk/programmes/po3tpv61; Stelzer, Cita. 2011. *Dinner with Churchill: Policy-Making at the Dinner Table*. London: Short, 122; CHAR 1/372/11.

20. Colville, John. 2005. *The Fringes of Power: Downing Street Diaries, 1939–1955*. London: Phoenix.

21. CHAR 1/362/18–25 WSC to RC 8 June 1941.

22. Hodgson, Vere. 1999. *Few Eggs and No Oranges: A Diary Showing How Unimportant People in London and Birmingham Lived Throughout the War Years 1940–1945*. London: Persephone Books, 74–75.

23. Anon. 1958. 'Recipes from No.10 Downing Street' (interview with Georgina Landemare). *Woman's Journal*, December 1958, 10–15.

24. *Daily Mail*, 27 June 1949, p.3; Interview with Georgina Landemare from T*imes Remembered: Below Stairs: Georgina Landemare* (BBC TV 1973). Available to watch at https://www.bbc.co.uk/programmes/p03tpv61.

25. Soames, Mary. 2002. *Clementine Churchill*. Rev. and updated ed. London: Doubleday, 328.

26. Holmes, Richard. 2009. *Churchill's Bunker: The Secret Headquarters at the Heart of Britain's Victory*. London: Profile, 81.

27. Colville, John. 2005. *The Fringes of Power: Downing Street Diaries, 1939–1955*. London: Phoenix, 233.

28. Soames, Mary. 2002. *Clementine Churchill*. Rev. and updated ed. London: Doubleday, 355.

29. Nel, Elizabeth, and Winston Churchill. 1958. *Mr Churchill's Secretary*. London: Hodder & Stoughton. 11, 27; Stelzer, Cita. 2011. *Dinner with Churchill: Policy-Making at the Dinner Table*. London: Short, 179.

30. Elizabeth Bright, Memories of 10 Downing Street in the WW2 People's War memory bank, consulted at https://www.bbc.co.uk/history/ww2peopleswar/stories/25/a5807225.shtml, January 2019.

31. As recounted, by her, to Edwina Brocklesby, her granddaughter. Harold Macmillan tells a different version, cited in Roberts, Andrew. 2018. *Churchill: Walking with Destiny: The Biography*. London: Allen Lane, 921, which involves models of the rations presented on a tray. It seems rather implausible to have gone to all that trouble. I passed the stories via Lady Williams, who thought the Macmillan version dubious and felt sure it was Georgina.

32. CHAR 20/21B; CHAR 20/2A-B.

33. CHAR 8/668 *Sunday Dispatch* 30 June 1940.

34. MCHL 1/1/2 Diary for 31 July 1940.

35. Rose, Jill. 2018. *Nursing Churchill*. Stroud: Amberley, 66.

36. CHAR 1/373/40.

37. Lough, David. 2015. *No More Champagne: Churchill and His Money*. New York; London: Picador/Head of Zeus, 252.

38. MCHL 1/1/6 Diary for 18 May–24 September 1942 (21 July); MCHL 1/1/8 Diary for 25 September–17 January 1943 (16 January); Hodgson, Vere. 1999. *Few Eggs and No Oranges: A Diary Showing How Unimportant People in London and Birmingham Lived Throughout the War Years 1940–1945*. London: Persephone Books, 230.

39. Rose, Jill. 2018. *Nursing Churchill*. Stroud: Amberley, 153.

40. CHAR 1/373/40.

41. *Times Remembered*, op. cit.

42. Lough, David. *No More Champagne: Churchill and His Money*, 292; CHAR 1/365/18–21.

43. CHAR 2/454 Gifts, A–C, letter of 16 December 1940.

44. CHAR 20/53C/256.

45. CHAR 1/361/39–40.

46. CHAR 2/454; Stelzer, Cita. 2011. *Dinner with Churchill: Policy-Making at the Dinner Table*. London: Short, 181; Nel, Elizabeth, and Winston Churchill. 1958. *Mr Churchill's Secretary*. London: Hodder & Stoughton, 175.

47. MCHL 5/7/22 5 July 1945.

48. MCHL 1/1/2 diary for 1940.

49. MCHL 1/1/5 diary for 16 February–28 March 1942.

50. MCHL 5/7/9 CSC to MS 6 September 1941; MCHL 1/1/4 Diary 22 July–16 October 1941.

51. CHAR /389/8; MCHL 1/2/12 Diary 7 June–5 November 1944.

52. Rose, Jill. 2018. *Nursing Churchill*. Stroud: Amberley, 159.

53. MCHL 5/7/14 CSC to MS 19 December 1943.

54. *Times Remembered* op. cit.

55. Stelzer, Cita. 2011. *Dinner with Churchill: Policy-Making at the Dinner Table*. London: Short, 69.

56. MCHL 1/1/16 Diary 18 May–24 September 1942.

57. MCHL 5/7/14 24th CSC to MS May 1943.

58. MCHL 5/7/12 CSC to MS 11 August 1942.

59. Landemare, Georgina, and Phil Reed. 2015. *Churchill's Cookbook (an Edited and Abridged Edition of Recipes from No.10)*. London: IWM, 13; Stelzer, Cita. 2011. *Dinner with Churchill: Policy-Making at the Dinner Table*. London: Short, 8.

60. MCHL 5/7/7 CSC to MS 2 November 1941.

61. *Times Remembered* op. cit.

62. Soames, Mary. 2002. *Clementine Churchill*. Rev. and updated ed. London: Doubleday, 380.

63. MCHL 5/7/11.

64. CSCT 4/10 Engagement diary 1941.

65. Stelzer, Cita. 2011. *Dinner with Churchill: Policy-Making at the Dinner Table*. London: Short, 174.

66. Soames, Mary. 2012. *A Daughter's Tale: The Memoir of Winston and Clementine Churchill's Youngest Child*. London: Black Swan, 328.

67. Shapiro, Laura. 2018. *What She Ate: Six Remarkable Women and the Food That Tells Their Stories*. New York: Penguin, 152.

68. MCHL 1/1/8 Diary 25 September 1942–17 January 1943.

69. Colville, John. 2005. *The Fringes of Power: Downing Street Diaries, 1939–1955*. London: Phoenix, 128; Soames, Mary. 2012. *A Daughter's Tale: The Memoir of Winston and Clementine Churchill's Youngest Child*. London: Black Swan, 306.

70. Stelzer, Cita. 2011. *Dinner with Churchill: Policy-Making at the Dinner Table*. London: Short, 74, 84; Shapiro, Laura. 2018. *What She Ate: Six Remarkable Women and the Food That Tells Their Stories*. New York: Penguin, 117–119.

71. MCHL 5/7/9 CSC to MS 10 September 1941; *Times Remembered* op. cit.

72. Rose, Jill. 2018. *Nursing Churchill*. Stroud: Amberley, 159.

73. MCHL 5/7/11.

74. Rose, Jill. 2018. *Nursing Churchill*. Stroud: Amberley, 181, 186.

75. Pawle, Gerald. 1963. *The War and Colonel Warden: Based on the Recollections of Commander C. R. Thompson, Personal Assistant to the Prime Minister 1940*. London: Harrap, 190.

76. MCHL 5/7/9 MS to CSC 11 September 1941.

77. Nel, Elizabeth, and Winston Churchill. 1958. *Mr Churchill's Secretary*. London: Hodder & Stoughton, 74; CSCT 1/26 CSC to WSC 14 January 1943.

78. Edwina Brocklesby, pers.comm.

79. Holmes, Richard. 2006. *In the Footsteps of Churchill*. London: BBC; Nel, Elizabeth, and Winston Churchill. 1958. *Mr Churchill's Secretary*. London: Hodder & Stoughton, 173.

80. Nicholson, Virginia. 2012. *Millions Like Us: Women's Lives in the Second World War*. London: Penguin.

81. *Times Remembered*, op. cit.; Soames, Mary. 2002. *Clementine Churchill*. Rev. and updated ed. London: Doubleday, 424.

82. Soames, Mary. 2012. *A Daughter's Tale: The Memoir of Winston and Clementine Churchill's Youngest Child*. London: Black Swan, 459; Edwina Brocklesby pers.comm.

83. CHAR 1/390/19.

84. Colville, John. 2005. *The Fringes of Power: Downing Street Diaries, 1939–1955*. London: Phoenix, 577.

7: Peace at Last

For a general overview of the period, see David Kynaston, *Austerity Britain*. Andrew Roberts's Churchill biography covers his second term in more detail than some other books, but the usual suspects are also vital: *Speaking for Themselves*, *First Lady* and others, all cited below. This chapter also draws on interviews and correspondence between myself and Edwina (Eddie) Brocklesby, Georgina's granddaughter, and a rather lovely lunch with Lady Williams, who, as Jane Portal, was one of Churchill's private secretaries from 1949 to 1955. Cita Stelzer's book on Churchill's dinners is also useful, especially for meals abroad, beyond the scope of this chapter.

1. Georgina Landemare, unpublished MS. Note that a 1950s cup was a teacup – approx. 150ml; and do not freeze – for Georgina, this was the shorthand for chill (if you do freeze it, the gelatine will collapse). '5–6 sheets of gelatine will set the mousse: soak them in cold water to soften, and dissolve in the hot syrup. The 1958 published version reads: for four people. 4 eggs, 1 pint cream, ½ oz gelatine, 1 cupful hot maple syrup. Separate the eggs and place the yolks in a basin over hot water. Pour in the hot maple syrup and the gelatine dissolved in a little of the syrup. Beat well until the mixture becomes thick. Remove from heat and allow to cool. Whip the cream until stiff and add this to the mixture. Finally add the stiffly whipped whites of egg.'

2. Stelzer, Cita. 2011. *Dinner with Churchill: Policy-Making at the Dinner Table*. London: Short, 169.

3. Soames, Mary. 2002. *Clementine Churchill*. Rev. and updated ed. London: Doubleday, 429.

4. Roberts, Andrew. 2018. *Churchill: Walking with Destiny: The Biography*. London: Allen Lane.

5. She would become attached mainly to Chartwell in the 1950s, and, after Winston's death in 1965, stayed with the house, as the first curator of the property when it opened to the public in 1966. By then, there was also Victor Vincent, the head gardener, who joined in 1947 and remained until 1979.

6. CHUR 1/30 CSC to WSC 5 December 1945.

7. Edwina Brocklesby pers.comm.

8. Barry Singer. 2012. *Churchill Style: the Art of Being Winston Churchill*: New York, Abrams Books.

9. CSCT 1/29 Cutting from the *Daily Mail*, 12 February 1945.

10. Purnell, Sonia. 2015. *First Lady: The Life and Wars of Clementine Churchill*. London: Aurum, 324.

11. Colville, John. 2005. *The Fringes of Power: Downing Street Diaries, 1939–1955*. London: Phoenix, 586 (1 May 1948).

12. Lough, David. 2015. *No More Champagne: Churchill and His Money*. New York; London: Picador/Head of Zeus, 357; Colville, John. 2005. *The Fringes of Power: Downing Street Diaries, 1939–1955*. London: Phoenix, 596.

13. McGowan, Norman. 1958. *My Years with Churchill*. [1st ed.]: London, Souvenir Press. After him came Walter Meyer (previously in the pantry from 1949, left 1953), and then a series of people whose first names I can't discover: Kirkwood (1953–1955), Rose (1955–1958), followed by Mr & Mrs Sheppard (1958), who were also nurses, and finally Roy Howells, also a nurse as well as a valet (1958–1965). See MCHL 5-7-7.

14. Ibid., 79.

15. Soames, Mary. 2002. *Clementine Churchill*. Rev. and updated ed. London: Doubleday, 428.

16. Purnell, Sonia. 2015. *First Lady: The Life and Wars of Clementine Churchill*. London: Aurum, 330.

17. The kitchen was later opened up under the National Trust, who restored the house roughly to its pre-war form and room usage, and it can still be seen today.

18. CHUR 1/31/129; CHUR 1/30 letter of 5 December 1945.

19. CHAR 1/371/29; CHAR 1/338/72; CHAR 1/318/34.

20. Delap, Lucy. 2011. *Knowing Their Place: Domestic Service in Twentieth Century Britain*. Oxford: OUP, 12.

21. McGowan, Norman. 1958. *My Years with Churchill*. [1st ed.]. London, Souvenir Press, 81; CSCT 9/3/14: family menus 1951 plus CSCT 9/3/3: staff menus 1949, and CSCT 9/3/15–17: staff menus 1951–1953.

22. CHUR 1/31/107–9.

23. White-Smith, Heather. 2010. *My Years with the Churchills: A Young Girl's Memories*. Ascot: Cotesworth Pub., 14.

24. MCHL 1/1/16, Diary January–March 1946.

25. MCHL 5/1/117, CSC to MS, 5 August 1945.

26. MCHL 5/7/27, GL to MS, 7 June 1968.

27. Soames, Mary. 2002. *Clementine Churchill*. Rev. and updated ed. London: Doubleday, 512; and conversation with Lady Williams (formerly Jane Portal), November 2018.

28. A collection of Mrs Dorgan's letters appeared on an episode of *Antiques Roadshow* in March 2019, together with various bits of Churchill-related memorabilia. Some are available here https://www.collectorsweekly.com/stories/250139-some-of-mr-and-miss-winston-churchill-item (consulted March 2019). The provenance is somewhat dubious – the letters seem real, but some of the other items are unlikely to be genuine. However, the presence of Mrs Dorgan had been confirmed by Edwina Brocklesby (pers.comm), and her name and probable position can be gleaned from genealogical work and the contents of the few letters available. At the time of writing I have sadly been unable to study the collection itself.

29. Ibid.

30. *The Times*, letter to the editor, 4 August 1947.

31. Edwina Sandys, Diana Churchill's daughter, quoted in *The Times*, 6 July 2004, 24.

32. Alexander Spearman to GL, 9 February 1977, in private papers belonging to Edwina Brocklesby.

33. White-Smith, Heather. 2010. *My Years with the Churchills: A Young Girl's Memories*. Ascot: Cotesworth Pub.; Mary Soames, quoted in Sue Corbett's 'Fighting them in the Kitchen', *The Times*, 5 April 2003, 11.

34. CHUR 1/64 staff file.

35. MCHL 1/1/7 Diary April–June 1946. Entry for 30 May.

36. MCHL 5/1/300 sales particulars for Hyde Park Gate, 1965.

37. CHUR 2/371.

38. Kynaston, David. 2007. *Austerity Britain, 1945–1951*. London: Bloomsbury, 246–7.

39. MCHL 5/1/130 letters of 17 January and 27 January 1946.

40. Buchan, Ursula. 2013. *A Green and Pleasant Land: How England's Gardeners Fought the Second World War*. London: Hutchinson, 276.

41. Soames, Mary. 2002. *Clementine Churchill*. Rev. and updated ed. London: Doubleday, 436.

42. White-Smith, Heather. 2010. *My Years with the Churchills: A Young Girl's Memories*. Ascot: Cotesworth Pub., 14; CHAR 2/308.

43. MCHL 5/1/141 Christopher Soames to WSC, 309 rabbits caught October–November 1948 (246 were sold to the local butcher).

44. McGowan, Norman. 1958. *My Years with Churchill*. [1st ed.]: London: Souvenir Press, 80.

45. White-Smith, Heather. 2010. *My Years with the Churchills: A Young Girl's Memories*. Ascot: Cotesworth Pub., 15.

46. CHAR 1/394/125.

47. https://winkleclub.org/. The Pathé news footage is particularly joyful.

48. CHAR 2/375.

49. This draws upon letters within CHUR 2/371; 2/383; 2/378; and 2/380.

50. CHUR 2/375, and for grouse, see Churchill, Winston, Mary Soames, and Clementine Churchill Baroness Spencer-Churchill. 1998. *Speaking for Themselves: The Personal Letters of Winston and Clementine Churchill*. London: Doubleday, 574.

51. CHUR 2/376.

52. CHUR 2/374.

53. Ibid.; CHUR 2/218.

54. CHUR 2/375.

55. Collingham, E. M. 2011. *The Taste of War: World War Two and the Battle for Food*. London: Allen Lane, 475; Patrick Sawyer, 'When Food Parcels from the US Brought Delight to British Families', *The Telegraph*, 18 October 2015, online at https://www.telegraph.co.uk/

history/11938214/When-food-parcels-from-the-US-brought-delight-to-British-families.html.

56. CHUR 2/274 and CHUR 2/375 – gifts July–December 1947, A–L and M–Z.

57. McGowan, Norman. 1958. *My Years with Churchill*. [1st ed.]: London, Souvenir Press, 80.

58. CSCT 9/3/2, staff menus from 1 April 1946 is the only book in Georgina's handwriting. Comparisons can be drawn to CSCT 9/3/3, staff menus at Chartwell 1949; CSCT 9/3/16 and CSCT 9/3/16, staff menus for 1951–1952.

59. CSCT 3/62.

60. CHUR 3/376 from Mme Baruk.

61. This section is drawn from CSCT 9/3/2.

62. McGowan, Norman. 1958. *My Years with Churchill*. [1st ed.]: London: Souvenir Press, 79.

63. Robbins, Ann Brolcaw Roe. 1951. *100 Meat-Saving Recipes*. London: Nicholas Kaye, 7.

64. Kynaston, David. 2007. *Austerity Britain, 1945–1951*. London: Bloomsbury, 246.

65. McGowan, Norman. 1958. *My Years with Churchill*. [1st ed.]: London, Souvenir Press, 81.

66. Todd, Selina. 2015. *The People: The Rise and Fall of the Working Class, 1910–2010*. London: John Murray.

67. Roberts, Andrew. 2018. *Churchill: Walking with Destiny: The Biography*. London: Allen Lane, 923.

68. Interview with Georgina Landemare from *Times Remembered: Below Stairs: Georgina Landemare* (BBC TV 1973). Available to watch at https://www.bbc.co.uk/programmes/p03tpv61.

69. Churchill, Winston, Mary Soames, and Clementine Churchill Baroness Spencer-Churchill. 1998. *Speaking for Themselves: The Personal Letters of Winston and Clementine Churchill*. London: Doubleday, 566.

70. Minney, R. J. 1963. *No.10 Downing Street: A House in History. [with Plates]*. London: Cassell, 419.

71. MCHL 5/1/231; CSCT 9/1/2 (this remains closed on data protection grounds, and I am grateful to the archivists at the Churchill Archive for providing as much information as they could).

72. Papers in the possession of Edwina Brocklesby.

73. Brocklesby, Edwina. 2018. *Irongran: How Triathlon Taught Me That Growing Older Needn't Mean Slowing Down*. London: Sphere, 9; and unpublished MS.

74. Interview with Edwina Brocklesby, October 2017.

75. MCHL 5/1/130, diary entry 15 February 1946.

76. Edwina Brocklesby. Nd. Unpublished MS.

77. Purnell, Sonia. 2015. *First Lady: The Life and Wars of Clementine Churchill*. London: Aurum, 338.

78. Ibid., 339.

79. Moran, Lord. 1966. *Winston Churchill, the Struggle for Survival 1940–1965*. London: Constable, 442.

80. Churchill, Winston, Mary Soames, and Clementine Churchill Baroness Spencer-Churchill. 1998. *Speaking for Themselves: The Personal Letters of Winston and Clementine Churchill*. London: Doubleday, 581.

81. Jenkins, Roy. 2002. *Churchill*. London: Pan Macmillan, 880. His BMI was 30.

82. CSCT 2/42 WSC to CSCT 5 June 1954.

83. CSCT 9/1/3 wages, April 1954–October 1957.

8: Retirement

Lucy Delap, *Knowing Their Place* brings the servant story up to date, from the 1950s to now. Nicola Humble, *Culinary Pleasures* is good on the publishing context of cookery literature in the era. People are mainly growing old and dying in this chapter, so there's not that much to add.

1. This cake, which was essentially that given to Dorothy Allhusen by Blanche Hozier (Clemmie's mother), did not make it to the published book, but it is amazing. Use six modern large eggs. The chocolate should be around 70 per cent cocoa solids, melted in a bain-marie or microwave before being added to the creamed butter with the (caster) sugar, plain flour and almonds. Sal volatile can be replaced most authentically with hartshorn (ammonium carbonate, or baker's ammonia, which is sold as a raising agent for use in traditional Dutch cookies, among other things. Otherwise use baking powder). Beat the yolks to a froth, beat the whites to stiff peak. Fold in yolks, then whites, put in a well-greased 8-inch(ish) tin, and bake in a conventional oven at 140°C for ninety minutes (fan 120°C).

2. CHUR 1/66/83–84: GL to WSC. That of 29 January 1955 was written from Eve's address in Chiswick, but by 29 July 1955 she was in Putney at Algy's address on Montserrat Road. See also MCHL 2/11, GL to MS, 20 July 1954, which has her at Algy's.

3. MCHL 2/11, GL to MS, 20 July 1954.

4. KBRM 2: Katharine Broome (née Anderson), memoir. Massive thanks to Katherine Thomson at the Churchill Archives for letting me know it existed and sending me a copy the day after she saw it for the first time (with a day to go before my cut off for any further changes on this book, phew).

5. Undated (probably 1958) newspaper article: 'She was Cook at No.10', from papers in the possession of Edwina Brocklesby.

6. Anon. 1958. 'Recipes from No.10 Downing Street' (interview with Georgina Landemare). *Woman's Journal*, December 1958, 10–15; Soames, Mary. 2002. *Clementine Churchill*. Rev. and updated ed. London: Doubleday, 495.

7. CHUR 1/66, GL to WSC, 29 June 1955.

8. MCHL 5/7/27 contains a list of cooks, valets and butlers with dates; CSCT /1/3, Wages 1954–1957 has payments to Georgina in October–December 1955. At Chartwell, Katharine Anderson was replaced by Mrs Schwarz, whose start date is noted at CSCT 4/24, CSC engagement diary for 1955. In London, Mrs Troger was eventually replaced by Mrs Skitt. See also CSCT 4/22, CSC engagement diary for 1954.

9. Based on Georgina's address book, plus data from the electoral registers and BMD.

10. Stelzer, Cita. 2011. *Dinner with Churchill: Policy-Making at the Dinner Table*. London: Short, 159–60; Getty Image search; *Time* magazine, 19 December 1951.

11. Purnell, Sonia. *First Lady: The Life and Wars of Clementine Churchill*, 345.

12. Letter from Fladgate & Co. to GL, 12 January 1978, confirming this amount to continue from CSC estate after her death according to her will. In papers in the possession of Edwina Brocklesby.

13. Marcel Boulestin, cited in Humble, N. 2005. *Culinary Pleasures: Cookbooks and the Transformation of British Food*. London: Faber & Faber, 170.

14. Anonymous article, *c.*1958, 'Cook at No.10', in papers in the possession of Edwina Brocklesby; Elizabeth Nel, cited in *The Times*, 8 January 2004, 33; Peavitt, Helen. 2017. *Refrigerator: The Story of Cool in the Kitchen*. London: Reaktion in association with the Science Museum, 79, 88.

15. Heath, Ambrose. 1953. *Small Meat Dishes*. London, Faber & Faber; Harben, Philip. 1948. *The Way to Cook*. London: John Lane/The Bodley Head.

16. Harben, ibid.

17. Humble, N. 2005. *Culinary Pleasures: Cookbooks and the Transformation of British Food*. London: Faber & Faber, 136–7.

18. Harben, Philip and Katharine Harben. 1951. *Entertaining at Home*. London, John Lane / The Bodley Head.

19. Spry, Constance, and Rosemary Hume. 1956. *The Constance Spry Cookery Book*. London: J. M. Dent & Sons. This edition, 1967, The Cookery Book Club, xi.

20. Humble, N. 2005. *Culinary Pleasures: Cookbooks and the Transformation of British Food*. London: Faber & Faber; Geddes, Kevin. 2017. 'Above all, garnish and presentation: an evaluation of Fanny Cradock's contribution to home cooking in Britain', in *Journal of Consumer Studies*, 2017, 1–9; thanks to Kevin as well for the insight into Fanny's wipe-clean gowns.

21. Bon Viveur (Fanny and Johnnie Cradock). 1955. *Cooking with Bon Viveur*. London: Museum Press, xi–xii.

22. Original typescript for *Recipes From No.10*, in papers in the possession of Edwina Brocklesby.

23. Anon. 1958. 'Recipes from No.10 Downing Street' (interview with Georgina Landemare). *Woman's Journal*, December 1958, 10–15.

24. Ibid. 'Recipes from No.10 Downing Street' (interview with Georgina Landemare). *Woman's Journal*, December 1958, 10–15; Steak and kidney pie noted as enjoyed by CSC in an email conversation with Nonie Chapman, February 2018.

25. CSCT 1/28 CSC to WSC 1944.

26. Anon. 1958. 'Recipes from No.10 Downing Street' (interview with Georgina Landemare). *Woman's Journal*, December 1958, 10–15; correspondence with Nonie Chapman, February 2018; conversation with Lady Jane Williams, November 2018.

27. Letter from Mark Bonham Carter to GL, 11 February 1958. In papers in the possession of Edwina Brocklesby.

28. *The Times*, 17 December 1958, 10; Maisie Fitter, 'Cooks at Home & Abroad', *Birmingham Daily Post*, 25 November

1958, 14; Helen Burke, 'Dining in: for your present list', *The Tatler & Bystander*, 12 November 1958, 421.

29. White-Smith, Heather. 2010. *My Years with the Churchills: A Young Girl's Memories*. Ascot: Cotesworth Pub., 15; Nicolas Soames, quoted in Sue Corbett, 'Fighting them in the Kitchen', *The Times*, 5 April 2003, 11.

30. Lethbridge, Lucy. 2013. *Servants: A Downstairs View of Twentieth Century Britain*. London: Bloomsbury, 292; Todd, Selina. 2015. *The People: The Rise and Fall of the Working Class, 1910–2010*. London: John Murray.

31. Nixon, Sean. 2015. 'Trouble at the National Trust: postwar recreation, the Benson Report and the rebuilding of a conservation organisation in the 1960s', in *20th Century British History* 26 (4), 529–550.

32. Delap, Lucy. 2011. *Knowing Their Place: Domestic Service in Twentieth Century Britain*. Oxford: OUP, 211.

33. MacLeod, Lily. 1958. *A Cook's Notebook*. London: Faber, 10.

34. MCHL 2/12.

35. Brocklesby, Edwina, unpublished MS; Brocklesby, Edwina. 2018. *Irongran: How Triathlon Taught Me That Growing Older Needn't Mean Slowing Down*. London: Sphere.

36. Anon, 'His servants bid goodbye', undated newspaper clipping from papers in the possession of Edwina Brocklesby.

37. Delap, Lucy. 2011. *Knowing Their Place: Domestic Service in Twentieth Century Britain*. Oxford: OUP, 211–213.

38. Wolens, Roger. 1973, 'Personal Glimpses', unattributed clipping in papers in the possession of Edwina Brocklesby.

39. Evelyn Battrum to GL, 15 December 1977.

40. Penelope Barwick (née Hampden-Wall) to GL, 29 December 1977.

41. Grace Hamblin to GL, 21 February 1978.

42. Last Will & Testament of Georgina Landemare and associated codicils, 10 November 1943; 20 February 1978.
43. Grace Hamblin to Edwina Brocklesby, 25 April 1978.

Epilogue

1. She definitely cooked for George VI, Edward VIII and Elizabeth II of the UK; Zog of Albania; Peter of Yugoslavia; Charles of Belgium; Wilhelmina and Juliana of the Netherlands; Haakan VIII and Olav of Norway; Constantine II and George II of Greece during the war; plus Frederick IX of Denmark after it. Grand Duchess Charlotte of Luxembourg wasn't a monarch, but was the ruler of the country (and in exile in Britain during the war), and Churchill was also very friendly with Prince Rainier III of Monaco. Given the level of society Georgina was cooking at, it's also pretty safe to add George V to the list. That makes sixteen.

References

Adam, Ruth. 2000. *A Woman's Place, 1910–1975*. London:
  Persephone Books.

Allhusen, Dorothy. 1927. *A Book of Scents and Dishes, Etc.*
  London: Williams & Norgate.

Baedeker, Karl. 1900. *London and Its Environs.* (Republished
  2002, Old House Books.)

Barr, Luke. 2018. *Ritz and Escoffier: The Hotelier, the Chef and
  the Rise of the Leisure Class*. New York: Clarkson Potter.

Battersea, Constance. 1923. *Reminiscences*. London:
  Macmillan.

Beeton, Isabella. 1888. *Mrs Beeton's Household Management.*
  London: Ward, Lock & Co.

Benson, John. 1989. *The Working Class in Britain, 1850–1939,
  Themes in British Social History*. London; New York:
  Longman.

Bonham Carter, Violet, and Mark Pottle. 1998. *Champion
  Redoubtable: The Diaries and Letters of Violet Bonham Carter,
  1914–1944*. London: Weidenfeld & Nicolson.

Boulestin, X. Marcel. 1931. *What Shall We Have Today?*
  London: William Heinemann Ltd.

—. 1936. *Myself, My Two Countries*. [S.l.]: [s.n.].

Brocklesby, Edwina. 2018. *Irongran: How Triathlon Taught Me
  That Growing Older Needn't Mean Slowing Down*. London:
  Sphere.

Buchan, Ursula. 2013. *A Green and Pleasant Land: How England's Gardeners Fought the Second World War*. London: Hutchinson.

Buczacki, Stefan. 2007. *Churchill and Chartwell: The Untold Story of Churchill's Houses and Gardens*. London: Frances Lincoln.

Burnett, John. 1989. *Plenty and Want: A Social History of Food in England from 1815 to the Present Day*. London: Routledge.

—. 2004. *England Eats Out: A Social History of Eating out in England from 1830 to the Present*. 1st ed. Harlow: Pearson / Longman.

Charpentier, Henri, and Boyden Sparkes. 2001. *Life À La Henri: Being the Memories of Henri Charpentier*: Modern Library.

Churchill, Randolph S. 1966. *Youth: Winston S. Churchill 1874– 1900*. London: Minerva, 1991.

Churchill, Winston, Mary Soames, and Clementine Churchill Baroness Spencer-Churchill. 1998. *Speaking for Themselves: The Personal Letters of Winston and Clementine Churchill*. London: Doubleday.

Collingham, E. M. 2011. *The Taste of War: World War Two and the Battle for Food*. London: Allen Lane.

Colville, John. 2005. *The Fringes of Power: Downing Street Diaries, 1939–1955*. London: Phoenix.

Cookery, Buckmaster's. *c.*1875. *Being an Abridgement of Some of the Lectures Delivered in the Cookery School at the International Exhibition for 1873 and 1874*. London: Routledge.

David, Elizabeth. 1978. *English Bread and Yeast Cookery*. London: Book Club Associates / Penguin.

Davis, Jean. 1988. *Aldbury People 1885–1945*. Aldbury: J. Davis.

de Salis, H. 1902. *À La Mode Cookery*. London: Longmans, Green & Co.

Delap, Lucy. 2011. *Knowing Their Place: Domestic Service in Twentieth Century Britain*. Oxford: OUP.

Escoffier, Auguste. 1919. *L'Aide Mémoire Culinaire*. Paris.

—. 2011. *Souvenirs Culinaires*. Paris: Mercure de France.

Francatelli, Charles Elmé. 1861. *A Plain Cookery Book for the Working Classes*. London: Bosworth and Harrison.

Gerard, Jessica. 1994. *Country House Life: Family and Servants, 1815–1914*. Oxford: Blackwell.

Gilbert, Martin. 1976. *Winston S. Churchill: Vol. V. 1922–1939*. [S.l.]: Heinemann.

—. 1982. *Winston S. Churchill*. London: Heinemann.

Gluckstein, Donny. 2011. *The Paris Commune: A Revolution in Democracy*. Chicago, Ill.: Haymarket Books.

Goiran, Joseph Henri. 1935. *Les Français à Londres: Etude Historique*. Paris.

Gouffé, Jules. 1873. *Le Livre De Pâtisserie*. Paris: Hachette.

Gray, Annie. 2017. *The Greedy Queen: Eating with Victoria*. London: Profile.

Greaves, Simon. 2014. *The Country House at War: Fighting the Great War at Home and in the Trenches*. Swindon: National Trust Books.

Harrison, Michael. 1977. *Rosa: Rosa Lewis of the Cavendish*. London: Corgi.

Harrison, Rosina. 1976. *Gentlemen's Gentlemen: From Boot Boys to Butlers, True Stories of Life Below Stairs*. London: Hachette.

—. 2011. *The Lady's Maid: My Life in Service*. London: Ebury.

Hodgson, Vere. 1999. *Few Eggs and No Oranges: A Diary Showing How Unimportant People in London and Birmingham Lived Throughout the War Years 1940–1945*. London: Persephone Books.

Holmes, Richard. 2006. *In the Footsteps of Churchill*. London: BBC.

—. 2009. *Churchill's Bunker: The Secret Headquarters at the Heart of Britain's Victory*. London: Profile.

Horn, Pamela. 2012. *Life Below Stairs: The Real Lives of Servants, the Edwardian Era to 1939*. Stroud: Amberley.

Hughes, Molly. 1979. *A London Family in the 1890s*. Oxford: OUP.

Humble, N. 2005. *Culinary Pleasures: Cookbooks and the Transformation of British Food*. London: Faber & Faber.

Jackman, Nancy, and Tom Quinn. 2012. *The Cook's Tale*. London: Coronet.

Jarrin, Guglielmo A. 1861. *The Italian Confectioner*. London: Routledge, Warne and Routledge.

Jenkins, Roy. 2002. *Churchill*. London: Pan Macmillan.

Jones, Stephanie. 1992. *Merchants of the Raj: British Managing Agency Houses in Calcutta Yesterday and Today*. Basingstoke: Macmillan.

Kynaston, David. 2007. *Austerity Britain, 1945–1951*. London: Bloomsbury.

Labouchère, Henri. 1871. *Diary of the Besieged Resident in Paris*. London: Bradbury, Evans and Co.

Lake, Nancy. 1930. *Menus Made Easy ... Revised and Extended Edition, the Thirty-Fifth*. London; New York: Frederick Warne & Co.

Landemare, Georgina. 1958. *Recipes from No.10: Some Recipes for Discerning Cooks*. London: Collins.

Landemare, Georgina, and Phil Reed. 2015. *Churchill's Cookbook (an Edited and Abridged Edition of Recipes from No.10)*. London: IWM.

Lethbridge, Lucy. 2013. *Servants: A Downstairs View of Twentieth Century Britain*. London: Bloomsbury.

Light, Alison. 2007. *Mrs Woolf and the Servants*. London; New York: Penguin/Fig Tree.

Lough, David. 2015. *No More Champagne: Churchill and His Money*. New York; London: Picador/Head of Zeus.

Lubbock, S. 1939. *The Child in the Crystal*. London: Jonathan Cape.

MacLeod, Lily. 1958. *A Cook's Notebook*. London: Faber.

Major, Norma, and Mark Fiennes. 2001. *Chequers: The Prime Minister's Country House and Its History*. London: Little, Brown.

Marcus, Sharon. 1999. *Apartment Stories: City and Home in Nineteenth-Century Paris and London*. Berkeley; London: University of California Press.

Marshall, A. *c.*1888. *Mrs A. B. Marshall's Cookery Book*. London: Marshall's Cookery School.

Marshall, Agnes. 1891. *Larger Cookery Book of Extra Recipes*. London.

McGowan, Norman. 1958. *My Years with Churchill*. [1st ed.]. London: Souvenir Press.

Mellish, Katharine. 1901. *Cookery and Domestic Management*. London: E. & F. N. Spon.

Minney, R. J. 1963. *No.10 Downing Street. A House in History. [with Plates]*. London: Cassell.

Moore, Lucy. 2009. *Anything Goes: A Biography of the Roaring Twenties*. London: Atlantic.

Moran, Lord. 1966. *Winston Churchill, the Struggle for Survival 1940–1965*. London: Constable.

Moran, Mollie. 2013. *Aprons and Silver Spoons: The Heartwarming Memoirs of a 1930s Kitchen Maid*. London: Penguin.

Morphy, Countess. 1935. *Recipes of All Nations*. London: Published for Selfridge and Co. Ltd by H. Joseph.

Muthesius, Stefan. 1982. *The English Terraced House*. New Haven; London: Yale University Press.

Nel, Elizabeth. 1958. *Mr Churchill's Secretary*. London: Hodder & Stoughton.

Nicholson, Virginia. 2012. *Millions Like Us: Women's Lives in the Second World War*. London: Penguin.

Pawle, Gerald. 1963. *The War and Colonel Warden: Based on the Recollections of Commander C. R. Thompson, Personal Assistant to the Prime Minister 1940*. London: Harrap.

Peavitt, Helen. 2017. *Refrigerator: The Story of Cool in the Kitchen*. London: Reaktion in association with the Science Museum.

Pépin, Jacques. 2003. *The Apprentice*. New York: Houghton Mifflin.

Perkin, Harold James. 1989. *The Rise of Professional Society: England since 1880*. London: Routledge.

Powell, Margaret. 2011. *Below Stairs*. London: Pan.

Purnell, Sonia. 2015. *First Lady: The Life and Wars of Clementine Churchill*. London: Aurum.

Rennie, Jean. 1977. *Every Other Sunday*. London: Coronet.

Robb, Graham. 2010. *Parisians: An Adventure History of Paris*. London: Picador.

Robbins, Ann Brolcaw Roe. 1951. *100 Meat-Saving Recipes*. London: Nicholas Kaye.

Roberts, Andrew. 2018. *Churchill: Walking with Destiny: The Biography*. London: Allen Lane.

Roscoe, Thomas, and Peter Lecount. 1839. *The London and Birmingham Railway*. London: Charles Tilt.

Rose, Jill. 2018. *Nursing Churchill*. Stroud: Amberley.

Rothschild, Miriam. 2008. *Walter Rothschild: The Man, the Museum and the Menagerie*. London: Natural History Museum.

Sambrook, Pamela. 2005. *Keeping Their Place: Domestic Service in the Country House*. Stroud: Sutton.

Saulnier, L. 1914. *Le Répertoire De La Cuisine*. Paris.

Searle, Geoffrey. 2004. *A New England: Peace and War 1886–1918*. Oxford: OUP.

Senn, Charles Herman. 1904. *The Century Cookbook: Practical Gastronomy and Recherché Cookery*. London: Ward, Lock & Co.

Shapiro, Laura. 2018. *What She Ate: Six Remarkable Women and the Food That Tells Their Stories*. New York: Penguin.

Singer, Barry. 2012. *Churchill Style: The Art of Being Winston Churchill*. New York: Abrams Books.

Soames, Mary. 2002. *Clementine Churchill*. Rev. and updated ed. London: Doubleday.

—. 2012. *A Daughter's Tale: The Memoir of Winston and Clementine Churchill's Youngest Child*. London: Black Swan.

Spang, Rebecca L. 2000. *The Invention of the Restaurant: Paris and Modern Gastronomic Culture*. Cambridge, Mass.; London: Harvard University Press.

Spry, Constance, and Rosemary Hume. 1956. *The Constance Spry Cookery Book*. London: J. M. Dent & Sons.

Steedman, Carolyn. 2009. *Labours Lost: Domestic Service and the Making of Modern England*. Cambridge: Cambridge University Press.

Stelzer, Cita. 2011. *Dinner with Churchill: Policy-Making at the Dinner Table*. London: Short.

Summers, Anne. 1998. 'Public Functions, Private Premises: Female Professional Identity and the Domestic Service Paradigm in Britain, *c.*1850–1930.' In *Borderlines: Genders and Identities in War and Peace, 1870–1930*, edited by Billie Melman, 353–376. New York & London: Routledge.

Suzanne, Alfred. 1904. *La Cuisine et Pâtisserie Anglaise et Américaine*. Paris.

Sweet, M. 2001. *Inventing the Victorians*. London: Faber & Faber.

Sysonby, Ria, Oliver Messel, and Osbert Sitwell. 1935. *Lady Sysonby's Cook Book*. London: Putnam.

Tinniswood, Adrian. 2016. *The Long Weekend: Life in the English Country House, 1918–1939*. London: Jonathan Cape.

Todd, Selina. 2015. *The People: The Rise and Fall of the Working Class, 1910–2010*. London: John Murray.

Trubek, Amy. 2000. *Haute Cuisine: How the French Invented the Culinary Profession*. Philadelphia: University of Pennsylvania Press.

Tschumi, Gabriel, and Joan Powe. 1954. *Royal Chef: Forty Years with Royal Households*. London: William Kimber.

Victorian Party-Giving on Every Scale. 2007. Stroud: Nonsuch.

Wadlow, Flo, and Alan Childs. 2007. *Over a Hot Stove: A Kitchen Maid's Story*. Norwich: Mousehold Press.

Ward, Humphry Mrs. 1895. *The Story of Bessie Costrell*. London.

Waterson, Merlin. 1985. *The Country House Remembered: Recollections of Life between the Wars*. London: Routledge & Kegan Paul.

White-Smith, Heather. 2010. *My Years with the Churchills: A Young Girl's Memories*. Ascot: Cotesworth Pub.

Acknowledgements

This book was not an easy thing to write, and there were times when hiding under the duvet seemed an entirely measured and appropriate response to yet another solid research wall. However, lots of people helped me see through it, as it were, and fulsome thanks are definitely due:

For various titbits, advice and answers to ridiculously specific enquiries on very obscure topics, thanks to buildings guru Olivia Horsfall-Turner, Chris Jones of the Tunbridge Wells History Society, Clemmie Fraser, Charlotte Molsey, Andrew Stevenson, Clemency Anderson and my reliably helpful Twitter followers (Creamola – what a joy). Thanks also to Kevin Geddes for his knowledge of all things Fanny Cradock, Adrian Tinniswood for letting me vent and sharing his footman's diary, Paul Couchman for showing me round the delightful Regency Town House in Hove, and David Heaton for sharing my perplexity about Downing Street. Stephen Kenny and his partner Roz hosted a wonderful afternoon (and evening) at their house in Exning, enabling me to crawl into cellars under the influence of Boodle's orange fool.

The Trustees of the Liddell Hart Centre for Military Archives, King's College London kindly gave me permission to use extracts from Lady Hamilton's diaries; and thank you too to Andrew Martin at the Irish Newspapers Archive, who was an absolute star; the French voluntary associations Fil d'Ariane and Entreaide Généalogique for accessing the Archives Nationales; Special Collections at University of Nottingham for information on Paul at Clumber; and Anna Towlson at LSE Special Collections when I was desperately seeking *Woman's Journal*.

The archivists at the Churchill Archive in Cambridge have all been absolutely amazing, and I owe them a huge debt of thanks: Allen Packwood, Andrew Riley, Natalie Adams, Katharine Thomson, Julia Schmidt, Heidi Egginton, Sarah Lewery and everyone else, I apologise for the dodgy chocolate cake, and I promise that the recipe in chapter 8 is way better. Thank you to Nonie Chapman for sharing memories of Georgina in the 1960s, and to Lady Williams for a memorable lunch and conversation. Emma Soames kindly allowed me permission to access her mother's papers, and to quote from them before the archive was opened to the public. Thank you all enormously.

Phil Reed at the Churchill War Rooms deserves massive thanks, especially for waiting patiently outside the ladies' loo in the former annexe, while I tapped on the walls and surprised the cleaner. Katharine Carter and Sarah McKeon showed me around Chartwell and answered my queries there, and Janet Clarke at Janet Clarke Books shared my excitement over Clemmie's recipe book collection, as well as sending therapeutic quinces.

I could not have even started this book without the enthusiasm and encouragement of Georgina's granddaughter, Edwina Brocklesby. Her influence also made sure I crawled into the gym and started doing yoga while writing (necessary). Thank you, Eddie, and also Anne Lewis, who went through the Landemare/Brocklesby family archive with me. Both also graciously allowed me to interview them when I was still clueless at the start, and Eddie has answered countless queries throughout the whole process. Vicki Lanceman transcribed that initial interview, and Georgina's TV appearance, and is an utter star.

My editor, Rebecca Gray, managed both a new baby and this book at the same time, so thank you to her, and also to Louisa Dunnigan. Thank you as well to Anna-Marie Fitzgerald, Jane Pickett, Penny Daniel, Valentina Zanca and everyone else at Profile Books for bringing *Victory* to life.

At PFD, Laura McNeill has been a stalwart, and my agent, Tim Bates, deserves every plaudit going for repeatedly dragging me kicking into the light, for beer and wine and food and so that I could swear and wave my arms about. I'd still be on chapter 3 without him.

Finally, my friends – Laura Gale, Kathy Hipperson, Rebecca Lane and Katharine Boardman-Hims – have both offered practical advice and stopped me going insane. Richard Gray, Jess Smith, Kristy Noble, Sean Griffiths and Angela and Mike Gray have also all been ready with solace through things that aren't Churchill

370 VICTORY IN THE KITCHEN

when I needed them. Last, and most of all, thanks to my partner, Matt Howling. You know how much I owe you. Winkle up.

Picture Credits

The author and publisher would like to express their thanks to the following for permission to use the photographs:

Alamy page 6 (top); Collage: The London Picture Archive page 5 (top); Churchill Archives Centre page 4 (bottom); Edwina Brocklesby page 1 (top), page 1 (bottom), page 3, page 4 (top left and top right), page 5 (bottom), page 7 (all photographs), page 8 (bottom); Getty Images page 6 (bottom), page 8 (top) Endpapers: Sample spread from the Chartwell menu book, showing both Georgina's and Clementine's annotations. Source: Churchill Archives Centre

While every effort has been made to contact copyright-holders of illustrations, the author and publishers would be grateful for information about any illustrations where they have been unable to trace them, and would be glad to make amendments in further editions.

Index